Mormonism and the Nature of God

In memory of my father,
Ernst Widmer,
1930–1998

Mormonism and the Nature of God

A Theological Evolution, 1830–1915

Kurt Widmer

Foreword by Irving Hexham

McFarland & Company, Inc., Publishers
Jefferson, North Carolina, and London

> The present work is a reprint of the library bound edition
> of Mormonism and the Nature of God: A Theological
> Evolution, 1830–1915, first published in 2000 by McFarland.

LIBRARY OF CONGRESS CATALOGUING-IN-PUBLICATION DATA

Widmer, Kurt, 1962–
    Mormonism and the nature of God : a theological evolution, 1830–1915 / Kurt Widmer ; foreword by Irving Hexham.
       p.   cm.
    Includes bibliographical references and index.

ISBN 978-0-7864-7402-8
softcover : acid free paper ∞

    1. Mormon Church—Doctrines—History—19th century.
2. God—History of doctrines—19th century.   I. Title.
BX8643.G63.W53   2012
230'.93'09034—dc21   00-25624

BRITISH LIBRARY CATALOGUING DATA ARE AVAILABLE

© 2000 Kurt Widmer. All rights reserved

No part of this book may be reproduced or transmitted in any form or by any means, electronic or mechanical, including photocopying or recording, or by any information storage and retrieval system, without permission in writing from the publisher.

Front cover: Statue of Jesus and background (iStockphoto/Thinkstock)

Manufactured in the United States of America

McFarland & Company, Inc., Publishers
  Box 611, Jefferson, North Carolina 28640
    www.mcfarlandpub.com

Contents

Acknowledgments	vii
Foreword by Irving Hexham	1
INTRODUCTION: MORMONISM YESTERDAY AND TODAY	3
1. YE MOUNTAINS ROLL DOWN YOUR THUNDER *Mormonism from Monotheism to Cosmic Henotheism*	14
2. OUT OF THE GROUND A VOICE SPEAKS *The Book of Mormon in Its Nineteenth-Century Religious Context*	23
3. KNOWING THE ONLY TRUE GOD *The Revelations of Moses, the Joseph Smith Translation, and the Rewriting of Genesis*	42
4. AMONG THE SCHOOL OF THE PROPHETS IN OHIO *Teachings from the Lectures of Faith*	57
5. IN THE GRAND COUNCIL OF THE GODS *Redacting the Writings of Abraham*	70
6. IF ANY MAN LACK WISDOM *The First Vision and the Mormon Quest for Legitimization*	91
7. AND YE SHALL BE GODS *Placing the King Follett Discourse in Its Historical Perspective*	108
8. ADAM OUR FATHER AND OUR GOD *Doctrinal Development During the Early Utah Period*	127
9. UNITY FROM DIVERSITY *Apostle James E. Talmage and the Birth of Mormonism*	143
Notes	161
Bibliography	191
Index	203

Acknowledgments

What began as a senior level college essay in history was added to, refined, enlarged and revised to become the work you now see. In the decade or more since I first began to research the topic of the Mormon view of the nature of God, and in the years that I have spent expanding the work, many individuals have made suggestions, made gracious offers to edit, and even provided moral support. It is with gratitude that I am now able to properly thank these individuals for their varying contributions over the years.

Inevitably some people who have made contributions will be overlooked. Therefore at the outset I wish to thank the nameless individuals who have helped in any way. This includes the library staff at several archives and universities in Canada and in the state of Utah.

As for those who have made significant contributions to the present work, the list begins with Dr. Marvin James Penton, retired professor of history at the University of Lethbridge. It was he who first expressed interest in what I was researching and gave a decade's worth of encouragement, editorial help, and intellectual conversation.

I would also like to thank Dr. Merlin B. Brinkerhoff, Dr. Brigham Young Card, and Dr. Irving Hexham, who all provided direction at critical points in the researching of the project.

Any list would be incomplete without giving special recognition to Dr. Thomas A. Robinson. Aside from being a sounding board for most of my theories over the last decade, he provided an example of how solid research and the application of critical analysis should be carried out in writing history. Many thanks.

And last but certainly not least I would like to thank Renée M. Clark. Renée, it was through your consistent encouragement and gentle prodding that the revisions to the manuscript neared completion. Once completed it was under your questioning editorial eye that areas of the manuscript I had glossed over would be fleshed out to make a consistent and coherent presentation. There was a time when I thought the manuscript would never see a printed page. Obstacle after obstacle brought delay after delay. Yet somehow you seemed to bring laughter in what were at times dark days, pushing me onward. All I can say is thanks.

Kurt Widmer
Spring 2000

Foreword

Following the lead of E. H. Carr in *What Is History?* (London: Macmillan, 1961), a generation of historians has paraded its ignorance by mocking the great German scholar Leopold Von Ranke, who is supposed to have argued that the task of the historian is to show "how it really was [*wie es eigentlich gewesen*]." Such an impossible ideal, the critics charge, distorted history for three generations.

Actually, anyone who has read Von Ranke's essays on history, or even his historical writings, knows that this is not what Von Ranke did or held up as an ideal. He was far too good a historian to be so foolish. Recognizing this fact prompts us to ask why modern historians have misunderstood Von Ranke's methods.

The answer is fairly straightforward. When Von Ranke penned his much-misquoted dictum in the preface to his *Histories of the Latin and Germanic Nations* (1824), the key item *eigentlich* had both the modern meaning of "actually" and the alternate meaning of "essentially" or "characteristically." From the context as well as the essays he wrote at the time it is quite clear that Von Ranke was using it in the sense of essentially, not actually. Mistranslation and the ease which with people read present meanings into the past have distorted the way many people understand Von Ranke's work.

This short discussion of the history of history may seem unrelated to Kurt Widmer's excellent work on the Church of Jesus Christ of Latter-day Saints. But Widmer shows that just as Von Ranke's words were misunderstood by later generations of historians (who really ought to have known better), many received interpretations of Mormon history rest on similar anachronisms.

Unlike most of his contemporaries, Widmer is not content to understand the history of Mormonism in terms of its later development while ignoring the subtle changes that have occurred in our language that alter perceptions of Mormon texts. Rather, following Von Ranke, he seeks to discover the essence of Mormon history by situating specific events in equally specific historical contexts. Therefore, unlike other writers, he does not assume that the meaning of the texts is self-evident, or that what was true in 1880 was equally true fifty years earlier in 1830. Instead he asks, What did this or that event or statement mean when it first occurred or was uttered? How did Joseph Smith's contemporaries understand his words and deeds?

To answer these and similar questions Widmer follows the classic historian's route of examining the available evidence in terms of its closeness to the events in question. He refuses to take the easy route of following later commentators or assuming that someone writing fifty years after an event accurately recalls that event. Therefore, he digs and probes until he comes up with arguments based on solid historical evidence contemporaneous with the issues he is discussing.

This book is a model of scholarship for religious studies that avoids the ever present traps of generalization and interdisciplinary mush. Of course not everyone will agree with the conclusions, but the author is too good a scholar to expect that. What is important is that the evidence he has unearthed receives consideration and the explanations he proposes fuel debate. If these goals are achieved then the book will have met all expectations. I urge everyone interested in the history of Mormonism or religion generally to read this outstanding work.

Irving Hexham
Dept. of Religious Studies
University of Calgary

Introduction: Mormonism Yesterday and Today

> Mormonism, a nickname for the real religion of the Latter-day Saints, does not profess to be a new thing, except to this generation. It proclaims itself as the original plan of salvation, instituted in the heavens before the world was, and revealed from God to man in different ages. That Adam, Enoch, Noah, Abraham, Moses, and other ancient worthies had this religion successively, in a series of dispensations, we, as a people, verily believe. To us, the gospel taught by the Redeemer in the meridian of time was a restored gospel, of which, however, He was the author, in His pre-existent state. Mormonism, in short, is the primitive Christian faith restored, the ancient gospel brought back again—this time to usher in the last dispensation, introduce the Millennium, and wind up the work of redemption as pertaining to this planet.
>
> Lorenzo Snow, *Millennial Star*, Vol. 61, 1901

The Church of Jesus Christ of Latter-day Saints, or Mormon Church,[1] is North America's largest indigenous religious group, with more than 10,000,000 Latter-day Saints worldwide. In reviewing the Church's history, and the development of Mormon doctrine, we see a religious movement in constant dialectic. As a result of several external and internal forces, the Church has changed its theological positions on many occasions. Through a modern prophet, modern with a direct line of communication with God, and the process of "continuing revelation," the beliefs of the Church can change, and have changed, suddenly.

This chapter has appeared in North American Religion, *Vol. 3 (1994): 51–70, under the title "An Introduction to Research in Mormon Studies."*

While the early Mormon Church of the 1830s was not significantly distinct from the rest of 19th-century Christianity, later Mormonism became quite distinct from the rest of 19th-century Christendom. For nearly a century, the Church underwent changes in its beliefs. The best example of these changes is seen in the development of the Mormon concept of God. This work is an attempt to document these changes and to add to the available literature on the historical development of the Mormon belief system.

Throughout its history, the Mormon Church has consistently defined itself as the only true Christian Church. Through maintaining doctrinal distinctiveness, the Church sought to disassociate itself from the rest of Christianity. For over 100 years the Church claimed to possess those "plain and precious parts of the gospel that have been held back by that abominable church."[2] While the rest of Christianity possessed some of the truth, the Mormon Church claimed to possess all of the truth pertaining to the nature and character of God. As well, the Church claimed to have restored the structure of the primitive Christian Church. The Church claimed to be a restoration of the New Testament Church in all of its facets and by virtue of this claim the only legitimate successor of primitive Christianity.

The claim of being restored Christianity expresses itself in the Mormon concept of the restoration. For many Mormons today this belief is historically founded on a concept that has come to be known as Joseph Smith's First Vision. Smith's vision relates his personal encounter with God and Smith's call to restore apostate Christianity. Yet this modern view of "the restoration" was not always held. In fact the concept of Smith's First Vision did not play an important role for the Church's first decade. The initial Mormon concept of "the restoration" was based on the belief that after 1,800 years God was again speaking to his people.[3] This belief gained prominence through the supernatural display of healings, prophecy, speaking in unknown tongues, and the introduction of the *Book of Mormon*.[4] As the Church matured, the charismatic gifts began to play less of a role, and belief and structure became paramount in maintaining the Church's claim to being restored Christianity.[5] In an attempt to maintain their claim of being true Christianity, Church leaders, through revelation, theological speculation, and scriptural interpretation, introduced new theological concepts. The result of this action contributed to the divergent, and sometimes opposing, streams of thought present in Mormonism for most of the 19th century and the early 20th century.

Presently there exist over 150 denominations, or sects, that place their faith in the teachings of the Mormon Prophet Joseph Smith, Junior. In the Church's history there have existed over 200 groups of believers that have laid claim to being the true and original Mormon Church restored by Joseph

Smith.[6] The individual beliefs of these groups reflect the divergent and often varied thought in existence throughout the Latter-day Saint's history. I have specifically chosen to limit this work to the history and development of thought in "The Church of Jesus Christ of Latter-day Saints," or the Utah Church. The Utah Church is the largest of the Mormon sects and the organization with which most people would be familiar.

The early Mormons, as a group, were continuously among the first people to move westward on the expanding American frontier. Early converts to the movement came from primitivist Christian sects and had followed many self-proclaimed prophets and seers prior to joining the Mormons. Holding to millenarian beliefs and apocalyptic expectations, the early Latter-day Saints gathered in specific geographic locations where they awaited the return of the Lord. This belief, called "the gathering to Zion,"[7] and a firm belief in the divine origin of the *Book of Mormon* formed the core of early Latter-day Saint doctrine. These two core tenets formed the basis for the Mormon's first missionary proclamation.[8] During the Prophet Joseph Smith's lifetime the Saints gathered collectively at four major centers: Kirtland, Ohio; Independence and Far West, Missouri; and Nauvoo, Illinois.[9] After the death of the Prophet Joseph Smith the Saints moved to the inter-mountain West in what was to become Utah, northern Arizona, and southern Idaho. Faced with ever-increasing political pressure, the Mormons soon abandoned their hope in the imminent return of Jesus and the establishment of the millennial kingdom of Zion. The shift from an immediate apocalyptic expectation allowed for the reinterpretation of the "Gathering" to that of a future Zion. The establishment of Zion in the future allowed the Church to reinterpret the concept and focus its attention on the whole of North America as being Zion.

The concept of the continent of North America as Zion, or the land chosen of God, has deep roots in American soil. John Winthrop, late 17th-century governor of Massachusetts Bay Colony, had proclaimed that the new land to which the Puritans had arrived was the chosen land for God's chosen people.[10] The Latter-day Saints stood firm with their Calvinistic countrymen in this aspect.[11] Yet, in Mormon ideology the belief that America was Zion was a later addition to their thought. The early Mormon Church saw specific sites as Zion. First it was Independence and then Far West, Missouri. In 1844 the Mormons expanded the concept of Zion and finally came to see all of America as Zion.[12] This view was only fitting, as early Mormons believed that Adam had lived, and that the Garden of Eden had originally been on the North American continent.[13] The Mormons also believed that during the Millennium the City of New Jerusalem, the city from which Christ would rule, would also be located on the American continent. The Mormons firmly believed that the City of New Jerusalem would descend from heaven to the geographical center of what had been the original location of the Garden of Eden (the counties of Jackson, Clay, and Caldwell, Missouri) to Independence.[14]

Latter-day Saint Church history can be divided into three distinct developmental periods which coincide with their residence in specific geographical locations. The first period of history coincides with the Saints' tenure in New York, Ohio, and Missouri. This period lasted from 1830 to 1838. The second, the Illinois period, coinciding with the Saints' residence in Nauvoo, lasted from 1839 to 1845. The third time period, the Utah period, encompasses the years 1846 to the present. Our historical inquiry will attempt to establish a chronology for the development of the Mormon concept of God coinciding with the three major periods of Latter-day Saint Church history.

The major aim of this work is to establish a proper chronology for the development of Mormon thought, specifically its concept of God. This is based upon the apparent development of Mormonism from its earliest theological position as a strict monotheistic Christian sect to the cosmic henotheistic[15] religion it is today. As a secondary conclusion, I will also establish that the modern Mormon doctrine of God is really the product of the 20th century with little resemblance to the original position of the Church in the early 19th century.

By placing the development of Mormon thought into its historical and cultural matrix, it will be shown that the Latter-day Saint movement is the product of an interaction with the larger American and continental culture, primarily its intellectual and social philosophies. Most of the major theological shifts occurred within the life of the movement's founder, Joseph Smith. It was during this first fourteen-year period, from 1830 to 1844, that the Mormon Church shifted from its earliest monotheistic belief to a nascent cosmic henotheism. The arrival at a henotheistic theology followed a progressive pattern. Mormon theology shifted from a modalistic form of monotheism to binatarianism within the first three years. Shortly before the death of the Prophet[16] in 1844, the Church held to a nascent cosmic henotheistic doctrinal position. The next half century following the Prophet's death would see Mormon leaders attempt to reconcile the divergent theologies of the early Mormon Church with the henotheistic position of 1844.

At the outset it must be stated that the shifts, which often took the form of prophetic revelations, were attempts to maintain Smith's position as "Prophet, Seer and Revelator." With a tradition rooted deep in intellectualism the Church's leaders saw all truth as God's truth regardless of its source. Borrowing concepts from various popular, cultural, philosophical, religious, and scientific sources, Mormonism would include these divergent streams within its developmental paradigm. It is for this reason that perhaps Mormonism is a perfect reflection of the development of American society and culture. Owing to its origins, not quite fifty years removed from colonialism, and at the time of strong anti-intellectual currents in America, Mormonism sought to address the chief problems of the day. Yet they addressed these problems not through public debate, intellectual argumentation, or violence. Rather, they chose to address the questions in a unique fashion, namely that God had spoken on these topics to 19th-century America. That the Mormons reflected the greater American society may also be seen geographically. As a result of being continuously on the American frontier they sought to establish a place were they could practice their faith in good conscience. This was not so unlike the early English dissenters who came to America.

The henotheistic doctrinal position of modern Mormonism is a refinement of concepts first introduced in 1844. At the Church Conference of April 1844, the Mormon Prophet Joseph Smith delivered a sermon now commonly called the King Follett discourse. This sermon provided the core for Latter-day Saint theology and speculative thought on the doctrine of God for the remainder of the 19th century. While some of the concepts expressed in the King Follett discourse had been alluded to in earlier sermons, other concepts were being introduced for the first time. Following the death of the Prophet Joseph Smith, the leaders of the Church continued to redefine the concepts that Smith had introduced to Mormonism in the King Follett discourse.

By the late 19th century the Mormon Church had moved to such an extreme theological position that no consistent or clear statement of Mormon beliefs existed. By the 20th century there existed competing definitions in Mormon theology, especially its Christology. It would be primarily through the work of Apostle James E. Talmage that the past seventy years of doctrinal speculation would be correlated. Talmage's work attempted to harmonize the fully developed concepts of 20th-century Mormonism with their 19th-century counterparts. The end product of the correlation provided the first clear doctrinal statements on the Mormon doctrine of God. James E. Talmage's correlation had resulted in the birth of a new Mormonism.

Historical Sources

In any reconstruction of Mormon doctrine several problems have to be considered. The field of Mormon studies is predominated by committed members of the Latter-day Saint community. This faith commitment often overshadows their research and finds expression in their apologetical style of writing. It is imperative that these secondary works be supplemented with primary and archival sources to document any reconstruction of Mormon doctrine.

There exist many primary and archival sources dealing with Mormonism. Since its organization in 1830, the Church has had a steady stream of Christian apologetical tracts, books, newspaper editorials, and articles directed against its membership, leadership, and its doctrines. Early polemical arguments against the Church, or anti–Mormon literature, often centered on the origin of the *Book of Mormon* and the Church's practice of the spiritual gifts, healings, prophecy, speaking in tongues, and the character of Joseph Smith. Newspapers of the time focused upon the Church's apparent abuses of the secular liberties of the Church's followers.

In addition to this external body of literature, members of the Church of Jesus Christ of Latter-day Saints have also provided numerous literary sources. Since its early years the Church has had an official Church historian who was to record a general history of the Church. The first official historian was John Whitmer, who was called by revelation in November of 1831.[17] The public discourses of the Prophet and other Church leaders were recorded by several individuals over the years. William Clayton, Thomas Bullock, William McIntire, and others served as personal scribes to Joseph Smith during his lifetime. These longhand accounts provided the majority of documents used to compile the official history of the Church.[18] In addition to this official history, the Prophet's own diaries and writings, the personal diaries of other members, which include references to the public sermons and private reflections of the Church's leaders, and official minutes from Church and city councils provide the core sources for a reconstruction of Mormon doctrine.

While many of these personal papers and private diaries have become part of the public domain, there is a reluctance by the Latter-day Saints' leadership to make all of these journals, diaries, and personal papers fully accessible to researchers. That reluctance placed certain limitations on this work. Yet, it is not any more limited than any other work dealing with Mormonism, either published or currently in progress, as no researcher in the field has special access privileges to the Church's archives. It is the Church's fear of embarrassing material being published that has caused it to restrict access to its collections. In light of the 1980s Mark Hoffman bombings and document forgery, the Church has restricted access to a case by case basis, dependent on the sensitivity of the materials requested from the collection.

For any researcher in Mormon history the Church's archives house most relevant documents. Yet the archives process for accessing materials is extremely strict. Forms and a personal interview by an archival assistant are required to access materials in the Church archives.[19] The Church's restrictions on materials have created a black market for early Mormon periodicals, personal papers, and diaries. Jerald and Sandra Tanner, directors of the Utah Lighthouse Ministry (based in Salt Lake City), have provided copies of extremely valuable and rare documents for over thirty years.

Canonical Sources

The Mormon canon has four major works which each Latter-day Saint believes to be the Word of God. These works are the Bible, *The Book of Mormon, The Doctrine and Covenants*, and *The Pearl of Great Price*. The *Pearl of Great Price* is comprised of several smaller works. Of these smaller works the *Book of Moses*, the *Book of Abraham*, and a short work entitled "Joseph Smith History" are the most relevant to this work. The four major works are collectively called "The Standard Works of the Church." The canon is comprised of works that were written primarily during the lifetime of the Prophet Joseph Smith. The Standard Works have, in one form or another, been available to Church members since the 1840s. While parts of Latter-day Saint scripture have been decanonized, several new revelations or "Sections" have been added to the *Doctrine and Covenants* since the 1840s.

Strangely, the central core of the Mormon belief system, the King Follett discourse, has never been canonized. Canonical support for the King Follett discourse is usually drawn from two sections of the *Doctrine and Covenants* (Sections 76 and 88), the *Book of Abraham*, and the First Vision recorded in "Joseph Smith History." Sections 76 and 88 are dated to the 1830s and allude to a plurality of Gods theology. In their original published formats, the sections omit the passages that support the plurality of Gods concept. The *Book of Abraham* was accepted as binding and canonized in 1876.

The Latter-day Saints' process of canonization has been problematic for establishing a chronology of the development of Latter-day Saint doctrine of God. The major problem area is the time difference between a document's first appearance in history and the date given for its acceptance as part of the canon. The earliest Mormon canon was comprised of the *Book of Mormon*, the *Doctrine and Covenants*, and the Bible. Except for editing of parts of the text, the *Book of Mormon* has remained substantially unchanged since 1830. This cannot be said of the *Doctrine and Covenants*. The modern version contains 138 sections, or revelations. The original *Doc-*

trine and Covenants, which first appeared in 1835, contained 102 sections. Major revisions to the *Doctrine and Covenants* were carried out in 1876 and 1921. In the 1876 revision, several revelations dated in the 1830s and 1840s were included in the work. The 1921 revision of the *Doctrine and Covenants* removed a large part of the work titled the *Lectures of Faith*.

For the researcher a major problem encountered in dealing with Mormon canonical sources is whether the revelation, as published, is accurate, or has undergone a textual revision to make the revelation congruent with later Latter-day Saint thought. The questions that need to be asked are: Did the original revelation from the 1830s, or 1840s, contain the same doctrinal material? If it did, did it then provide the base in which the later thought is rooted? As well, did individuals within the Church see that revelation as important between the dates of origin and canonization? Or, did the canonization of the revelation merely add a historical legitimization for a concept that already existed, while having no roots in the original revelation? Fortunately, we are able to access the original source in either a Church periodical or a private diary.

A preliminary assessment of Mormon doctrinal development shows that it did not develop in a logical linear fashion. Holding to a linear view would oversimplify the way in which Mormon doctrine developed. In a later chapter we will deal with this problem at greater length.

Throughout this work we will concentrate primarily on the canonical and published works of the Latter-day Saints. As well, we will refer to the public discourses and lectures of the Church's leaders. All speeches of the Church's leaders, or "General Authorities," will be considered as true expressions of Latter-day Saint thought. Our concentration on the documents available to the public is related to our concern with what the Saints believed and taught at specific times in their history. By doing this it is hoped that a fuller understanding of the development of the Mormon doctrine of God can be attained.

It is not the intention of this work to discredit the Church, or its leaders. It is also not my intent to show that the leaders deliberately deceived the members of the Church. When examining any faith community care must be given in allowing the sources to speak for the faith community. This work is in no way intended to discredit Joseph Smith's claims to having received revelations from God. This claim of Smith lies beyond the scope of objective historical criticism, and can in no way be proved or disproved according to scientific criteria. For the researcher, Smith's claims must be taken into account in so far as they significantly shaped the Latter-day Saint movement.

Before any investigation of the development of Mormon doctrine can be undertaken some important groundwork must first be established. It is hoped that by giving attention to several primary points, some shaded areas can be cleared, providing a solid background for our investigation.

Church Structure and the Process of Revelation

The Church's hierarchy is comprised of three groups, or quorums, known collectively as the General Authorities. The Church of Jesus Christ of Latter-day Saints claims to have a living Prophet at its head. The Prophet, or President of the Church, has two Counselors who aid him and give advice when called on to do so. This group of men constitutes the First Presidency of the Church.

In the Church hierarchy, beneath the First Presidency is the Quorum of the Twelve Apostles. This group, often referred to as the Twelve Apostles, is ranked according to seniority within the group. Seniority is not based on years of membership within the Church, but is based upon length of continuous unbroken service as a member of the Twelve Apostles. Succession in the Church leadership is carried out in the following manner. Upon the death of the current Prophet the Church's power structure reverts to the Twelve Apostles, with the Senior Apostle becoming the Church's interim head. This precedent was set in 1845 when Senior Apostle Brigham Young became the second Prophet of the Church. Since that time the Senior Apostle within the Church has always succeeded to become the Prophet of the Church upon the death of the present Prophet.

The third group of individuals within the Church hierarchy is the Quorum of the Seventies (or Seventy). This group is designated to preside over specific geographic regions within the Church.

Under the present system the three groups are empowered to receive prophetic revelation for the entire Church. This act usually occurs during General Conference. The General Authorities' power to receive revelation from God has great implications for the general membership. In this regard, when the Church gathers at General Conference the words that are spoken by the General Authorities are spoken under the direction of, or inspiration of, the Holy Spirit, and are to be considered as valid as scripture. Both Joseph Smith and Brigham Young claimed the right to produce scripture. In Smith's case, the majority of his revelations have been included in the *Doctrine and Covenants*. As for Brigham Young, the best example of this authority to produce scripture is seen in a sermon found within the *Journal of Discourses*. Brigham said:

> I have never yet preached a sermon and sent it out among the children of men that they may not call scripture. Allow me the privilege of correcting a sermon, and it is as good a scripture that they deserve.[20]

Brigham Young had most of his sermons recorded in Church periodicals of the time. Brigham Young appears to be echoing a revelation given initially to Joseph Smith in 1831. The revelation, now part of the *Doctrine and Covenants*, stated:

> whatsoever they shall speak when moved upon by the Holy Ghost shall be scripture, shall be the will of the Lord, shall be the mind of the Lord, shall be the word of the Lord, shall be the voice of the Lord, and the power of God unto salvation.[21]

The statements of the Mormon Prophets create several problems for students of the Mormon tradition. Given the broad definition of Mormon scripture, which teachings are to be considered authoritative? As well, who has the authority to speak for the Church? In 1835, Joseph Smith claimed that the First Presidency, the Twelve Apostles, the Quorum of the Seventy, the High Councils of Kirtland and Missouri were all equal in authority.[22] The revelation allowed each of the groups to speak, officially and authoritatively, on doctrinal matters. This may have contributed to the competing theologies that existed in Mormonism during the 19th century. The Latter-day Saint's canon incorporates the entire canon of Christianity. The *Authorized Version* of the Bible is the preferred Bible translation. In addition to this they also have the Standard Works. Changes have been made to most of the Standard Works, the Bible being no exception.

In the current Mormon canon we find doctrinal statements from various times in Latter-day Saints' history. The present canon also provides us with clear examples of Mormon doctrinal development. The divergent theologies present in the Mormon canon are currently interpreted as developing in a line upon line fashion. This is to say that presently held beliefs existed as a central core of doctrine at the Church's founding in 1830. Over time, when the membership was deemed ready, parts of this core would be revealed to them. These new concepts would be delivered as either revelations, translated works, or sermons. The new works would then need to be accepted as binding, or authoritative, by a unanimous vote in a General Conference of the Church. This process often leaves large gaps between the introduction of the concept and its canonization at a later date.

Within the current Mormon Church we have two avenues through which the general Church receives guidance. One, through the canon, or Standard Works. The second way is through continuing revelation. The eighth and ninth *Articles of Faith* sum up the Mormon position on these points quite adequately:

> We believe the Bible to be the Word of God as far as it is translated correctly, we also believe the Book of Mormon to be the Word of God.
> We believe all that God has revealed, all that He does now reveal, and we believe that he will yet reveal many great, and important things pertaining to the Kingdom of God.[23]

Mormonism has a built-in mechanism by which new doctrinal concepts can be introduced. As new concepts are introduced, old concepts can be, and often are, discarded in favor of the newer concepts. As we progress through this work, this point will be stressed at greater length. While the mechanism for change is in place, the changes were often not greeted with the expected or desired results.

As with any Church's history, problems often arise between the objective history, and the official recorded history of that religious organization. Mormonism is no exception. For the purposes of our discussion we will not dwell on the historical inconsistencies of Mormon origins. From this author's perspective the origins of the Mormon Church are rooted in the experiences of Joseph Smith and his claim to having had received visitations from divine beings. Joseph Smith chose to interpret these experiences within the greater context of a call from God to restore Christianity to the pristine condition of the first century. Joseph Smith was not the first North American religionist that can lay claim to being a restorationist. The Mormons as well cannot lay claim to being the first restoration movement. The ground from which the Church sprang was ripe for new religious movements. Originating in an area in the eastern United States that had seen many revivals, the Mormons were one of many groups that had their origin in the same geographic area, and in the same time period. Of the several groups which originated in the early 19th century the Mormons eventually became the largest.

The stories and myths surrounding the origin of the Mormon Church have often been debated. Explanations for the origins of the Church, such as the official Church's position that a fourteen-year-old boy was visited by supernatural beings[24] to an elaborate scheme by Smith to secure riches, have all been promoted.[25] Perhaps we will never know the real reasons for the origin of the Church, or for the publication of *Book of Mormon*. One thing can be certain, Joseph Smith had a religious experience which shaped his self-view and his worldview. The precise time in history of this experience has been and probably will continue to be debated.

1. YE MOUNTAINS ROLL DOWN YOUR THUNDER

Mormonism from Monotheism to Cosmic Henotheism

> God is in the still small voice. In all these affidavits, indictments, it is all of the devil—all corruption. Come on! ye prosecutors! ye false swearers! All hell, boil over! Ye burning mountains, roll down your lava! for I will come out on top at last. I have more to boast of than ever any man had. I am the only man that has ever been able to keep a whole church together since the days of Adam. A large majority of the whole have stood by me. Neither Paul, John, Peter nor Jesus ever did it. I boast that no man ever did such a work as I. The followers of Jesus ran away from Him, but the Latter-day Saints never ran away from me yet.
>
> Joseph Smith, May 26, 1844

On April 7, 1844, approximately 20,000[1] Saints had gathered in Nauvoo, Illinois, to hear the Prophet Joseph Smith's General Conference address. The address is now commonly called the King Follett discourse. The teachings of the sermon would have a tremendous impact on the development of Mormon doctrine. Those who were present heard their Prophet Joseph Smith reveal the great mystery of the ages, the true nature and character of God. After 1900 years the teachings of true Christianity were at last fully disclosed to 19th-century America, and the world. Many present at the April Conference did not view the teachings of the sermon as the lost truths of Christianity restored to the world by their Prophet. Key members

Parts of this chapter have appeared in an earlier article titled "Turbulence in Early Mormonism and the Death of Joseph Smith: The Nauvoo Expositor *(1844),"* North American Religion, *Vol. 2 (1993): 135–201.*

of the Latter-day Saint community opposed the teachings of the sermon.[2] They saw the teachings as blasphemous and the leader of the Mormons, Joseph Smith, as a fallen prophet. The dissenters voiced their opposition to the Prophet in a paper called the *Nauvoo Expositor*. For taking action against the opposition from within, Joseph Smith would be arrested and held over for trial at the county seat in Carthage, Illinois.[3]

Many members of the Church had entertained similar sentiments to the Nauvoo dissenters. The dissent in Nauvoo was led by Joseph Smith's Second Counselor in the First Presidency, William Law. The leaders of the dissenting party also included William's brother Wilson, Robert and Charles Foster, and Chauncey and Francis Higbee. For the dissenters the sermon of April 7, 1844, was the final proof needed to show that Smith was indeed a fallen prophet. The Nauvoo dissenters found the teachings of the sermon difficult to accept as revelations from God. While the dissenters opposed Smith on many theological points brought out, or touched upon in the sermon, their greatest opposition was reserved for the concept of a plurality of Gods. In light of previous teachings believed to be true by the Saints the concept of a plurality of Gods was especially difficult to reconcile with the teachings of the *Book of Mormon*.

When the sermon was over the dissenters more now than ever sought to separate themselves from the Latter-day Saints. Many of the Saints continued on in the faith, believing that Joseph Smith was a prophet sent by God. Those that remained in the Church believed that the sermon of April was part of the eternal plan of God, and a glimpse of what would be revealed at a later time. Some members saw the sermon in a distinctly positive light. Elder Joseph Fielding, a convert from Canada, in his Nauvoo diary relates that the sermon was evidence to him that the Prophet had not fallen.[4]

William Law and the others were not content to quietly withdraw from the Church. The dissenters took upon themselves a moral responsibility to outline their points of contention and publicly confront the Prophet. On June 7, 1844, the first and only edition of the *Nauvoo Expositor* was published. Through the pages of the *Nauvoo Expositor* the Nauvoo dissenters, led by William and Wilson Law, made their disaffection with the Prophet known. Among the key points of disagreement with the Prophet were the very concepts that Joseph had taught in April of that year, that a hierarchical Council of Gods existed and that men could become Gods.

Joseph saw the dissent rising through the ranks of the Church and took quick action. On June 10, 1844, Joseph Smith declared the *Expositor* to be a public nuisance, and had the paper and its presses destroyed.[5] Joseph Smith as mayor of Nauvoo had far-reaching powers granted to him under the Nauvoo Charter.[6] The Nauvoo Charter was issued by the Illinois State

Legislature in December of 1840 to compensate for perceived democratic inequalities. Section 11 of the charter had given the mayor and council: "all power and authority to make, ordain, establish and execute, all such ordinances, not repugnant to the Constitution of the United States or this State, as they may deem necessary for the peace, benefit, good order, regulation, convenience, and cleanliness of said city." Section 16 of the charter provided the judicial powers granting, that:

> The Mayor and Aldermen shall be conservators of the peace within the limits of said City, and shall have all the powers of Justices of the Peace therein, both in civil and criminal cases, arising under the laws of the State: they shall as Justices of the Peace, within the limits of said City, perform the same duties, be governed by the same laws, give the same bonds and Security as other Justices of the Peace, and be commissioned as Justices of the Peace in and for said City by the Governor.

The original intention of the charter had been to create equity for the Mormons as a minority in Hancock County. By 1844 the Mormons had become the majority in the county and dealt with any opposition to them with the same measure that they had endured during previous tenures in Ohio and Missouri. From a Mormon perspective the actions taken by the Nauvoo city council were not without precedent. The Saints had had similar action taken against them in 1833, by the citizens of Independence, Missouri. The actions against the Mormons in Missouri came after the Mormons failed to act upon the ultimatum that had been issued. The ultimatum had called for the Mormons to leave the area and to cease publication of their newspaper *Evening and Morning Star*. The actions of the Independence town council had been carried out with no legal ramifications enacted towards them.[7] It was a benevolent act on behalf of the Illinois legislature that the charter had been issued to circumvent another Missouri incident with the Mormons again being the victims. Seeing the power of the elected government in the actions taken against them in Missouri, and on the basis of the Nauvoo Charter, perhaps Smith believed he had a right to destroy the press.

Mormon history contains various incidents of opposition against the leadership, the Church's policies, and practices, and against the Mormons in general. Dissent in Mormon history takes on two varied forms. It occurs both from within the Church and is expressed often from an external point. The latter is especially true with regards to the older inhabitants of regions to which the Mormons had migrated en masse. The earliest major external dissent occurred with the Mormon arrival in Jackson County, Missouri, in the early 1830s. The Mormons had begun to arrive in Independence in 1832.

Ezra Booth was one of the first persons sent from Kirtland, Ohio, to help Oliver Cowdery with missionary work in Independence and the Indian territory lying just west of the Missouri border in present-day Kansas. Booth recalled the early troubles in Missouri in a series of letters written to the *Ohio Star* shortly after his apostasy. These letters were reprinted in E. D. Howe's *Mormonism Unvailed* in 1834. Booth had often been seen as the first apostate from Mormonism. Early Mormon Church historian John Whitmer records that some apostatized before the Church had left New York, and arrived in Kirtland in June of 1831.[8] Ezra Booth's place in Mormon history is that he is the first apostate to publish tracts against the Church.[9]

The escalation of tension between the older Missouri settlers and the Mormons began shortly after the Mormons' arrival in Independence. The tensions caused by the large influx of Mormons into Missouri began with several violent incidents and peaked with the destruction of the Mormon newspaper *The Evening and Morning Star*. The Church had began to publish its paper in Independence in March of 1832. In addition to publishing the paper, the presses were used for Mormon books and tracts. The Missouri incident would be a contentious point between the Mormons, and state and federal governments over the next decade. The Mormons sought compensation for the violent incidents in Jackson County, and for their final expulsion from the state in the late 1830s. Sadly, the compensation that the Mormons so desperately sought after never materialized. By 1834 the Mormons had left the Center Stake of Zion, at Independence in Jackson County, and had moved to the northern Missouri counties of Clay and Caldwell.

The *Expositor* incident proved to be fatal for Joseph Smith. On June 12, two days after the destruction of the press of the *Nauvoo Expositor*, a writ calling for the arrest of Joseph Smith, mayor of Nauvoo, was issued at the county seat of Carthage, Illinois. The initial charge was for the destruction of private property—the press of the *Nauvoo Expositor*. Before Joseph would face trial in Carthage, additional charges, including treason against the state of Illinois, would be added.[10] On June 27, 1844, Joseph Smith was shot to death in a gun battle.[11]

The destruction of the *Expositor's* presses struck at the very core of individual freedoms guaranteed by the Constitution of the United States. Miscalculating his position among the Saints, Joseph sought to override these constitutional guarantees without fear of repercussion. By virtue of the power invested in the mayor and council, Joseph stood as Moses before God and his people: lawgiver, judge, and executioner. Joseph, secure in his own position as leader of the Nauvoo Legion, a militia larger than the Illinois state militia, could not have foreseen the outcome of the writ of destruction he had issued.

As Prophet, Priest, and King, Joseph stood as a unique figure in American social history. Seldom has one man wielded as much power in the physical and spiritual realm over his followers.[12] Joseph was more than an obscure country boy with dreams of grandeur. He saw himself as an individual that had spoken to God and firmly believed that he was empowered to deliver the restored Gospel to the world. It is perhaps this role that Smith took on that made some of his followers begin to doubt him. Smith had joined together Church and state in an unholy marriage. Not only was Smith endowed by God in spiritual matters, he was also responsible for the temporal affairs of the Church and its members.

For those who saw the Constitution of the United States as an inspired document the marriage of Church and state would indeed cause a clash in their ideologies. If indeed there was dissent over economic control between Smith and Law it could possibly be that Law saw a sharp distinction between the temporal and the spiritual. In that case then Smith, in Law's eyes, would deal only in terms of practices that would affect the hereafter and not the present. Yet this seems unlikely given that the very core of Mormon structure and belief was based on an apocalyptic understanding. For them the return of Christ was imminent and not distant and so preparing for the kingdom was foremost, not preparing for some future state of bliss. At best this is only speculation, for we are limited in our sources as to what actually caused the rift between Smith and Law. We are certain that a rift between Smith and Law did occur and the end resulted in the death of the Prophet Joseph Smith. Yet one (temporal) is not mutually exclusive of the other (spiritual). Both appear to have been welded together in an unusual degree in Mormon Nauvoo. The evidence points that both did play an important part in the rift between Smith and Law.

Yet several central questions still remain, what had caused the dissension between Smith and his followers to reach such a point in 1844? What series of events had brought Joseph to his end? The chief opposition to Smith came from his second counselor, William Law. Perhaps it was as Lyndon Cook points out, that the rift between the two was based on economic opportunities and the rights of individual freedoms rather than on religious grounds.[13] However, if the pages of the *Nauvoo Expositor* are to be believed, the sermon of the April Conference and its teachings on a plurality of Gods had been the spark that ignited the powder keg. It was the theological concepts advocated by Smith at the April Conference which Law and the others found so offensive.[14] In the eyes of the Nauvoo dissenters, the sermon of April 7, 1844, was new doctrine and they considered it to be blasphemous.[15]

The Nauvoo dissenters were not from the lower ranks of the Church, or recent converts to Mormonism, they were faithful members of the

Church.[16] Many of the Nauvoo dissenters were members of the inner circle. This would have given them knowledge of any new revelations and teachings before their public dissemination.[17] Other high-ranking officials had apostatized while the Church had resided in Kirtland. Earlier apostasy had even included some of the Twelve Apostles.[18] The earlier dissent, however, had never unified around a central figure or cause.

If the King Follett discourse did not contain new teachings, as some scholars contend,[19] then why the reaction of Law and the others through the pages of the *Nauvoo Expositor*? If we review Smith's response to the allegations of the *Nauvoo Expositor*, the sermon of June 16, 1844, Joseph Smith contends that he had never taught any other concept, except a plurality of Gods.[20] Smith seemed amazed that the Saints had reacted to his April 7 sermon in such a way. Perhaps then the teachings were not new revelations from Smith's perspective. Could the Saints have simply misunderstood Smith, or not paid attention to what Smith had said in the past, or on April 7, 1844? Members of the Church by 1844 should have been familiar with many of the concepts expressed in the discourse. The Saints should have been familiar with the plurality of Gods concept through previous works, like the *Book of Abraham*, and through isolated statements over the years. The Saints, at the very least, should have been familiar with the concepts expressed on April 7, but that does not necessitate that they believed them to be truth, or an important part of the restored Church's message. After all, the Church's canon made no mention of a plurality of Gods.

Smith's previous references to a plurality of Gods were speculative statements. No claims were made that these statements should be believed as revealed truth. Yet, when Joseph delivered the sermon of April 7, he claimed to be speaking by the power of God. The words spoken on April 7, 1844, from the Mormon perspective, were not those of a man, but those of God. In the eyes of the Latter-day Saints, the living God had chosen that day to reveal the great truths that had been hidden from the world for the past two millennia.

A possible observation to make from the available data is that in the King Follett discourse Smith would illuminate, clarify, and tie together concepts that he had hinted at during his tenure as the Prophet. As well, Smith could have been attempting to silence the voices that had cried false prophet once and for all. By delivering a radical sermon, with biblical texts to support his position, Smith could appeal to an established and accepted work to retain his prophetic status.

Over the years, many of the Saints had heard Joseph reveal many new truths. Many had been with him since Fayette, New York, and Kirtland, Ohio. They had seen Joseph Smith develop and firmly believed him to be a great prophet. Yet Joseph Smith and his theological convictions were a product of his time. As a Prophet of God, the pressure to reveal new, or previously unheard of, concepts becomes paramount to retaining his status as Prophet. Once the claim is made that God has spoken through him, and people come to believe in that message, then one must follow that course of events. If the claim to being a Prophet was to be upheld, then revelations from God must accompany this claim. God must be seen as still being active among his people. With each stage of his personal development and maturity, a new expanded theology would emerge finally peaking in the King Follett discourse. An excerpt from the King Follett discourse gives us a glimpse of the new theology. The following excerpt also shows the tension between the religious environment of the 19th century, and the Mormon claim to prophetic revelation:

> I have the truth of God, and show that ninety-nine out of every hundred professing religious ministers are false teachers.... I will prove that the world is wrong, by showing what God is.... God himself was once as we are now, and is an exalted man, and sets enthroned in yonder heavens!... That is the great secret.... We should understand the character, and being of God, and how he came to be so. We have imagined, and supposed that God was God from all eternity. I will take away the veil that you may see.... The scriptures say it, and I defy all the learning, and wisdom, and all the combined powers of earth and Hell together to refute it.... You have got to learn to be Gods yourselves, and to be Kings, and Priests to God the same as all other Gods have done before you.[21]

Those who had followed Joseph Smith since the early years in New York and Ohio had seen changes in the Church's doctrines. Converts to early Mormonism were drawn by its newness and its emphasis on the power of God. They had joined because in Mormonism they saw the heavens opened, and God speaking and working through his people. Early converts saw the elders of the Church perform healings and miracles, prophesy, and speak in tongues. They did not join the Church because of the doctrines that were taught.

As James Allen has outlined, early converts would not have had to alter their theology in order to join the Church.[22] If belief in the *Book of Mormon* was a prerequisite to joining the Church, it was a belief in the book's divine origin rather than in the doctrinal content of the book. The *Book of Mormon* taught nothing different from what early 19th-century religious seekers would have already been familiar with.

The theology of the *Book of Mormon* was monotheistic. Early Mormon theology then would not have been unique in comparison to other beliefs of the day. There do exist several historical parallels for their Christology. Early Mormons attempted to explain how three persons can be called God and yet there still is only one God. They explained this in the language of the common person, language that the uneducated and the less philosophical minded could understand. They attempted to explain a complex theological and philosophical problem, void of theological and philosophical language. This attempt resulted in the confusion of the Mormon concept of God. While early Latter-day Saint theology as presented in the *Book of Mormon* is monotheistic, by 1844 the theology would become henotheistic.

Documenting the development of the Mormon concept of God from 1830 to 1930 has been a difficult task. Many scholars have set out on this same course and their findings are well documented.[23] In the last several years, new publications have removed some of the haze surrounding Mormon doctrinal development. Yet, the haze is still present within Mormon doctrine. Presenting a complete history of Mormon belief is a task that will require a great amount of time and effort. Perhaps it is better to speak of what Mormons did not believe, rather than what Mormons have believed. Mormonism is a religion that concerns itself with practice, rather than belief.

There are no professional theologians within the Mormon Church. Mormon theology is the speculative reasonings of individuals called from various walks of life. The Mormon Church is a theological corporation whose CEO, the Prophet, has the final say on doctrinal matters. Mormonism is at the same time a liberal religious movement and an extremely conservative one. By liberal we mean that the Church has a mechanism in place, an open canon, to alter or change their doctrinal positions in accordance with society's changes. These changes can be effected without any fear of opposition from the membership. Yet, at the same time it is hesitant to do so. Since the days of Joseph Smith, the Mormons have changed little in the way of doctrine, officially that is. Within the Mormon canon there exist competing views on the godhead. Both monotheism and henotheism are contained in the canon with apparently no hermeneutical contradiction. In an attempt to deal with this problem the older theologies are interpreted in light of the newer theological understanding. Several of Mormonism's intellectuals, Orson Pratt, B. H. Roberts, James E. Talmage, and John A. Widstoe, made attempts to resolve the theological difficulties. Yet, these attempts were often stifled by a hierarchy who chose to place a heavier emphasis upon revelation than reason. This is the great Mormon paradox.

The Mormon Prophet Joseph Smith, in his early years, relied heavily on revelation. Smith had used divine revelation to produce the *Book of Mormon* and to revise the Bible. In Smith's early years, revelations from God, with the familiar "thus saith the Lord," were part of the Mormon religious experience. Once Joseph had acquired a solid secular education, he used every opportunity available to him to display this new knowledge. Later Mormon works, like the *Book of Abraham*[24] and the King Follett discourse,[25] both show evidence of Smith's reliance on secular learning. Once Smith had acquired secular knowledge, the revelations from God appeared to have become less frequent.[26]

The early modalist position of Mormonism is connected to revelation. The later henotheistic thought is the result of reason. Mormon doctrine began from a modalist position and with the introduction of the King Follett discourse it became henotheistic. If, as Van Hale points out, there were no new concepts in the King Follett discourse, and each of the four separate doctrines can be found in earlier Latter-day Saint publications, then our task of establishing a chronology for the changes in the Mormon doctrine of God will be simple.[27] But, if the concepts of April and June of 1844 were radically new concepts, something the Saints had never heard before, then a reconstruction of Mormon doctrine is in order.

Our examination of Mormon doctrine must then begin with the earliest Mormon publication, the *Book of Mormon*, and move chronologically forward. In order to understand the Latter-day Saint's belief system, as its followers would have understood it, we will concentrate on the published works of the Church and the public discourses and writings of Mormon leaders. It is hoped that this will bring us to a fuller understanding of the birth and the growth of the Latter-day Saint movement.

2. Out of the Ground a Voice Speaks

The Book of Mormon *in Its Nineteenth-Century Religious Context*

> And now Abinadi saith unto them, I would that ye should understand that God himself shall come down among the children of men, and shall redeem his people; and because he dwelleth in flesh, he shall be called the Son of God: and having subjected the flesh to the will of the Father, being the Father and the Son; the Father, because he was conceived by the power of God; and the Son, because of the flesh; thus becoming the Father and the Son: and they are one God, yea, the very Eternal Father of Heaven and of Earth; and thus the flesh becoming subject to the Spirit, or the Son to the Father, being one God, suffereth temptation, and yieldeth not to temptation, but suffereth himself to be mocked, and scourged, and cast out, and disowned by his people.
>
> *The Book of Mormon*, 1830

For the early Latter-day Saints, the *Book of Mormon* was their chief missionary tool carried to a doubting world in the age of reason. Since its first publication in 1830, many things have been written regarding its origin. The Church's official position on the book's origin is found in the canonical work entitled *The Pearl of Great Price*. In the section "History of Joseph Smith," Joseph Smith describes how God appeared to him as a young boy in response to a prayer for guidance. A subsequent visit by an angel named Moroni directed the young Smith to a set of golden plates which had been buried underground for several centuries. These plates, it is claimed, were the basis from which Smith translated the *Book of Mormon*.

In an 1842 letter to *Chicago Democrat* editor John Wentworth, Joseph Smith briefly described the contents of the *Book of Mormon*, and how he had acquired the book.¹ Smith stated that the golden plates were divided into two sets which he referred to as the larger and smaller Plates of Nephi.² The smaller plates of Nephi were inscribed by nine authors, among which Nephi and Jacob, both pre–Columbian American prophets, are the major writers. The larger plates are an abridgment of the writings of Nephi, completed by another ancient prophet, Mormon the father of Moroni, and Moroni's abridgment of the Jaredite record. Moroni was the last of the Nephites, a people that inhabited pre–Columbian America. The Nephites, along with the Jaredites, Mulekites, and Lamanites were descendants of peoples who had migrated to the American continent from the ancient Near East.

From the Mormon perspective the *Book of Mormon* documents the history of the inhabitants of pre–Columbian America. Arriving in three successive migrations, and landing in various parts of North and Central America, these pre–Columbian immigrants soon spread out over the entire western hemisphere. The first migration, under their leader Jared, left the ancient Near East at the time of the tower of Babel. Under the prophet Lehi a second group had left the Near East during Nebuchadnezzar's invasion of Palestine, around 650 B.C.E. The last migration, under Mulek son of King Zedekiah of Judea, left the Near East around 600 B.C.E. In time, the descendants of these inhabitants populated the land, built cities, and achieved a high degree of civilization.

The *Book of Mormon* tells us that over time and through several wars the people were eventually separated into two remaining groups, the Nephites and the Lamanites. The Lamanites, as a result of their disobedience to God, became dark skinned. The Lamanites were considered to be the ancestors of the Amerindian nations. The Nephites remained obedient to God, and therefore remained white. Eventually the Nephites and the Lamanites clashed in a final battle that resulted in the annihilation of the Nephites.

The history of the ancient American continent was compiled and inscribed on golden plates and buried in upstate New York, only miles from the Smith family farm at a place called the Hill Cumorah. It was from this hill that Joseph Smith retrieved the buried record of ancient America. On September 22, 1827, under the direction from the resurrected Moroni, the last of the Nephites, Joseph Smith retrieved the golden plates and began to translate what was to be published as the *Book of Mormon*.

The origin of the *Book of Mormon* has provided interest for its detractors since its first publication. The uniqueness of the work is that it attempts to explain prominent questions of the day within an absolutist framework, the origin of the Amerindians being one of them. The disappearance of the Hopewell cultures, or the Mound Builders, had left many questions unanswered in the minds of 19th-century America. The exploration of the Hopewell burial mounds and their archaeological remains left many questions still to be answered. Popular culture had also been introduced to the findings of Alexander von Humboldt on his explorations in the Americas. While perhaps not the central topic of debate in the early 19th century, Amerindian origins certainly were discussed to some degree. In this light then the *Book of Mormon* can be seen as an attempt to answer the question of the origin of the Amerindians, specifically the Hopewell culture.

Yet the *Book of Mormon*, while not being a scholarly or scientific treatment, presented itself as the definitive answer on a host of topics. The authority for the work did not rest on the careful gathering of evidences and an interpretation of that evidence. Rather, the authority for its premises and conclusions rested on the foundation that the book was of divine origin and that Joseph Smith had been chosen to reveal its long hidden truths. As a result of this the work became a focus point for many spiritual searchers, and scientific researchers. As attention was drawn away from the central questions of the day it became focused on a work that claimed to answer those questions. Secret societies, responsible government, individual freedom, anti-intellectualism, romanticism, as well as numerous theological topics prevalent in early 19th-century America were all addressed in the *Book of Mormon*. It becomes plain to see then that the work would be significant to all of America, not only those involved in a search for truth. Its claims could not go unanswered, the book had to be addressed. The starting point for those who sought to address its context began with its origin.

Early 19th-century explanations for the origin of the *Book of Mormon* and the formation of the Church of Christ[3] would be provided by clergymen, newspaper editors, neighbors of the Smiths, and apostate Mormons. The largest of these early anti–Mormon works was compiled by apostate Mormon Philastus Hurlburt. When Hurlburt failed to secure a publisher for his work, the collection was published by E. D. Howe. Howe's *Mormonism Unvailed*[4] provided a base for all future anti–Mormon writings. Howe's work included a collection of affidavits from several individuals familiar with the Smith family. The work also includes early Mormon apostate Ezra Booth's letters to the *Ohio Star*. Booth's letters to the *Star* are generally regarded as the earliest writings directed against the Church by a former member. The general argument made by Howe's work was that the *Book of Mormon* was a product of the 19th century.

Howe maintained that the *Book of Mormon* was a collection of various stories that were circulating, in oral and printed form, during the early 19th century. Howe points specifically to Ethan Smith's *View of the Hebrews*[5] and an unpublished romantic novel by Solomon Spalding titled *The Manuscript*

Story as possible foundational texts for the *Book of Mormon*. Ethan Smith had published his work in 1825. In brief Ethan Smith's *View of the Hebrews* was an account of how the Ten Lost Tribes of Israel had migrated to America. In response to the second part of the Howe thesis, how did Joseph Smith gain access to an unpublished Spalding manuscript? It has been speculated that Sidney Rigdon on a trip to Philadelphia had acquired the manuscript and it had been used by Smith and Rigdon in writing the *Book of Mormon*. The Spalding theory became the dominant theory regarding *Book of Mormon* origins for most of the 19th century. The theory is still widely held today and is disseminated by many anti–Mormon groups.[6]

In the early 20th century, Latter-day Saint apologist B. H. Roberts also entertained the idea that Joseph Smith had it within his capabilities to produce the *Book of Mormon*.[7] Roberts' manuscripts contained a detailed account of the parallels between the *Book of Mormon* and several of its contemporary works dealing with Amerindian origins.[8] Roberts' works, compiled between 1922 and 1927, were expansions of his earlier apologetical work on the *Book of Mormon*, the three-volume set *New Witnesses for God*.

One of the most insightful explanations regarding the origins of the *Book of Mormon* comes from Disciples of Christ founder Alexander Campbell. Campbell, in his *Millennial Harbinger*, stated that the *Book of Mormon* contained:

> every error and almost every truth discussed in New York for the past ten years. [It] decides all the great controversies; infant Baptism, ordination, the Trinity, regeneration, repentance, justification, the fall of man, the atonement, transubstantiation, fasting, penance, church government, religious experience, the call of the ministry, the general resurrection, eternal punishment, who may baptize and even the question of Free Masonry, Republican government, and the rights of man.[9]

Interaction between the early Campbellites, or the Disciples of Christ, and the Mormons was extensive. The *ordo salutis* of Campbell and Smith are identical. Both groups believed that faith, repentance, baptism, and the laying on of hands for the reception of the Holy Ghost were important parts of the Gospel.[10] Campbell lost one of his finest ministers in the Western Reserve area of Ohio to the infant Latter day Saint Church in Sidney Rigdon.[11] Several other early Mormon leaders, like Parley Parker Pratt, also came from Campbell's churches.[12] The influx from other churches to early Mormonism was broad. Ezra Booth and John Taylor were Methodist preachers.[13] Orson Spenser had been a Baptist minister.[14] The large

Whitmer family, which figured prominently in early Mormonism, were of Pennsylvania German background and had belonged to the German Reformed church.[15]

Many other converts had been members of New England primitivist movements.[16] In any society when social upheaval occurs, people begin to search for answers. Converts to early Mormonism were religious seekers. They were first and foremost believers who had passed through other churches, they were not from the rolls of the unchurched, or unbelievers.[17] In turn, the *Book of Mormon* was the new convert's first introduction to the thought and to the practices of the Latter-day Saints.[18]

Alexander Campbell's comment on the *Book of Mormon* provides us with a great insight into early 19th-century American religion. It gives us a solid understanding of the *Book of Mormon* in its historical matrix. The 1830 edition of the *Book of Mormon* is a reflection of Joseph Smith's, and therefore the Mormons', earliest theological convictions. These convictions revolved around a single tenet, faith in the age of reason. Frederick J. Voros, and Thomas Alexander, contend that Smith's theological heritage was rooted in a strong biblical literalist tradition.[19] Philip Barlow as well[20] strongly argues that Joseph Smith's early theological convictions were rooted in biblical literalism. By comparing the Prophet's quotations taken from the biblical text to those taken from the *Book of Mormon*, Barlow indicates that the use of the Bible, as texts for sermons and doctrinal exposition, outweighs the *Book of Mormon* quotes significantly. One can agree with Barlow's conclusion in principle, that Smith used *Book of Mormon* material sparingly, and that Smith's theological convictions were rooted in the biblical literalism of the day. The almost complete absence of *Book of Mormon* quotations in Smith's sermons would not however be centered, as Barlow contends, on Smith's preference for the biblical text. Could not this absence be accounted for by stating that the *Book of Mormon* contains no theological material not already present in the biblical text? If we accept the text of the *Book of Mormon* as a valid historical text the differences between the biblical text and the *Book of Mormon* become not theological, but rather historical and geographical. The relationship between the Bible and the *Book of Mormon* would be similar to a comparison between the Koran and the Bible and not vastly different, such as a comparison between the Bible and the Vedas.

As well, if we view the work as a product of the 19th century then it would be limited in its scope with regard to the topics of controversy or concern that it would address. The biblical text was compiled over at least 2,000 years giving it a broader scope with which to address specific and immediate concerns and controversies within a historical reoccurrence paradigm. Once questions specific to early 19th century were addressed adequately, either by the work or by an external source, then the work becomes obsolete until those specific concerns occur once again.

Whitney Cross as well pointed out that the earliest theological convictions of the Prophet Joseph Smith were both evangelical and revivalist.[21] This connection is more likely the result of the influence left by the Second Great Awakening, which swept through the northeastern United States in the early part of the last century, than of any conscious effort on Smith's part. While Smith, like his father, never formally belonged to a church, he had made overtures to join the Methodists. Members of the Smith family—his mother Lucy as well as sister Sophronia and brothers William, Hyrum, and Alvin—had belonged to the Methodist and Presbyterian churches. After the Church of Christ was organized on April 6, 1830, in Fayetteville, New York, the entire Smith family converted to Mormonism.[22]

An extremely cynical approach to Mormon origins is Fawn Brodie's *No Man Knows My History: The Life of Joseph Smith the Mormon Prophet*. Brodie argues that Smith constructed the religious dimensions of Mormonism as an attempt to secure riches. She goes on to say that only with the passage of time did Smith begin to take himself seriously as a religious leader.[23] While one could agree with Brodie's premise that Smith became more aware of his prophetic calling over time, this change was a result of external events causing him to interpret his life within a larger historical framework rather than any self-directed change of conscience on his part. This point can be seen by comparing Smith's early writings and sermons with those of his later life. Brodie's assertion that Smith consciously sought to defraud individuals and found religious fraud to be the best method of attaining his goal cannot be supported by the evidence.[24]

The Restoration of Plain and Precious Truths

Since it was first made available to the public in March of 1830, the *Book of Mormon* has gone through several revisions. Anti-Mormon writers Jerald and Sandra Tanner cite that over 3,900 changes have been made to the *Book of Mormon* between 1830 and the present.[25] The majority of these changes have been to correct grammatical and spelling mistakes. However, several key doctrinal points were either removed or revised during that same time period. The revisions seem also to have been an attempt to deal with the changing theology over the years. Early Mormon thought, as reflected in the *Book of Mormon*, is strictly monotheistic. Mormon writer Milton Backman has alluded to the fact that *Book of Mormon* Christology has a certain similarity to the Christology of Unitarian William Ellery Channing.[26]

William Ellery Channing had delivered the sermon "Unitarian Christianity" in Baltimore in 1819. In it Channing would outline what would become the central creed of Unitarianism. Channing's foremost principle was the use of reason as the central force to discern all phenomena, spiritual and natural. Channing saw the divine as one being, person and mind, and not as a divine society of agents performing different functions. As well, Channing dismissed the concept of Christ as having a dual nature. Rather, he saw Christ as a distinct person from God, an angelic being more divine than human, but a man nevertheless. In his "Likeness of God" (1828) Channing presented his views on Christian humanism. Channing believed in human perfectibility. Yet not in the same sense that Ralph Waldo Emerson spoke of, or in the sense that would become part of Mormon thought in the 1840s. Instead Channing saw a close connection between the nature of the divine and human nature. He saw in man the capability to develop, to become all that he was capable of becoming, a divine human but never a God. In his view of man the preoccupation with total depravity, sin, corruption, and misery which characterized Calvinistic Christianity had to be rejected. Channing spoke of the great inner conflict as not being between God and the devil but rather the struggle between mankind's lower and higher nature. This conflict arose as one progressed from the lower to the higher nature. He defined his central tenet of faith as God willing to perfect the human soul.[27]

While Backman may be correct in noting a similarity between the Christology of William Ellery Channing and modern Mormon Christology, Channing's thought bears little to no resemblance to early Mormon Christology. Nowhere within the pages of the *Book of Mormon* can one find the concept of human perfectibility, or that the Christ was not divine. In fact, early Mormon Christology appears to counter the Channing argument by maintaining that Jesus and the Father were the same person, not distinct individuals.

In contrast to Channing the thought of Ralph Waldo Emerson[28] and the Transcendentalists took the concept of the human perfectibility to newer heights. In several of Emerson's works the concepts of the human perfectibility and the divinity of man begin to emerge.[29]

Emerson's thought began to emerge after his resignation from the Second Church of Boston. In works such as *Nature, An American Scholar, Self Reliance*, and *The Over Soul*, Emerson would proclaim that in his core essence and nature man is divine. Holding to an all-permeating concept of the divine, Emerson saw a pantheistic universal soul contained in all things. This kernel of the divine resided in the very soul of humankind. It would emerge if allowed to but only through confident self-awareness and a following of its leadings. The divine in man would express itself in creativity and through intuitive action. With the divine in each person as the guide for moral and ethical action, each person had an infallible guide. Through following the intuitive leadings, the divine would be able to act through each person and therefore the world.[30]

Yet *Book of Mormon* thought, primarily its Christology, is substantially different from other early 19th-century theologies and thought streams. Other Christologies of the early 19th century, such as Channing's, sought to remove the substance of divinity from all other persons except the Father. The Transcendentalists saw the divine in man. Ironically it would be this concept of the divine in man that came to characterize later Mormon thought. Yet early Mormonism did not find either Unitarian or Transcendentalist thought to be a suitable option. Rather, Mormonism, in order to maintain the divinity of Jesus, confounded the three persons of the Christian Trinity, that same Trinity which Channing called a vulgar tritheism. Even with taking this alternative course of action, Mormonism did not do so consistently. Mormonism follows none of the historical Christological models with which we are familiar on a consistent basis. Early Mormonism is neither consistently tritheistic or modalistic. Neither is early Mormon thought consistently Sabellian[31] or Noetic.[32] Rather, *Book of Mormon* thought maintains a unique Christological position. The work contains pieces and portions of many historic Christological and Trinitarian interpretations, both heterodox and orthodox.[33]

Perhaps the best description of *Book of Mormon* thought is that it is a layman's Trinitarianism. *Book of Mormon* thought can best be explained as a simplistic interpretation of the godhead void of philosophical or theological terms. The thought of the *Book of Mormon* is a solid attempt to explain the complex problem of how three individuals can be called God (within the construct that there exists only one God). In this attempt it is neither consistent nor adequate in addressing the problem it hopes to solve.

Defining Mormon thought, based upon textual evidence, is difficult. No clear or consistent thought exists in the 1830 *Book of Mormon*. What is apparent is that early Mormons were reacting against a heavily intellectualized and theologized Trinitarian concept of God.

In many people's eyes the philosophical language of the Nicene formula was difficult to grasp. The thought expressed in the *Book of Mormon* then can be seen as a reaction to Trinitarianism. The reaction is expressed in both modalistic and Patripassian terms.

Early Mormons employed rational arguments to defend their beliefs. Yet Jacksonian American rationalism had become common sense rationalism. Joseph Smith would later use this common sense approach to defend his plurality of Gods theology in 1844.[34]

Mormonism fits well into the Jacksonian ideal of the common man.[35] Through the revolution political ties had been severed with the continent. Yet ideological ties still remained intact. The ideology of 18th-century American culture was still rooted in the old world thinking of a privileged class and government control of the economy. With the defeat in 1828 of John Q. Adams by Andrew Jackson, a new age of individualism would emerge as the dominant ideology in American culture. Seeing themselves as self-made individuals rather than collaborators in the maintenance of the paternalistic privileged class, Jacksonians contributed to the transformation of American culture. Gone were the old rules of the privileged, the rules of the American aristocracy. Old notions, old institutions, and economic monopolies, all would make way for individual choice, and self-regulating laissez-faire economics. In this era of the death and rebirth of institutions, individual freedom loosened from the bonds of state, economy and family came to be glorified. The concept of a favored elect of God, rooted deep in American culture, yielded to a notion of individualism regulated only by a person's will.

By rejecting what they perceived as undue speculation and theologizing on the part of the established clerics, early Mormons defined God in terms that all, including those who lacked formal education, would understand.[36] The concept of the restoration, in Mormon terms, meant that the time had come for God to speak directly to his people, with signs and wonders following. This God had done, through Joseph Smith, and the *Book of Mormon.*

No longer were the mysteries of the nature and power of God the special domain of the Christian church's clergy.[37] The mysteries of the kingdom of God were now available to everyone. The move towards a personal experience of the power of God, and away from rationalism, can be seen in the Methodists, and through the teachings of the Presbyterian revivalist Charles Finney.[38]

The early Mormons grappled with the same questions that the church fathers had sought to answer in the ecumenical councils between Nicea and Chalcedon. The early church answered these questions with a Trinitarian Christology. The Mormons in turn chose an alternative, a strict monotheistic position, and interpreted the divine as one person with varying modes.

Yet what had originally began as a modalistic expression of the divine eventually would develop into tritheism. Over time, the roles of the Father and the Son would become distinct from each other. If we take 1830 as our starting point, the farther we move away from that date, the less the newer revelations continue to equate the Father with the Son. By 1833 we see Smith's early modalism evaporate. After May of 1833, Smith never referred to Jesus as the Father.[39] The major Mormon publications to show this shift were the 1835 *Lectures of Faith* and the 1837 revision of the *Book of Mormon*.

In a period of five years a drastic shift had developed with the Latter-day Saints conception of the divine. It proved to be problematic. While a new interpretation of the divine had emerged the central document of the Church, the *Book of Mormon* still reflected the earlier thought. A new edition of the major work was in order.

In 1837 a new edition of the *Book of Mormon* was offered to the public. Many, it can be supposed, thought the new edition was merely a reissue of the 1830 version. Perhaps as well, the typographical, spelling, and grammatical mistakes would be removed. Yet what was offered to the public in 1837 was a newly revised work. The new work, in keeping with the recently emerged Mormon concept of the divine, removed the passages that reflected the earlier modalistic position of the Church.

The 1837 edition of the *Book of Mormon* revised several passages that directly referred to the Father and the Son as modes of the same being. Yet not all of the *Book of Mormon* passages containing the earliest Mormon Christology were revised. Modern versions of the *Book of Mormon* still contain several passages showing Mormonism's earliest modalistic thought.

There is no doubt that the earliest Mormon concept of God is modalistic.[40] This strict monotheistic concept was the new converts' first introduction to Latter-day Saint thought. In the following passages we will see clearly the theological leanings of the early Latter-day Saints.

The 1830 *Book of Mormon* confuses the individuals in the godhead. This can be seen through the three main groups into which the *Book of Mormon's* Christological passages can be divided. The groups are 1) modalistic or Sabellian passages, 2) Patripassian passages, 3) traditional Christological, Trinitarian or anti-modalistic passages.

Using *Book of Mormon* history as parameters we find that there appears to be a consistent use of the various types of Christological positions. The historical setting for the first two types of Christological positions show the pre-incarnate Jesus revealing himself through visions to the inhabitants of ancient America. In these passages, no distinction is made between the Father and the Son. The setting for the third set of passages shows Jesus in a postresurrection phase, in which he appears bodily to the inhabitants of the North American continent. The third set of passages all have contextual parallels in the Christian canon. As well the third set uses the same language and imagery as that found within their parallels. These passages present the Father, Son, and Holy Ghost as distinct individuals.

Several passages in the 1837 edition of the *Book of Mormon* were revised from their 1830 counterparts. The revisions reflect the changes in

Mormon thought between 1830 and 1837. The changes show the Father and the Son as distinct individuals.

In a modalistic passage found on page 25, in 1 Nephi Chapter II,[41] Mary, the mother of Jesus, is seen as the Mother of God because she provided a physical body for God the Father. The passage reads: "Behold the virgin which thou seest, is the mother of God after the manner of flesh." In 1837, this passage was changed to read "the mother of the Son of God after the manner of flesh." Further on, Nephi adds: "behold the Lamb of God, yea even the eternal Father." In the 1837 revision, this passage was changed to read, "behold the Lamb of God, yea even the Son of the Eternal Father."[42]

The 1830 *Book of Mormon* addresses Jesus with many names that all point to the fact that He is being equated with the Father. The "Eternal God" and "the Everlasting Father" were epithets consistently used to identify Jesus. This can be seen from the following passage in 1 Nephi. In 1 Nephi Chapter III, found on page 28 of the 1830 *Book of Mormon*, the prophet Nephi, receiving a revelation from God, hears an angel say to him:

> And a great and terrible gulf divideth them; yea, even the word of the justice of the Eternal God, and Jesus Christ, which is the Lamb of God, of whom the Holy Ghost beareth record, from the beginning of the world until this time henceforth and forever.

Beginning with the 1837 edition[43] of the *Book of Mormon* this passage was revised to read:

> And a great and terrible gulf divideth them; yea, even the word of justice of the Eternal God, and the Messiah who is the Lamb of God, of whom the Holy Ghost beareth record, from the beginning of this world until this time henceforth and forever.

The *Book of Mormon's* Patripassian Christology is seen in two passages from 1 Nephi. In Chapter III, on page 26, Nephi records an angel foretelling the future passion and crucifixion of Jesus as saying:

> And I looked and beheld the Lamb of God that he was taken by the people; yea the everlasting God; who was judged of the people, and I Nephi saw that he was lifted upon the cross, and slain for the sins of the world.

In later editions, beginning with the 1837 *Book of Mormon*, this passage was revised to read "the Son of the everlasting God."[44] The revision removed the Patripassian implications from the passage. A second passage, found on page 32, reads:

> And the angel spake unto me saying: These last records which thou seest among the Gentiles, shall establish the truth of the first, which is of the twelve apostles of the Lamb, and shall make known the plain and precious things which have been taken away from them; and shall make known to all kindreds, tongues, and people, that the Lamb of God is the Eternal Father and the Saviour of the world; and they must come unto Him, or they cannot be saved; and they must come according to the words which shall be established by the mouth of the Lamb; and the words of the Lamb shall be made known in the records of thy seed, as well as the records of the twelve apostles of the Lamb; wherefore, they shall be established in one, for there is one God and one Shepherd over all the earth.

This passage, found in modern versions (which use Arabic numerals for chapters) at 1 Nephi 14:41–42, is an extremely important passage for the Latter-day Saints. The passage is seen as an ancient prophecy concerning the *Book of Mormon*. The passage appears to be Patripassian, as it claims that the "Eternal Father" is the "Saviour of the world." In 1837, "the Lamb of God is the Eternal Father and the Saviour of the world" was changed to read that "the Lamb of God is the Son of the Eternal Father and the Saviour of the world."

A modalistic trend is continued in other *Book of Mormon* passages. For instance, 2 Nephi Chapter 8, found on page 86, Nephi writes:

> For if there be no Christ, then there be no God; and if there be no God, we are not, for there could have been no creation. But there is a God, and he is Christ; and he cometh in the fullness of his own time.

In the book titled Mormon, Chapter IV, page 536 in the 1830 *Book of Mormon*, Moroni writes:

> But behold, I will shew unto you a God of miracles, even the God of Abraham and the God of Isaac, and the God of Jacob; and it is that same God which created the heavens and the earth, and all things that in them is. Behold he created Adam; and by Adam came the fall of man. And because of the fall of man, came Jesus Christ, even the Father and the Son; and because of Jesus Christ came the redemption of man.

In the Book of Ether, Moroni, who makes an abridgment of the record of the Jaredites, records a vision that the brother of Jared received from the preincarnate Jesus. The vision is found on pages 544, 546, and 547. In the vision, Jesus, who is speaking to the brother of Jared, states:[45]

> Behold, I am he which was prepared from the foundation of the world, to redeem my people. Behold I am Jesus Christ, I am the Father and the Son.

> In me shall all mankind have light, and that eternally, even they which shall believe on my name; and they shall become my sons and my daughters. And never hath I shewed myself unto man whom I have created, for never hath man believed in me as thou hast. Seest thou that ye were created in mine own image. Behold, this body, which ye now behold, is the body of my spirit; and even as I appear unto thee to be in the spirit, will I appear unto my people in the flesh.

On page 546 the text continues:

> [T]hen will I manifest unto them the things which the brother of Jared saw, even to the unfolding unto them all my revelations, saith Jesus Christ, the Son of God, the Father of the heavens and of the earth, and all things that in them is.

On page 547 Jesus again proclaims:

> I am the same that leadeth men to all good: he that will not believe my words, will not believe me, that I am; and he that will not believe me, will not believe the Father which sent me. For behold, I am the Father, I am the light, and the life, and the truth of the world.

The passages quoted above are found, unchanged, in modern editions of the *Book of Mormon* in Ether 3:14–16, 4:7, 5:12.

The general revision of the *Book of Mormon* in 1837 added the word "Son" to many passages where the Father and the Son were portrayed as the same individual. This is seen from the passages in 1 and 2 Nephi, Alma, and Mormon. The revision was not carried out consistently throughout the *Book of Mormon*. This is seen from the Ether passages that have remained unchanged. Many other modern *Book of Mormon* passages still reflect the Church's earliest modalistic theology.[46] The following modern *Book of Mormon* quotations show the early modalism quite clearly.

Passage 2 Nephi 31:21 reads: "this is the only true doctrine of the Father and of the Son and of the Holy Ghost which is one God." Mosiah 7:27 leads us to the same conclusion: "Christ was the God, the Father of all things that he should take upon him the image of man and that God should come down among the children of men; and take upon flesh and blood."

The following list of Christological passages can still be found in modern editions of the *Book of Mormon*. Modalistic, or Sabellian passages, can be found in Mosiah 3:5, 4:2, 7:27, 13:34, 16:15; Ether 4:7–12. Patripassian passages are found in Mosiah 15:1–5, Alma 11:38–41, and Ether 3:14. Anti-modalistic passages are still seen in 3 Nephi 11:6–8, 32; 15:1, 18, 19; 18:27; 26:2, 5, 15.

The evidence clearly shows that the 1830 *Book of Mormon*, and subsequently the early Mormon Church, held a modalistic, Christological position. At the same time, the *Book of Mormon* also contains passages that seem to present an anti-modalistic Christology.

The theology of the *Book of Mormon* refers to the preincarnate Jesus as: "the Father," "the Eternal God," "the everlasting God," "the Father of heaven and earth," "the Father and the Son," and "the Father of all things." When Jesus is speaking, the terms "I Am," "the light," "the truth," "the Messiah," "the Christ," and "the Lamb of God" are used. In the 1830 *Book of Mormon*, "the Son" is used only to refer to the incarnate Jesus. This appears to be the case in several passages found on page 537, in Ether Chapter 1, where Jesus Christ is called "the Son of God." Despite the selected Ether passages no clear, consistent, distinction is made between "the Father" and "the Son" within the *Book of Mormon* prior to its revision in 1837. In 1837, the term "Son" was interpolated into several texts making the Father and the Son distinct persons.

Between 1830 and 1837, Mormon thought underwent a shift from modalism, to making a distinction between the Father and the Son. Joseph Smith's introduction to the Hebrew epithets, Elohim and Jehovah, during the winter of 1835 to 1836, played an important role in this development.

Boyd Kirkland, in several articles, states that a major shift occurred in 1835 to 1836, during the Hebrew sessions of the School of the Prophets in Ohio. Kirkland maintains that from this time on, the terms Elohim and Jehovah began to appear more readily in Latter-day Saint publications when referencing Jesus and his Father. Yet, the epithets Elohim and Jehovah continued to be used interchangeably for several years after that date.[47]

Between 1830 and 1835, several revelations would continue to promote the early modalistic view of God. The revelations were originally published in official Church newspapers. Later, several of the revelations would be collected and bound into volumes and offered to the public. The major Mormon theological works having their origins in this time period were the *Book of Moses*, the *Book of Commandments*, several revelations of the *Doctrine and Covenants*, and Joseph's revision of the Bible, *Joseph Smith Translation*. These works would continue the modalistic tradition of the earlier *Book of Mormon*.

One of the most significant documents to be produced in the months following the publication of the *Book of Mormon* was the Church's statement of faith. The document is entitled "The Articles and Covenants of the Church of Christ." There exists some speculation as to the exact month in which the document was produced. The document's publication, in the Church's *Book of Commandments for the Government of the Church of Christ* in 1833, gives the date as June of 1830.[48] Lyndon W. Cook places the origin of the document several months earlier, to April of 1830.[49] The earliest publication date for the document is in 1832, in the *Evening and Morning Star*.[50] The document, reproduced below, was edited and revised prior to its inclusion in the 1835 edition of the *Doctrine and Covenants*.[51] "The Articles and Covenants" is the earliest Mormon creed.

> [F]or the Lord God hath spoken it; for we, the elders of the church, have heard and bear witness to the words of the glorious Majesty on high, to whom be glory forever and ever. Amen. Wherefore by these things we know there is a God in heaven, who is infinite and eternal, from everlasting to everlasting the same unchangeable God, the maker of heaven and earth, and all things that in them is; and that he created man, male and female, after his own image and after his own likeness created he them; And that he gave unto the children of men commandments that they should love and serve him the only being whom they should worship.... Wherefore, the Almighty God gave his only begotten Son, as it is written in those scriptures, which have been given of him, that he suffered temptations, but gave no heed to them; That he was crucified, died, and rose again the third day, and he ascended into heaven to sit down on the right hand of the Father, to reign with Almighty power according to the will of the Father. Therefore, as many would believe and were baptized in his holy name, and endured in faith to the end, should be saved; Yea, even as many as were before he came in the flesh, from the beginning, who believed in the words of the holy Prophets, who were inspired by the gift of the Holy Ghost, which truly testified of him in all things, as well as those who should come after, who should believe in the gifts and callings of God, by the Holy Ghost, which beareth record of the Father and of the Son; which Father, and Son, and Holy Ghost is one God, infinite and eternal, without end. Amen.[52]

Early critics of the Mormon Church did not concentrate on its theology. Early Apostate Ezra Booth makes no mention of the *Book of Mormon's* thought in his criticisms against the Church. Booth points to the failure of Smith's revelations, and the abuse of spiritual gifts as his chief points of contention. Early anti–Mormon literature addressed the personal character of Joseph Smith, and the Mormon's emotionalism, rather than its teachings.[53] Even Alexander Campbell, in his critique of the *Book of Mormon* in 1831, did not level charges against the modalism of the work. He concluded that the work sought to resolve contemporary theological and social problems, including Trinitarianism. Major doctrinal arguments against Mormonism, by members of the mainline churches, appear to have been a phenomenon of the 1840s and later, rather than the 1830s.

This is not to imply that the *Book of Mormon* was not singled out for its modalism by critics. Opposition to the Mormon Church in the 1830s used varying approaches. Mainline, non-experiential movements concentrated on the Mormon's emotionalism. Experience oriented movements, like the Methodists, appear to have concentrated on doctrinal issues. Lucy Mack Smith, the Prophet's mother, recalls an incident where she was berated by Methodists for her beliefs.[54] Dan Vogel, as well, cites a series of letters that were exchanged between Oliver Barr, of the Christian Connection, and Mormon Elder Stephen Post. The exchange of letters appeared in the *Christian Palladium* in January and August of 1838.[55] Judging from his polemical arguments, Barr must have drawn his data from an 1830 *Book of Mormon*.

The Earliest Mormon Concept of the Restoration

The *Book of Mormon* taught nothing substantially different, theologically, than many other groups in early 19th-century Christianity. It did, however, emphasize certain additional aspects in its proselytizing message.

Given the social and religious backgrounds from which the Latter-day Saint movement rose, it is not surprising to find a modalistic tendency in early Mormonism. Current with the introduction of the *Book of Mormon*, American thought and culture was undergoing drastic changes. It was in a time of the new order when rugged individualism and access to equal opportunity made each person responsible for this life and the life to come. William Ellery Channing had delivered his inaugural address at the First Church of Boston proclaiming the perfectibility of man; Ralph Waldo Emerson and Theodore Parker had announced the divine within man; David Millard was engaging in theological debates with Trinitarians in New York, and the Campbellite and Christian Connection movements had rejected the historic Christological interpretations. As well, Charles Finney spoke of the individual's response to the call of God and of the religion of the heart. Many options existed, it was the dawn of a new age, freedom of choice coupled with the responsibility for that choice. When countless options presented themselves, how is one to know which option is correct? It was precisely in answer to the questions that plagued early 19th-century Americans that the *Book of Mormon* proved to be such a timely work.

The *Book of Mormon*, a revelation from God, presented itself as the definitive work on the nature of God and the role of man to early 19th-century Americans. The message found in its pages was the message of the restoration of precious truths removed from the world by the establishment, the evil clerics. In a new order that concentrated on the free choices of an individual in the temporal realm, and with the old order's paternalistic guidance no longer of any value in the temporal, or spiritual realm, the message of the *Book of Mormon* restored faith to the individual in something beyond themselves. Institutions had fallen and with them the interpreters of reality. All of this had created an age of social upheaval and for individuals this meant a dissociation from a world that they had come to know. The age called for a reinterpretation of an individual's value system and a creation of a new worldview. Some would be able to adjust making the transition smoothly and capitalizing on the newly emerging world of opportunity. Others would need a little shove, or some form of guidance from beyond. For many this guidance from beyond took the shape of a simple message. The message proclaimed first and foremost that there was a God, and that God had not abandoned creation. It also would proclaim that this God had chosen to reveal himself once again, and speak to creation once again. To creation, God would proclaim that there existed only one God, and that Jesus was God the Father. In the words of the *Book of Mormon*:

> And the angel spake unto me saying: These last records which thou seest among the Gentiles, shall establish the truth of the first, which is of the twelve apostles of the Lamb, and shall make known the plain and precious things which have been taken away from them; and shall make known to all kindreds, tongues, and people, that the Lamb of God is the Eternal Father and the Saviour of the world; and they must come unto Him, or they cannot be saved; and they must come according to the words which shall be established by the mouth of the Lamb; and the words of the Lamb shall be made known in the records of thy seed, as well as the records of the twelve apostles of the Lamb; wherefore, they shall be established in one, for there is one God and one Shepherd over all the earth.[56]

The restored message of the early Mormons proclaimed that God had not changed, God was still the God of miracles:

> But behold, I will shew unto you a God of miracles, even the God of Abraham and the God of Isaac, and the God of Jacob; and it is that same God which created the heavens and the earth, and all things that in them is. Behold he created Adam; and by Adam came the fall of man. And because of the fall of man, came Jesus Christ, even the Father and the Son; and because of Jesus Christ came the redemption of man ... O all ye have imagined up unto yourselves a god which can do no miracles, I would ask of you, have all these things past, of which I have spoken? Has the end come yet? Behold, I say unto you, Nay; and God has not ceased to be a God of miracles. Behold, are not the things that God hath wrought, marvelous in your eyes? yea, and who can comprehend the marvelous works of God? Who shall say that it was not a miracle, that by the power of his word the heaven and the earth should be; and by the power of his word, man was created of the dust of the earth; and by the power of his word, hath miracles been wrought. And who shall say that Jesus Christ did not do many mighty miracles? And there was [sic] many

mighty miracles wrought by the hands of the apostles. And if there was miracles wrought, then why has God ceased to be a God of miracles, and yet be an unchangeable being. And behold I say unto you. He changeth not: if so, he would cease to be God; and he ceaseth not to be God, and is a God of miracles. And the reason why he ceaseth to do miracles among the children of men, is because they dwindle in unbelief, and depart from the right way, and know not the God in whom they should trust.... For behold, thus saith Jesus Christ, the Son of God,... These signs shall follow them that believe: In my name shall they cast out devils; they shall speak with new tongues; they shall take up serpents; and if they drink any deadly thing, it shall not hurt them; they shall lay hands upon the sick, and they shall recover; and whosoever shall believe in my name, doubting nothing, unto him will I confirm all my words, even unto the ends of the earth. And now behold, who can stand against the works of the Lord.[57]

The message presented to the American people by the Mormon elders in 1830 was the message that the age of miracles had not ended with the death of the apostles in the first century. The *Book of Mormon* was clear, to those that believed, signs and wonders would follow. Converts to early Mormonism were drawn by the promises of the book, as was Ezra Booth who joined after witnessing a healing.[58] The earliest Mormon concept of the restoration was not the concept of the restoration commonly perceived by 20th-century Latter-day Saints; the restoration of new doctrines, and of the New Testament Church structure. The concept of the restoration, presented in the *Book of Mormon*, was that God was alive and was speaking again in the age of reason. Miracles, tongues, and reported healings were evidences to the early Mormon Church that God was once again among God's people.[59] In an age that was dependent on free choice and strong individualism, it proved to be a powerful message for those that were forced into the realities of the new age.

It was not that the *Book of Mormon* taught new truths about God which drew the early converts. Rather, the *Book of Mormon* presented a God who was active in the world. The God revealed through early Mormonism was a God who was more concerned with practicing what was believed, than with theorizing about what is to be believed.

The concentration on practice, instead of belief, has forced the Church to make several attempts at harmonizing their past leaders' doctrinal statements with those introduced in more recent periods. The revision of the *Book of Mormon* is such a case in point. The early, modalistic *Book of Mormon* passages presented problems for Church leaders in the 20th century. In 1916, the Church issued a doctrinal statement which attempted to reconcile contradictory *Book of Mormon* passages with current doctrinal views.[60] The doctrinal statement, written by James E. Talmage, attempted to explain how Jesus could be called the Father. Talmage took the contradictory theological statements of the *Book of Mormon* and reinterpreted them in light of the current doctrinal understanding. By doing this, Talmage gave the impression that Mormonism had never held a modalistic position.

Several explanations can account for this reinterpretation. A mechanism is present within Mormonism that would allow for changes to be implemented without need of an explanation, the ninth *Article of Faith*.

It seems likely that a stronger, and much older, hermeneutic tradition overrides the Church's ninth *Article of Faith*.[61] This hermeneutic is seen in the early Latter-day Saint belief that the entire Gospel is as old as Adam, and was known throughout history by select persons.[62]

As has been pointed out, earliest Mormonism taught nothing substantially different from the rest of mainstream Christianity. In turn then, the Church's claim to being the restored Church of Christ was not centered on its doctrinal claims, or in having additional knowledge of the nature of God. Neither can the claim to being the restored Church of Christ be found in the early Mormon Church's structure. The Church's concept of the restoration was a reaction to the social and religious environment from which it emerged.

The claim to being the restored Church of Christ for the early Mormons meant that the Bible could be believed, and that the *Book of Mormon* validated the truths of the Bible. The truths that the early Mormons claimed to possess were: that there was only one God, that Jesus was that God, and that God was still a God who took an active role in and through creation. The message of the restoration was a simple message. This simple message would proclaim that God was still able to act in the world in the age of reason and rugged individualism.

3. Knowing the Only True God

The Revelations of Moses, the Joseph Smith Translation, and the Rewriting of Genesis

> [F]or the Lord God hath spoken it; for we, the elders of the church, have heard and bear witness to the words of the glorious Majesty on high, to whom be glory forever and ever. Amen. Wherefore by these things we know there is a God in heaven, who is infinite and eternal, from everlasting to everlasting the same unchangeable God, the maker of heaven and earth, and all things that in them is; ... the only being whom they should worship.... Wherefore, the Almighty God gave his only begotten Son, as it is written in those scriptures, which have been given of him, that he suffered temptations, but gave no heed to them; That he was crucified, died, and rose again the third day, and he ascended into heaven to sit down on the right hand of the Father, to reign with Almighty power according to the will of the Father. Therefore, as many would believe and were baptized in his holy name, and endured in faith to the end, should be saved; Yea, even as many as were before he came in the flesh, from the beginning, who believed in the words of the holy Prophets, who were inspired by the gift of the Holy Ghost, which truly testified of him in all things, as well as those who should come after, who should believe in the gifts and callings of God, by the Holy Ghost, which beareth record of the Father and of the Son; which Father, and Son, and Holy Ghost is one God, infinite and eternal, without end. Amen.
> "Articles and Covenants of the Church of Christ," 1830[1]

Between the months of June and December of 1830, Joseph Smith claimed to have received a series of revelations from God. These revelations, originally given to Moses, would later be compiled into a single text known as the *Book of Moses*. In 1851 the majority of these revelations were published, collectively, in the first edition of *The Pearl of Great Price*.[2] At the General Church Conference, of October 10, 1880, Second Counselor Joseph F. Smith moved that the writings contained in *The Pearl of Great Price* be added to the Church's canon.[3]

The series of revelations are authentic expressions of early Mormon thought given their provenance in the history of the Church. Only two major theological documents predate the revelations of Moses. These are the *Book of Mormon*, published in 1830, and the "Articles and Covenants of the Church of Christ," written in April of 1830. The "Articles and Covenants" were first published in the first edition of the *Evening and Morning Star* in June of 1832.

The press of the *Evening and Morning Star* was the first printing press established by the Mormons. The press was established in Independence, Missouri, in early 1832, and in February of 1832 a prospectus was issued for the new paper. The press served as the official publisher of Mormon literature until its destruction on July 20, 1833.[4] No press existed in Kirtland prior to December of 1833, when the *Evening and Morning Star* resumed publishing, after the return of the Mormons from Missouri. The press of the *Evening and Morning Star*, on which *A Book of Commandments* was being printed, was destroyed in July of 1833 along with many of the extant copies of *A Book of Commandments*. This was the first collection of the revelations given through Joseph Smith. The majority of these revelations were first published in the *Evening and Morning Star* and later were included in the first edition of the *Doctrine and Covenants* in 1835.

With the establishment of the printing press in Missouri in 1832, the Mormons began a long tradition of publishing their own works. In the case of the "Articles and Covenants," and the *Book of Moses*, we may assume that the content of the materials were known by members within the church at least two years prior to their official publication dates. The Church at this early date, 1830, would have been relatively small, comprising less than 200 people. The contents of the two documents contain nothing that the members would have found to be controversial. The two documents represent streams of thought that were already taught by the *Book of Mormon*, which would have been considered the primary source document of the early Mormon belief system.

The Rewriting of Genesis

The revelations of Moses[5] appear early in Mormon literary history. The first published accounts of the revelations appear shortly after the publication of the Church's statement of faith. The writings of Moses would also predate the majority of revelations contained in the *Book of Commandments* and the *Doctrine and Covenants*.

The 1851 *Pearl of Great Price* is the first complete publication of the revelations given to Joseph Smith in the early 1830s. Various sections of the revelations had been published in the Church's periodicals before 1851. The *Evening and Morning Star* in 1832 to 1833 and the *Times and Seasons* in 1844 carried parts of the revelations. As well, in 1853 the *Latter-day Saints Millennial Star* would also publish parts of the revelations.

The earliest of these published sections was "The Prophecy of Enoch," which first appeared in the *Evening and Morning Star*, in August of 1832.[6] This section is now Moses 6:1–42; 7:1–69. Moses Chapter 6:43–68, or "A Revelation of the Gospel to Adam," appeared in March of 1833.[7] Parts of the "Revelation to Moses Concerning This Heaven and This Earth" (Moses 5:1–16), along with the "History of Noah" (Moses 8:1–30), were published in April of 1833.[8] The remainder of the "Revelation to Moses Concerning This Heaven and This Earth" (Moses 2:1–5:17–59) was not contained in the 1851 edition of *The Pearl of Great Price*. The complete revelation was first published in the *Latter-day Saints Millennial Star* in 1853.[9] The final section, "The Visions of Moses," now Moses 1:1–42, first appeared in the *Times and Seasons* in January of 1844.[10]

The *Book of Moses* contains several theological and cosmological concepts. Our primary focus in this investigation is with the *Book of Moses'* view of the nature of God. If we review the earliest Mormon creation account, as recorded in the present passage of Moses 2:1–5, 29,[11] we see that the text follows very closely the *Authorized Version* of the Bible, with only a few minor changes. The text is as follows.

> 1. And it came to pass that the Lord spake unto Moses saying; Behold, I reveal unto you concerning this heaven and this earth; write the words which I speak. I am the Beginning and the End, The Almighty God; by mine only begotten I created these things; Yea in the Beginning I created the heaven and the earth upon which thou standest.
> 2. And the earth was without form, and void; and I caused darkness to come upon the face of the deep; and my Spirit moved upon the face of the water; for I am God.
> 3. And I, God, said; Let there be light; and there was light.
> 4. And I, God, saw the light and that light was good. And I, God, called the light Day; and the darkness, I called Night; and this I did by the word of my power, and it was done as I spake; and the evening and the morning were the first day. —*Moses 2:1–4*

While the text closely follows the *Authorized Version*, there appears to be a conscious attempt to flesh out ambiguous parts of the biblical text.

The above passage attempts to show that God, the Father, is the sole agent in creation. In an attempt to clarify the ambiguous passages of the creation text of Genesis, the personal pronoun I is added. A plausible explanation for this is that Smith saw the *Authorized Version* of the biblical text as being ambiguous in its reference to the nature of God. This makes perfect sense given that the earliest Mormon literary work, the *Book of Mormon*, had explicitly portrayed the Father and the Son as identical persons.

The *Book of Moses* also includes minor references to other individuals being present at creation. This point may be difficult to reconcile given that in other period documents, like the *Book of Mormon*, Jesus is the physical manifestation of the Father. One should not see this as support for a nascent plurality of Gods concept. Given the contents of the majority of period documents, Mormonism in this early period was still strictly modalistic. The reference to the "only begotten" and "the beginning and the end" as active agents in creation with the Father in the *Book of Moses* passage can be seen as a Christian interpolation by Smith. It must be kept in mind that Smith in this early period of Mormon history was still closely linked to the textual heritage of his age. The *Book of Mormon*, as we have seen, clearly sought to answer questions of the day. It was not intended in any way to supersede the historical biblical text but rather its common 19th-century interpretation. It was an attempt to apply common sense and reason to historical theology and to reinterpret the theology in terms of the common man.

There exists no doubt that early Mormon theological documents were modalistic. The *Book of Moses* is no exception. While the revelations of Moses continued to be published separately, they remained an unconnected group of theological curiosities. With their collective publication in 1851, and their canonization in 1880, they became literary expressions of a theology that had existed in the Church's formative years. The contribution of the *Book of Moses* to Mormon thought is not its concept of the nature of God. Its place as an important theological document is the result of two additional concepts that have roots in the work.

The first of the two concepts, that the Gospel was taught to Adam, is of primary importance to any understanding of the history and development of Mormon structure and belief. The concept forms the primary hermeneutic to which all future concepts are related. The syllogy of the hermeneutic runs like this. If the Gospel is as old as Adam, then any new revelation is merely a reintroduction of something that had been removed over the centuries. This then allows for an open system by which new concepts can be introduced without any correlation to any previous thought stream.

The second concept is the existence of inhabitable worlds. While the concept of inhabitable worlds was introduced into Mormon thought at a very early time, it remained a dormant stream of thought. It would not be until the 1840s that this concept would gain any significance, and then only with regards to its wedding to the concept of a plurality of Gods.

The *Book of Moses* also makes a distinction between the two creation accounts of Genesis. The work states that the two narratives are accounts of the creation of this earth and this heaven, first in a spiritual and then in a physical form. This may be an attempt to harmonize the Elohist and Yahwist creation narratives of Genesis.

While the *Book of Moses* forms part of the Church's canon, its impact on Mormon doctrinal development is minute. There exist documents from the same time period that had a greater impact on Mormon theology. The *Joseph Smith Translation*, while never published during Smith's lifetime or made part of the Mormon canon, appears to have made a greater contribution to Mormon doctrinal development.

The Joseph Smith Translation

During the Saints' tenure in Ohio two significant theological works would be added to the growing body of Mormon theological literature: the *Joseph Smith Translation* (or the *Inspired Version* of the Bible) and the *Lectures of Faith*. The *Joseph Smith Translation* was never published during the life of the Prophet. The *Lectures*, in turn, became part of the *Doctrine and Covenants* in 1835, and remained part of that work until 1921. During the life of the Prophet excerpts of the Bible translation were published in various Church periodicals.[12] The Utah Church has also included brief annotated references to the work in its current editions of the Bible.

The *Joseph Smith Translation* was first published in 1866, by the Reorganized Church of Jesus Christ of Latter Day Saints, headquartered in Independence, Missouri. At that time, the publishers did not have in their possession the entire original manuscript.[13] The *Joseph Smith Translation* has been accepted as authoritative by the Reorganized Church of Jesus Christ of Latter Day Saints since 1878.[14] The text for the *Joseph Smith Translation* was taken from the original manuscript prepared by the Prophet, which currently is in the possession of the Reorganized Church. The *Joseph Smith Translation* also contains the *Book of Moses*, in its proper historical setting, by including it in the text of Genesis.[15]

In terms of chronology, the *Joseph Smith Translation* follows closely the *Book of Mormon*, and is simultaneous with the *Book of Moses*. The revision of the biblical text was an early project for the Prophet Joseph Smith. On October 8, 1829, Joseph Smith and Oliver Cowdery purchased a pulpit-sized *Authorized Version* of the Bible, with Apocrypha. Joseph Smith would use this Bible as the source text for his revision of the biblical text.

The earliest date given for the commencement of the revision is June of 1830. Joseph Smith began the revision of the biblical text with Genesis. Several key developments have their roots in this formative period in Mormon history. It would be while translating Genesis that Smith received the revelations that became the *Book of Moses*.

Joseph Smith and Oliver Cowdery continued their revision of Genesis until March 7, 1831. According to Smith, on March 7, he received specific instructions in a vision to begin translating the New Testament. Smith and Cowdery would return to complete the Old Testament at a later date. On March 9, 1831, Smith inquired of the Lord regarding the correctness of the Apocrypha. God's reply became Section 91 of the *Doctrine and Covenants*. In the revelation, the Lord told Smith that the Apocrypha was sufficiently translated in its present form.

Smith and Cowdery continued to work on the translation of the New Testament until it was completed in July of 1833. Smith had used several scribes in his translation of the biblical text. Former Campbellite preacher Sidney Rigdon appears to have been the scribe used for the majority of the textual revisions.

Smith's translation of the Bible was not a translation from the original Hebrew and Greek texts as one would suspect. Smith had no knowledge of either of the biblical languages at this time. Rather, Smith would use an alternative method to restore lost passages and clarify ambiguous ones: Smith revised the Bible through divine revelation.[16] Smith would begin translating by reading from the English text. When he came upon certain passages, the Spirit of God would lead him to make the necessary clarifications in the English text. The passages, according to Smith, had been tampered with during their transmission from the original writing of the manuscripts. Smith sought to clarify the misinterpreted and mistranslated portions of the English text. Through the spirit of inspiration, Smith would make the appropriate changes to the text. The newly revised text was then copied onto sheets of paper by the scribes Smith had at his disposal.

Originally, two methods were used to revise the text. The first method was used to translate Genesis Chapters 1–24 and the New Testament books of the Gospel of Matthew to John's Gospel Chapter 5. This method involved copying the complete passage from the Bible and then making appropriate changes to the copied text. This method soon became tedious and Smith decided to record only the changes. This second method was used for the remainder of the biblical translation, from Genesis Chapter 24 to the end of Malachi, and John 6 through to the Book of Revelation.

The entire revision of the Bible totaled 3,410 verses. The Smith revisions consist of contextual changes to the *Authorized Version* of the Bible. In keeping with Smith's original mandate to restore the teachings of primitive Christianity, the changes were necessary to restore those "plain and precious truths" that had been removed from the biblical text.[17]

A number of biblical books received little or no revision. In the Old testament a total of 1,314 changes were made. The books of Ruth, Ezra, Esther, Lamentations, Haggai, and Malachi received no revisions. The entire Song of Solomon was deleted. Of the 2,096 verses altered in the New Testament, the majority of changes were made to the Gospels. Only 2 and 3 John were not altered.

The contribution of the *Joseph Smith Translation* to Mormon theology is not as minute as one would at first believe. The changes in the text, as well as the doctrines that were introduced as a result of revising the text, are significant. It was during the early Kirtland period, particularly during the time in which the *Joseph Smith Translation* came into being, that Mormonism made its first departure from its earliest roots. Curiously lacking in this early work are the distinctive theological ideas that are characteristic of later Nauvoo theology. Joseph would have had ample opportunity to translate the monotheistic passages of the Bible as polytheistic passages, yet he did not. In fact, he did the opposite; he removed all references to a plurality of Gods from Old Testament passages.

Robert Millett sees the *Joseph Smith Translation* as an attempt to illuminate difficult passages in the *Book of Mormon*. Millett has stated that major points of Mormon doctrine were introduced as a direct result of Joseph's biblical revision.[18] The five points that he considers important are: the premortal existence of humankind; no original sin; that the Gospel of Jesus was known by Adam and the patriarchs; the concept of a three-tiered Heaven; and the pattern for Zion. Millett states that of the five points, the premortal existence of humankind had probably the largest impact upon LDS theology. Also, in an attempt to harmonize the two creation accounts of Genesis, the *Joseph Smith Translation* would see the first creation account as a spiritual creation, while the second was the physical creation.[19] The *Joseph Smith Translation* gives us our first glimpse of the concept of a council in heaven, the earliest Mormon concept of creation, and the way in which God's plan for humankind came into being.[20]

The Mormon concept of a preexistence in heaven has become an important part of LDS theology. The "Vision of the Glories," now *Doctrine and Covenants* Section 76, is an early reference to this concept. The origin of *Doctrine and Covenants* Section 76 can be traced to a revelation received by Joseph Smith on February 16, 1832. The revelation came in response to a prayer regarding the meaning of John 5:29. The revelation was first published in July of 1832, in the *Evening and Morning Star*, and was included as Section 91 in the 1835 *Doctrine and Covenants*. The vision has often been seen as the first textual reference to the concepts of a plurality of Gods, and that humans may become Gods.[21]

Drawing on the text of Section 76, it appears that the reference to "gods," or "the sons of god," is a secondary point made by the revelation. The revelation begins by stating that "the Lord is God, and beside him there is no Savior." The reference to "gods" in Section 76 appears to be a quote taken directly from Psalm 82. The central focus of Section 76 is not the concept of apotheosis, but rather an elaborate description of the premortal existence of man, and the rebellion of Lucifer. These concepts were to be fleshed out in the *Joseph Smith Translation*.

We have additional information to support our claim that Mormonism did not hold to a plurality of Gods concept this early in its history. Joseph Smith was preparing the text of his biblical revision at the same time as section 76 was given. In several passages from the Hebrew Bible, Smith would remove references making reference to a plurality of Gods. In Exodus 7:1, the passage was changed from the original which read, "And the Lord said unto Moses, See, I have made thee a god unto Pharaoh." Smith would alter the passage in his revised text to read "And the Lord said unto Moses, See, I have made thee a prophet unto Pharaoh." The word "gods," in Exodus 22:28, is changed to read "God" and in I Samuel 28:13, "gods" is changed to "words." In a passage from Revelation 1:6, the passage is altered from "and hath made us kings and priests unto God and his Father," to read "and hath made us kings and priests unto God, his Father."[22]

The strongest modalist passage is found in Luke 10:23. Joseph Smith would alter what he saw as an ambiguous passage, concerning the identity of the Father and the Son. Smith would revise the text to read: "All things are delivered to me of my Father; and no man knoweth that the Son is the Father, and the Father is the Son, but to him whom the Son will reveal it." The altered passages of the *Joseph Smith Translation* remove any ambiguity from the biblical text concerning a plurality of persons in the godhead, the existence of a plurality of Gods, as well as the concept of the human as divine. Smith's revision makes no attempt at reconciling multiple persons in the godhead within the context of monotheism. Rather, Smith follows a line of interpretation first introduced by the modalism of the *Book of Mormon*, that the Father and the Son are the same person.

To say that the concept of apotheosis, or that a plurality of Gods concept, existed in Mormon thought as early as 1832 cannot be drawn from the sources. The existence of such a concept would not be harmonious with Joseph's early theology, nor his later theology as contained in the 1835 document, the *Lectures of Faith*. We cannot take an ambiguous statement, like that found in Section 76, and dismiss the clear statements, as found in Smith's revision, to support a nascent concept of apotheosis. The revised passages of the biblical text, quoted above, were all revised following the vision now contained in Section 76. It is on these grounds that we must insist that the reference to men becoming Gods in Section 76 cannot be used to support the theory that a plurality of Gods concept existed in Mormon thought in the early 1830s.

The *Joseph Smith Translation* was Smith's attempt at restoring several lost truths of the Bible.[23] The work was never published in the lifetime of the Prophet. While the *Joseph Smith Translation* is used by the Reorganized Church, the Utah Church has never acknowledged the validity of the work. The Utah Church's rejection of the work is based on the assumption that it was never completed, and therefore it could never be published. However, the revision had reached a point of completion and was considered for publication as early as 1841.[24]

The Utah position cannot be supported from the historical evidence. The revision of the Bible was begun on March 7, 1831, by Joseph Smith and Sidney Rigdon. Beginning with Genesis, the pair began a thorough revision of the Old Testament. After working in Genesis, the pair turned their attention to the New Testament, which they completed by February 2, 1833.[25] Smith and Rigdon would return to the Old Testament, completing their revision of it by July 2, 1833.[26] In fact, Joseph continued to plead for funding on a continuous basis in order to have the completed revision published.[27]

The *Joseph Smith Translation* is a completed revision of the biblical text. Joseph Smith, by revising the text, intended to restore the lost parts of the Bible that he assumed had been removed through transmission. The work contains no concepts that are contrary to those already contained in other period documents. The document is Christologically modalistic. Like the earlier *Book of Mormon*, it attempts to restore lost teachings of the biblical text. Again, like the *Book of Mormon*, these restored teachings of the Bible reveal to the world that the Father and the Son are the same person. Owing to its size, apart from the *Book of Mormon*, no other Church document gives us as much of an insight into the theological mind of the Prophet Joseph Smith.

Smith's intention, in revising the Bible, is clear. The Bible contains many ambiguous passages that can be misinterpreted. With his revision, Joseph sought to remove these ambiguous passages and replace them with what he felt the original authors intended. The intent of the original authors was drawn from the theology of the *Book of Mormon*, its modalistic view of the divine. Beginning with the Genesis creation accounts, Joseph replaced the passages containing the words "us" and "we," with reference to God, with the phrase "and I, God."

Yet, it is a daring move on the part of Smith, who at this time had not yet been introduced to the original Greek or Hebrew of the biblical text. Smith as translator used common sense to legitimize his reasons for revising the text. Smith sought to restore, through revelation, what he perceived to be the original author's intent. While this may be the core reason, he also sought to restore the scriptures of the apostate church, wrestling them from the hands of the ruling priestly order, and return them to their rightful heirs, the laity.

Smith can be seen as a 19th-century Martin Luther, with a direct line to God. In the age of reason, the individual seekers were asked to choose from a host of theological options that were available to them. The Second Great Awakening had put out a call for the individual to experience God personally. Smith, riding on the tail of the spirituality of the Second Great Awakening, took the aspect of this new spirituality one step further.

Protestantism, since the Reformation, had revolved around "Sola Scriptura." Joseph Smith coming from a background in the Protestant tradition retained a reverence for the scriptures, but used a different hermeneutical approach.[28] The reinterpretation had come through Joseph's view of himself and his mission. Unlike Luther, Joseph claimed to have spoken with God personally. God had called Joseph Smith to restore the true teachings of Christ. These teachings were revealed through the early Mormon documents. These documents attempted to reduce the theological options in early 19th-century America by claiming to be ancient documents restored in this age. The documents were not theological commentary or academic arguments, but rather the words of God and the prophets which had been lost for centuries. With this calling, Joseph Smith would embark upon a career as the Prophet of God, standing as a mediator between God and the people.

Early Mormon David Whitmer cites that Joseph Smith was only called to translate the *Book of Mormon*, not to receive revelations as a prophet.[29] David Whitmer was one of the original witnesses to the *Book of Mormon* and the third person baptized into the Church. Whitmer would later apostatize. Whitmer firmly believed that the Church strayed from its original mission when Joseph began to take on the role of Prophet, Seer and Revelator. While Whitmer did apostatize he never denied the validity of the *Book of Mormon*. From the two documents we have reviewed in this chapter we have seen that Joseph's theology, and that of the Church, was not radically different from the rest of American religion. This, perhaps, allowed apostates the privilege of leaving the Church, but still having a belief in the *Book of Mormon*.

The complete *Book of Moses* and the *Joseph Smith Translation* were never made public documents in the Kirtland period. Parts of the documents were published at various times during that period. The documents are expressions of Smith's and the Mormons' theological leanings. Converts to the early Church did not find the concept of God radically different from that expressed by the majority of Protestants.[30] Recalling the statement of Smith's contemporary, Alexander Campbell,[31] we see that Mormonism offered an alternative to the religious pluralism and theological options of its day. Mormonism was an attempt to resolve theological difficulties that had emerged based on variant readings of the biblical text. The early Mormon documents would resolve these difficulties by appealing to the original words of the text, which had now been restored through Joseph Smith.

If strict modalism was the dominant theology of Kirtland-era Mormonism, when and how did the Church move to the henotheism that exists today? It would be during the Kirtland period, particularly after the introduction of Hebrew during the fall and winter of 1835-36 that the first steps were taken. By 1837, the *Book of Mormon* would become obsolete as a document outlining Latter-day Saint beliefs on the godhead. Early Mormon documents, through revelation, sought to reintroduce a strict monotheism into the Christian tradition. This was done through the *Book of Mormon*, and by removing passages referring to a plurality of persons, beings, or Gods, within the biblical text.

The early Mormon Church held to a strict monotheistic interpretation of the divine. Smith was convinced that God was only one being, who manifested himself in varying modes. What seems like confusion, on Smith's part, is really nothing more than an honest attempt at an interpretation of radically opposed theological lines presented in the cultural milieu of 19th-century America. Thomas Paine and his writings had exerted a great influence on the mind set of 19th-century America. Trinitarianism had come under fire on many fronts. The Baltimore sermon of William Ellery Channing had popularized Unitarianism.[32] As well, the Stone-Campbell movement, particularly the wing led by J. Barton Stone, had expressed some concern regarding the validity of Trinitarianism.[33] It may be impossible to establish clear lines of influence from these two cases, but we cannot dismiss their influence, particularly in the age of printing, upon the religious and cultural milieu of 19th-century America.

We must also not discount the idea that Smith, coming to grips with his calling, sought to define God in whatever terms he had available to him. As we are well aware, the complexity of philosophical Trinitarianism is rooted in the Christological debates of the Nicean and Chalcedonian councils of the fourth and fifth centuries. The creeds that evolved from those debates have become part of the nature of the Christian Church. The formulators of the creeds attempted to deal with a complex philosophical idea in precise language. Smith, on the other hand, had very limited formal education. As is often the case, in explaining Trinitarianism, one has a tendency to go to two extremes, either tritheism or some form of modalism. Neither explanation of the divine is in accordance with the rulings of the Church councils, which in turn formed the basis for the majority of Western Christianity's belief systems.

With Smith we see a man who is attempting to reconcile his perceived calling, restorer of lost truths and prophet of God, his background in New England revivalism within the overall paradigm of the common sense revolution. This mixing of self-perception and the cultural milieu of the 19th-century apears to have contributed to Smith's concept of the divine. As this is an individualistic attempt on the part of Smith, it is only fitting that his definition fits none of the historic models of oneness—modalism, Patripassian, Sabellian, or Arian, on a consistent basis. Smith's concept of the divine is an early 19th-century layman's interpretation of Trinitarianism. The revolution had created a new country, Thomas Paine and Andrew Jackson had created a new man, and Joseph Smith would create a new God. Perhaps this definition was no different than the rest of the laity's, that sat in both Catholic and Protestant churches in the early 19th century. Given that early converts to Mormonism were neither from the upper classes, or from the marginalized classes,[34] Mormonism then drew to itself individuals that had entertained the same thoughts as Smith had.

Joseph Smith, in the early 1830s, attempted to remove the excessive theological language surrounding the concept of God. With a belief in one God entrenched in Smith's belief system, Smith set out to answer the same questions that the Church fathers had in the early centuries of the first millennia. Whereas, the Church fathers had accepted Trinitarianism as the most suitable response to the Christological controversy, Smith, in the 19th century, chose his own version of modalism as the most suitable option. Early Mormon documents clearly express that it was the modalist interpretation of the divine that had been lost by the Christian Church over the centuries.

Early Mormon documents, the *Book of Mormon*, the *Book of Moses*, and the *Joseph Smith Translation*, are attempts at restoring "plain and precious truths." The great mystery of the ages, the plain and precious truths removed from the Bible, was that "the Son is the Father, and the Father is the Son." Early Mormon documents are a response to the theological debates that existed in the early 19th century. In time the questions that prompted the foundation of the Church were answered. As the teachings of the early Mormons were accepted as valid interpretations by its converts, the Church moved into new directions. From its initial phase, as a reaction to early 19th-century theologies, Mormonism would introduce new thought conditioned by external and internal forces. Responses to external and internal dissent became characteristic for Mormon doctrinal development, and of its official policy. As Mormonism grew, the likelihood for dissent became greater. Of the many beliefs that caused dissension within the Church, as well as those which drew the ire of citizens and the U.S. government, none played as great a role as plural marriage, or polygamy as it is more commonly known.

The Origin of Plural Marriage

As a practice polygamy has become synonymous with the Mormon Church. Laws have been enacted to curb Mormon polygamy in Canada and the U.S. Books, tracts, and movie scripts have been written about its practice. For many outside of the Church, it is the sole doctrine that they are aware of that Mormons believed, or in some cases still believe. The quest for the origin of polygamy or "plural marriage," as practiced by the Mormons, is murky at best. We have conflicting reports about its purpose, its nature, its origin and its demise. We have attempts to conceal its practice, and then to risk loss of property and freedoms in defense of it. As well, we have the major problem confronting us that it was not officially sanctioned or practiced among the Mormons until 1852. All of this contributes to the problems surrounding the practice of plural marriage among the Mormons, and its importance to the mainstream believers. In simple terms plural marriage formed such an integral part of late 19th-century Mormon belief that no person could achieve exaltation to the position of being a God without entering into the practice. Whether this was always believed is another matter. There appears little evidence to support the notion that polygamy was an important part of the heavenly plan during the 1830s and 1840s.

Throughout the Church's history, anti–Mormons have made the allegation that polygamy was being practiced. The criticisms against the Mormons surface very early. Perhaps these early anti–Mormon allegations were an attempt to label the Mormons as immoral individuals. This could be an accurate assessment, if Mormon leaders themselves would not have admitted to the practice of polygamy as early as 1832. Despite all of this, in 1835 the Church issued a statement that proclaimed that the Church was not practicing polygamy.[35]

Again at Nauvoo the same scene would be played out as allegations would be made that the Church was practicing polygamy. Again the Church would deny that it was practicing polygamy. The section of the *Doctrine and Covenants* authorizing plural marriage is dated July 12, 1843. One year later, in June of 1844, allegations were made by William Law in the *Nauvoo Expositor* that polygamy was, in fact, a doctrine sanctioned by Joseph Smith and the Church. Smith dismissed the charge as spurious.

In the 1880s the U.S. government disenfranchised the Church and its leaders through the passage of the Edmunds-Tucker Act. President John Taylor went underground. Taylor sent emissaries to Canada to find a safe refuge for the Saints. The hoped for reprieve from American intervention by the removal of the Saints to Canada never materialized. It would be by the issuing of what has been called the "Manifesto" or "Official Declaration 2" by President Wilford Woodruff that the Church would be received back into the fold. Woodruff assured the U.S. government that the Church would cease to practice polygamy, on U.S. soil anyway. Yet a belief that had become central to the Church's teaching had forced the Church into an unenviable position. Which should man obey, the laws of God or human laws?

On the surface Woodruff chose the latter while secretly continuing to follow the former. The Church continued to perform plural marriages both within the U.S. and in Canada and Mexico. In 1912, Senator Reed Smoot was denied his seat in Washington for continuing the practice of polygamy. Before the Senate investigation committee Smoot, as well as Joseph F. Smith, admitted that polygamy was still being practiced. Smith, just days after appearing before the Senate, took another plural wife. Yet at its core the early belief in polygamy does not carry the same implications as its later counterpart. While the practice appears early in Mormon history there is no reason to suspect that its practice was tied to the concept of exaltation.

Church leaders—B. H. Roberts, Orson Pratt, and Joseph F. Smith—all claimed that the contents of the revelation on plural marriage, dated to 1843, were known to Smith and a few close associates as early as 1832.[36] The question over the origin of plural marriage, and the date of its introduction into the belief system, has proved to be a contentious one throughout the Church's history. With the lines drawn, to practice it or not to practice it has divided many of the sects that claim Joseph Smith as their founder.

Of the numerous groups, the two largest, the Utah Church and the Reorganized Church, divided over this issue in the early 1860s. In 1905, future President Joseph Fielding Smith engaged in a letter-writing campaign with Richard Evans, counselor in the Reorganized Church's presidency. The contents of the debate were carried out through the pages of the *Toronto Star*. Then Apostle Smith, representing the Utah Church, entered evidence that the revelation on plural marriage was in fact carried out while the church was in Kirtland.[37] No major, known, anti–Mormon literature from the 1830s concentrates on plural marriage as a practice among the Latter-day Saints.

Rumors were perhaps circulating among non–Mormons that the Saints were practicing plural marriage. It is difficult to assess these statements, as they could have been used by the Church's detractors as part of a polemical argument, having little basis in fact. The 1835 *Doctrine and Covenants* included an official declaration on marriage. In all probability, the revelation on plural marriage had its origins while Joseph Smith was revising the biblical text. This is the argument that Robert Matthews makes.[38]

While the origins for the revelation on plural marriage can be placed in the Kirtland period, it is difficult to determine the actual reasons for the practice being introduced. One thing, however, can be assured. The practice of polygamy in Kirtland did not carry with it the same theological implications as it would in Nauvoo or Salt Lake theology. But given Joseph's development in one area, that the Gospel preceded Jesus, Joseph may have thought that polygamy was an important part of the Gospel.

During the early Kirtland period Joseph's theology would expand in certain areas as two new documents would be added to the body of Mormon literature. With the *Book of Moses* and the *Joseph Smith Translation,* Mormonism would flesh out concepts alluded to in the Bible and *Book of Mormon*. The concepts introduced to Mormonism during the early Kirtland period took on a greater significance as Mormonism began to expand its doctrinal teachings. During the early Kirtland period we saw the introduction of a council of spirits, polygamy, and the eternal nature of man. While in their early forms these concepts may only be speculative statements, these concepts contributed to the text and body of Joseph's greatest sermon, the King Follett discourse. During the Salt Lake period these concepts would be expanded upon, redefined, and eventually become the core for the Mormon belief on the nature of God. The teachings of the Kirtland period, in a later refined state, would influence the formation of the doctrine of eternal progression or "as man is God once was, as God is man may become."

4. Among the School of the Prophets in Ohio

Teachings from the Lectures of Faith

> There are two personages who constitute the great, matchless, governing and supreme power over all things—by whom all things were created and made, that are created and made, whether visible or invisible: whether in heaven, on earth, or in the earth, under the earth, or throughout the immensity of space—They are the Father and the Son: The Father being a personage of spirit, glory and power: possessing all perfection and fullness: The Son, who was in the bosom of the Father, a personage of tabernacle, made, or fashioned like unto man, or being in the form and likeness of man, or, rather, man was formed after his likeness, and his image—he is also the express image and likeness of the personage of the Father; possessing all the fullness of the Father, the same fullness with the Father; being begotten of him, and was ordained before the foundation of the world to be a propitiation for the sins of all those who should believe on his name, and is called the Son because of the flesh.
>
> *Lecture Fifth of Faith*, 1835

Having its origin in New York State, the infant Mormon Church would soon move from that state carrying with it two primary concepts rooted deep in 19th-century American society. The two concepts were both evangelical in nature: the concept of the establishment of the millennial kingdom, and that God spoke to individuals bypassing any church hierarchy. The arrival of the Saints in Ohio saw the infant Mormon Church make the first attempt at a central "Gathering." The Saints were called to come to Kirtland and to await the coming of the Messiah to establish his reign on the earth.

The first missionary endeavors in Ohio had centered around the small town of Mentor, Ohio. By the mid part of 1831, Joseph Smith and a part of his followers had left New York for the town of Kirtland, Ohio. There they joined with a large number of Saints that had converted to the Church through the efforts of ex–Campbellite minister Sidney Rigdon.

The Gathering of the Saints in Ohio was not a secular attempt to carve a piece of the American dream on an expanding Western frontier. Rather, the call to gather the Saints was a direct commandment of the Lord. The revelations, dated late in 1830 and early 1831, are recorded as *Doctrine and Covenants*, Sections 37, 38. The purpose of the move, as outlined in the revelation, was to escape the persecutions that the Church had endured in both Pennsylvania and New York.

Not all of the Saints had left New York and Pennsylvania for Kirtland with Smith. Some of the Saints had remained in Colesville and Fayette, in New York, and in Harmony, Pennsylvania. Kirtland, Ohio, would become the central destination for the majority of Mormons during the early 1830s. A large part of the early converts to the Church would remain in Kirtland, neither following the Prophet to Missouri in 1832, nor to Nauvoo, Illinois, in 1839. It would be during what can be termed as the Kirtland period of Mormon Church history that the Church would be divided into two main geographic regions. Independence and Far West in Missouri, and Kirtland, Ohio, would become the main destinations for any Mormon wishing to join the brethren and await the return of the Messiah.[1] It was only as a result of difficulties with his followers in Kirtland that the Prophet would spend time in both Missouri and Ohio during the 1830s.[2] The difficulties with the Kirtland Saints would lead Smith to attempt to gather all of the Saints into one cohesive body, in Independence. By claiming that Independence, not Kirtland, was the Center Stake of Zion, and the locale to which the City of New Jerusalem would descend, Smith had placed a divine sanction on locating to Independence and all faithful Saints should relocate there or face eternal judgment.

With the establishment of the Saints in Ohio, a new chapter in the Church's history was about to begin. While in Kirtland, several significant political, economic, and theological events began to take shape. It would be from the theological developments shaped during the late Kirtland period that a distinct, new theology would emerge by the early 1840s. Several factors contributed to the development of the future Nauvoo theology, but none were as significant as Joseph Smith's learning of Hebrew in the School of the Prophets.[3] Joseph's introduction to biblical Hebrew, in the mid–1830s, impacted the theology of two future documents, the *Book of Abraham* in 1842, and the King Follett discourse in 1844. The School of the Prophets would also provide the academic setting for a set of seven theological treatises known as the *Lectures of Faith*.[4]

The School of the Prophets was an instruction center designed to educate the Saints on various academic topics. Formalized instruction in writing, reading, science, geography, history, and religion were all included in the curriculum. The Mormon preoccupation with higher learning would become part of its very soul, establishing future, additional schools in Nauvoo and in Salt Lake City. The Kirtland School of the Prophets had been initiated through a revelation dated January 3, 1833. The revelation is now contained as Section 88 in the *Doctrine and Covenants*.

The School of the Prophets was intended to offer instruction in various subjects to the members of the Church in Kirtland and the surrounding area during the winter months.[5] During the four winters, 1833 to 1837, that the school was in operation, the Saints received instruction in English grammar, mathematics, geometry, history, and penmanship.[6] A second instructional school called the School of the Elders operated under Parley P. Pratt's direction in Independence, Missouri, during the summer of 1833.[7] The winter sessions of the Kirtland School of the Prophets provided a broad spectrum of education to the Latter-day Saints. During the winter session of 1835-36, Hebrew was offered and was taught by Joshua Seixas of Hudson Seminary. The following year, H. M. Hawes taught Greek and Latin to 150 students.[8] The Prophet Joseph Smith, as well as several of the elders, took full advantage of this academic instruction on the American frontier.

The secular topics taught at Kirtland were intended to compliment the primary purpose of the school, which was theological instruction. The School of the Prophets was originally designed to teach the present and future Church leaders the principles of the Gospel.[9] It would be during the winter of 1834-35 that the theological treatises which became known as the *Lectures of Faith* were introduced to the Saints in Kirtland.[10]

Early Mormon thought had been characterized by its modalism, or its layman's Trinitarianism. By the close of the Kirtland era, in 1839, the Church would have shifted from modalism to a binatarian position on God. This does not imply that Mormons did not see three persons, the Father, Son, and Holy Ghost, as being divine. Rather, what is meant by binatarianism in this case is that, while there exist three persons called God, they are no longer defined in terms of their modes of operation. The binatarianism present in Mormonism during the mid–1830s can be described in the following way. While Mormonism did not have a clear definition of the nature of God, it did make a distinction between the Father and the Son. The Father and the Son were no longer seen as the same person with different modes of operation and purpose.

At this time in Mormon theological development the concept of the Holy Ghost and the Holy Spirit still lacked a clear definition. At this time the two, Holy Ghost and Holy Spirit, were synonymous, unlike later Mormon thought which would see the two as separate and distinct persons. The thought during the Kirtland period defined the Holy Ghost as an extension, a shared asset, of the Father and the Son, and not a distinct person or being. During the Kirtland period, Joseph made his first attempts to move away from his early modalism, and gain a newer, broader, theological understanding of the nature of God. The *Lectures of Faith* provided the vehicle through which Joseph Smith presented this new understanding of God to his followers.

Joseph Smith's first step towards a new theological understanding had begun in 1833. This important first step was characterized by Smith rejecting his early modalism by no longer seeing the Father and the Son as the same person.[11]

In moving from his earlier theological position, Smith began to refer to the beings in the godhead as individuals or persons. Joseph Smith uses the title God, singularly, to address both Jesus and the Father; he does refrain from addressing the two beings as individual Gods. Upon learning Hebrew, Joseph Smith would make further distinctions between the Father; and the Son by applying the Hebrew names Jehovah and Elohim to Jesus and the Father.

By designating Jesus as Jehovah and the Father as Elohim, Smith made it expressly clear that Jesus and the Father were distinct individuals. While Smith may have used proper names to differentiate the individuals, he did not use them consistently in addressing the two individuals. In fact, designating Jesus as Jehovah and the Father as Elohim was not done consistently during the 19th century by any Mormon leader. The only consistent use of the term Jehovah we find throughout the 19th century was to designate the God of the Old Testament. Beginning in the mid–1840s Elohim was used to designate the Father of Jesus, as well as the head of the Council of Gods. With no consistent use of the terms Elohim and Jehovah many problems could, and did, evolve. The problems carried on throughout much of the 19th and early 20th centuries eventually being resolved in 1915. By resolving who Jehovah was one could then assume who Elohim was. The central problem then became who is Jehovah? Is Jehovah the preincarnate Jesus, or is He the Father of Jesus? The problem was fully resolved by James E. Talmage in 1915, when he stated, with official Church sanction, that Jehovah was the preincarnate Jesus, the God of the Old Testament.[12]

The inconsistency, evidenced in the application of the term Jehovah, caused many problems for the Church throughout the 19th and early 20th centuries. As well, the use of Elohim caused as many problems for Mormon leaders, and the Church in general. During the same time in which the Jehovah controversy was being played out, Mormon leaders would use the term Elohim to designate the Father of Jehovah, to designate the Council of Gods, or even a God superior to Jehovah.[13] With the resolution of the Jehovah controversy Elohim would become the Father of Jesus.

In the following pages we will look at the most significant theological document produced during the mid–1830s, the *Lectures of Faith*.

The Lectures of Faith

The theological lectures, prepared to educate the Saints in theology, were introduced during the winter of 1834-35. The purpose of the lectures? The lectures were "to be used as doctrinal aids by members, and missionaries."[14] The *Lectures of Faith* consisted of a series of catechismal discussions on seven theological topics. The topics of discussion included faith, miracles, sacrifice, the existence of God, the attributes and character of the Father and the Son, and the Gift of the Holy Ghost. The seven lectures were first published collectively in the 1835 *Doctrine and Covenants*, and remained part of the *Doctrine and Covenants* until their removal in 1921.

The significance of the *Lectures of Faith* to Mormon doctrinal history has been debated over the years. The focus of some of the debates have centered around the provenance of the lectures, their authorship, and the authority of the *Lectures of Faith* as true expressions of Latter-day Saint thought during the period in question.[15] In recent years word analysis patterns have sought to determine the authorship of the *Lectures of Faith*. Findings have revealed that Joseph Smith, Sidney Rigdon, Frederick G. Williams, and the Prophet's brother Hyrum all contributed to the writing of the *Lectures*. While the lectures give us a glimpse into a formative period of the Church's theological development, in this study we are mainly concerned with *Lecture Fifth of Faith*, the lecture dealing with the nature and character of God. This lecture was first published in the *Messenger and Advocate* in May of 1835.[16] According to the word analysis results, parts of this lecture definitely show the influence of the Prophet Joseph Smith on the lecture. At the very least, even if we cannot ascertain that he was its author, we are certain that he had some form of influence regarding its content.[17]

The arguments for the authenticity and the authorship of the *Lectures* are relegated to secondary points in this discussion. Their inclusion in the 1835 *Doctrine and Covenants*, a canonized work, proves beyond a doubt that they were subjected to the Prophet's final approval before publication. By virtue of their inclusion they would have had to have met certain criteria, one of them being that they were in fact authentic expressions of Smith's own thought. There is strong evidence to suggest that the *Lectures* were the Church's officially recognized doctrinal treatises, or expanded statements of faith. In that capacity they would have definitely contained the thought of Joseph Smith, and in a farther reaching conclusion constituted what was to be believed by any faithful Saint.[18]

Additional controversy has also centered around the doctrinal authority of the *Lectures of Faith* and the reasons for their inclusion in the 1835 *Doctrine and Covenants*. Echoing conservative Mormon historical consensus, historian Milton V. Backman has said:

> Though lectures were not regarded as equal in authority to the revelations, they were considered profitable for the gaining of a better understanding of the doctrines of the kingdom.[19]

Backman's argument follows an argument made earlier by historian B. H. Roberts. Roberts, in his *History of the Church*, contends that the *Lectures of Faith* inclusion in the 1835 *Doctrine and Covenants* should not be seen as binding expressions of faith for the Church's membership. Roberts goes further and states that the lectures should be relegated to a lower level of doctrinal authority than the revelations of Joseph Smith. Roberts bases his argument on a statement made by Elder John Smith, who was President of the Kirtland High Council during the publication of the 1835 *Doctrine and Covenants*. Roberts explains that John Smith made a clear distinction between the doctrines expressed in the revelations and the theology contained in the theological lectures.[20] The implications of the Roberts and Backman arguments seem to cast a doubt around the purpose and the authority of the lectures. Both Roberts' and Backman's arguments seem to suggest that the *Lectures of Faith* were never intended to be part of the Church's canon.

In reviewing the source for the Roberts and Backman arguments we see another perspective. Citing the August 17, 1835, General Assembly, the Church unanimously voted to accept the book, the 1835 *Doctrine and Covenants,* as the "doctrine and covenants of their faith."[21] B. H. Roberts is quite correct in his citation; Kirtland High Council President John Smith did make a distinction between the theology of the lectures, and the revelations from God. The minutes of the Assembly record Smith as saying "that the revelations were true, and that the lectures were judiciously arranged and compiled and profitable for doctrine." But Roberts fails to continue his quotation. The Kirtland High Council, including John Smith, accepted the book as the "doctrine and covenants of their faith."

At the August 1835 General Assembly, every major ecclesiastical official, including the Twelve Apostles and the Quorum of the Seventy, accepted the book as presented to the Assembly as true, and as the "doctrine and covenants of their faith." From the minutes of the August 17 Assembly, there can be no doubt that the complete 1835 *Doctrine and Covenants,* including the *Lectures of Faith*, were accepted as authentic doctrine, and binding upon the Church members.

There is an argument that would allow for the Roberts-Backman interpretation to be upheld. The work, the *Doctrine and Covenants*, had not yet been published by the August Conference date, and therefore the Assembly would not have known what was contained in the new edition of the *Doctrine and Covenants*. The new *Doctrine and Covenants* would not have been available to the Saints until September.[22] Some of the *Lectures* had been published earlier than September of 1835, therefore the Saints would have had access to these.[23] The lecture on the nature and character of God, Lecture 5, had been published in May of 1835, at least two months prior to the August General Assembly. That the Saints voted blindly in accepting the new *Doctrine and Covenants* is difficult to accept. The Saints, at the August Conference, should have been fully aware of what the *Doctrine and Covenants* would contain. A committee had been appointed in 1834 to make selections from several sources, which were to be included in the new work.

The Prophet Joseph Smith's history records that the High Council appointed a committee on September 24, 1834, to "arrange items of the doctrines of Jesus Christ" for inclusion in the new edition of the *Doctrine and Covenants*.[24] The items for inclusion were to be taken from the Bible, *The Book of Mormon*, and the revelations. The members of the committee were Second Counselor Oliver Cowdery, Oliver; First Counselor Sidney Rigdon, Sidney; and prominent publisher Frederick G. Williams.[25] The committee, upon selecting items for inclusion, presented the contents of the volume to the Church membership for final approval at the August Conference. The finished work became the *Doctrine and Covenants.*

The 1835 *Doctrine and Covenants* was originally a two-part work, as its name would indicate. If we look at a current edition of the *Doctrine and Covenants*, we see that the work contains 138 revelations, or sections. In the 1835 edition, the work is divided into two distinct parts. The first part of the work is titled "Theology: Lecture First of Faith on the Doctrine of the Church of the Latter Day Saints."[26] Subsequent lectures are simply titled "Lecture Second of Faith," "Lecture Third," and so on. The revelations were included in a second part titled "Covenants and Commands of the Lord," which begins on page 75. That the seven *Lectures of Faith* originally comprised the doctrine part of the *Doctrine and Covenants* there can be no doubt. The revelations in turn comprised the "Covenants and Commands" portion of the work. The two parts, collectively, were called the *Doctrine and Covenants of the Church of the Latter Day Saints.*

For many of the Saints in Kirtland, and for Mormons of subsequent generations until 1921, the *Lectures of Faith* were Mormon doctrine. For the members of the Church in the late 1830s, the *Lectures of Faith* were the doctrines of the Church to which they belonged. The decanonization of the *Lectures of Faith* brought about a serious revision of Latter-day Saint theology. The *Lectures of Faith* by 1921 were representative of a theological position that the Church had not held for nearly a century. Their continued inclusion, in post–1921 editions of the *Doctrine and Covenants*, would have presented an additional problem for the Church by providing an older, rejected, theological option for the membership of the Church. Having just resolved the Jehovah-Elohim controversy, a new thorn in the flesh was not needed.

Scholars have attempted to legitimize the reasons for the removal of the *Lectures* in 1921.[27] Reasons for the decanonization of the *Lectures* follow an apologetical line of logic. Reasons such as they contain imperfect doctrines on the godhead, they were not received as revelations by the Prophet, and they were only given as instructions, form the core of the apologists' arguments.[28] The opinions surrounding the decanonization have never been fully explained. Why then were the *Lectures* originally included as part of the canon? It seems odd that a religious movement that holds to beliefs not contained in its canon (the King Follett discourse) would include in that canon teachings which it did not believe to be authoritative. In what must have been an embarrassing position for the Church to be in, removing part of its canon, reasons for the removal were needed. This was accomplished by arguing that the *Lectures* were never part of the canon.

Regardless of the reasons for the *Lectures'* removal in 1921, an important fact cannot be denied. By virtue of their inclusion in the *Doctrine and Covenants*, from 1835 to 1921, the *Lectures of Faith* shaped the theological views of the Latter-day Saints during that period. The *Lectures of Faith* were to be tools of theological instruction.[29] The *Lectures of Faith* addressed the central tenants of the Latter-day Saints doctrine, and "gave the most studious attention to the all important object of qualifying themselves as messengers of Jesus Christ."[30]

The contents of the *Lectures of Faith* express a slightly different theological perspective than earlier Mormon works. In the *Lectures of Faith* Joseph Smith expressed, in a major document, what he had been considering as early as 1833, that the Father and the Son were distinct persons.[31]

Lecture Fifth of Faith[32] describes the godhead as containing three persons, the Father, Son, and Holy Ghost.[33] The *Lecture* states:

> There are two personages who constitute the great matchless, governing, and supreme power over all things ... by whom all things were created and

made.... They are the Father and the Son: The Father being a personage of Spirit, glory and power.... The Son ... a personage of tabernacle made or fashioned like unto man ... possessing all the fullness of the Father; or the same fullness of the Father; and is called Son because of the flesh ... possessing the same mind with the Father, which mind is the Holy Spirit ... and these three are one; or in other words these three constitute the great matchless and supreme power over all things: by whom all things were created and made ... and these three constitute the Godhead, and are one.[34]

The Holy Spirit is defined in the *Lectures* as being the mind of the Father and the Son. In 1841, Smith began to see the Holy Spirit as a separate and distinct person.[35]

The *Lecture* continues in its catechismal style by asking the question:

Q. How many personages are there in the Godhead?
A. Two: The Father and the Son.
Q. How do you prove that there are two personages in the Godhead?
A. By the Scriptures Gen. 1:26; 2:6 "and the Lord God Said unto the only begotten who was with him from the beginning, Let us make man in our own image—and it was done." Gen. 3:22—"and the Lord said, Behold, man is become as one of us."[36]

It should be noted that the quotes from the biblical passages are taken from Smith's own translation.

In the *Lectures*, Joseph taught that the Father was a personage of glory and power. The Son was declared to be a personage of tabernacle, or flesh. Smith, quoting John 14:9 to support his claim of divine unity, states that the Son was "in the form and likeness of man."[37]

Conservative Mormon approaches to historical documents often produce a skewed interpretation of Mormonism's doctrinal past.[38] Conservative Latter-day Saint scholars often make an attempt to interpret a post Kirtland theological understanding of concepts into earlier Church concepts. The underlying hermeneutical principle for this is connected to the concept that the Gospel is as old as Adam. In order to maintain this hermeneutical approach, there can be no variance in teachings between the present belief system and the early belief system. The syllogism for this hermeneutical principle is such. If a variance of thought did exist, then the claim of Smith to have restored primitive Christianity would be open to attack. If a variance exists between the earliest Mormon concepts, those restored by Smith, and later concepts, how could Smith claim to have restored primitive Christianity, when these concepts were not present at the foundation of the Mormon Church?

The result of this interpretive approach to the historical development of Mormon doctrine is problematic for any researcher dealing with Mormon documents or secondary source material. The result of this apologetic approach often leaves the reader with a perspective that is skewed. This skewing is evidenced in Milton V. Backman's contention that while the doctrines of the Saints regarding the Father and the Son are not clear, they do point to the fact that more than one God is still present.[39] Backman is attempting to place the concept of a plurality of Gods, a distinct characteristic of Nauvoo Mormonism, into an earlier historical context. However, a more appropriate historical reconstruction would give us a different perspective. This perspective is, that while the *Lectures* do make a distinction between the Father and the Son, they are clear that there exists only one God. This one God consists of three personages, the Father, Son, and Holy Spirit.

Milton V. Backman contends that the *Lectures* teach that God the Father has a physical body. Backman's argument is based on Smith's comment that Jesus is "also in the likeness of the Father."[40] The *Lectures* clearly state to the contrary. God is described as a being distinct from the Son. The Son, being in the image and likeness of the Father, is seen as the Son possessing all the power of the Father. Smith quotes Paul's letter to the Colossians, 1:19, 2:9, and Ephesians 1:23, in support of his argument. The *Lectures* are clear. The Son is called the Son because he has a physical body, not that he bears any physical resemblance to the Father.[41]

It does appear likely that the *Lectures* were precursors to the early 1840s' Mormon thought, which taught that God the Father had a material body. The distinctiveness between the Father and the Son, evidenced in the *Lectures*, allowed for new theological definitions to take place in Nauvoo. The *Lectures* are a departure from the Church's earlier modalist doctrines on the godhead. With Joseph's introduction to Hebrew in 1835-36, and the Hebrew epithets of Elohim and Jehovah, Mormon theology would begin its progression towards cosmic henotheism.

The Kirtland Hebrew School

During the winter of 1835-36, Joseph had contracted Dr. Daniel Piexotto of Wiloughby Medical College to instruct the Saints in Hebrew. Smith had contacted Piexotto after hearing him deliver a lecture in a nearby town. Soon after, Joseph Smith sent Oliver Cowdery to New York to purchase a book bindery for the Saints.[42] Cowdery returned from New York with a Hebrew Bible, grammar, and lexicon, as well as a Greek lexicon.[43]

Further contact with Piexotto had led Smith, and others, to believe that Piexotto was unqualified to teach Hebrew.[44] Smith desired to be released from the Saints' obligations to Piexotto and dispatched emissaries to New York to find another teacher.[45] When Piexotto failed to arrive in Kirtland at the designated time, the contract was voided and a new Hebrew instructor, Lucius Parker, was contacted.[46] Parker was not hired. Instead, Smith hired Joshua Seixas of Hudson Seminary in Hudson, Ohio. Seixas was hired to teach forty students for seven weeks at 320 dollars.[47] Joshua Seixas had been referred to Joseph Smith as a capable Hebrew scholar by Eliza R. Snow. Snow had heard of Seixas from her brother Lorenzo, who had studied Hebrew with Seixas at Oberlin College.

Joshua Seixas came to Kirtland on January 26, 1835, with a supplement to his recently published *Manual Hebrew Grammar: For Beginners*.[48] Seixas had taught Hebrew at Oberlin College, at the Western Reserve College in Hudson, Ohio, and in Andover, Massachusetts. The Kirtland Hebrew lectures, under Seixas, lasted for about 12 weeks.[49]

The contribution of the study of Hebrew to Mormon theological development is evidenced through the introduction of, and in the use of, the epithets Elohim and Jehovah. Prior to the study of Hebrew, Smith had used Jehovah as a generic term for God, which he had used to designate both the Father and the Son.

The use of the proper names Elohim and Jehovah began to appear in 1836 in Mormon literature and thought. The proper name Jehovah appears to have been used more often after this date as well. Jehovah appears in two of the Church's standard works, the *Book of Mormon*, and the *Book of Abraham*. Elohim appears nowhere in the Latter-day Saints' canon.[50] During the 1830s, and prior to 1844, Smith consistently used Jehovah to refer to the Father. Elohim was often used interchangeably with Jehovah. There was no attempt by Smith to explain who Elohim was until the spring of 1844. In the King Follett discourse, Elohim was seen as the Council of Gods, or a God superior to Jehovah, who Smith saw as the God of Israel.[51]

By the close of the Kirtland era the Mormon Church had moved from its earliest modalistic position to a binatarian position. The new thought stream produced during this time found expression in the *Lectures of Faith*. The Kirtland period also saw Smith introduced to Hebrew and with that a new era of speculative thought would begin. The introduction to Hebrew in the winter of 1835-36 would prove to be one of the most significant influences to emerge during the Kirtland period. As a direct result of his Hebrew lessons, Smith was introduced to concepts that became important parts of his future theological speculation. Smith, now familiar with the meaning of Elohim and Jehovah, coupled with an already cynical view of biblical translations, had created an environment from which the distinct henotheism of the Nauvoo period could emerge. Smith's use of Hebrew would play an important role in two future documents, the *Book of Abraham* and the King Follett discourse.

Summary

In the early years, Mormon theology remained relatively stable and the concept of God remained relatively modalistic. During the Kirtland era several key developments would radically alter Mormon thought. While little theological differences existed between the majority of Christian sects and Mormonism during the early years, we begin to see a gradual shift occurring in Mormonism during the Kirtland period. The Church soon began to search out a new identity for itself among an expanding pluralistic religious environment.

Several new doctrinal developments would emerge in the years 1832 to 1838. By 1833, the earliest, the modalist concept of the divine began to decline, and a new thought stream began to emerge. In this new stream the Father and the Son attain a distinct identity from each other. The new stream would gain enough prominence that the 1837 *The Book of Mormon* would have some of its modalist passages revised.[52] The 1835 *Lectures* are the first major public record we have of the Kirtland theology. While the *Lectures* reflect a binatarian concept of the divine, the belief in one God is still firmly entrenched in Mormon thought. Yet, while the new stream, binatarianism, has emerged and is being proclaimed in public and in private, the older stream of thought, modalism, still forms a core part of the Mormon belief system.

The learning of Hebrew provided Joseph with a new understanding and a new set of terms with which to define God. As a result of the new information, the Father and the Son were now given the Hebrew epithets of Elohim and Jehovah. With the introduction of the epithets, just cause for a new theological interpretation became evidenced. This new interpretation would soon become reality as between 1839 and 1844 Mormon theology moved from monotheism to henotheism.

The concepts expressed in the King Follett discourse can not be divorced from the background laid for them during the Kirtland period. Without a move from modalism to binatarianism, cosmic henotheism would have been a difficult jump in logic. In a period of 14 years, Mormonism shifted from modalism to binatarianism to cosmic henotheism.

Many factors came into play, causing this shift from modalism to cosmic henotheism. Joseph's self-concept as a prophet of God, as well as several external forces contributed to the shift. As the Mormon Church began to move from its early textual-based roots, new ideas and speculative doctrines were introduced. In 1833, the Father and the Son began to take on distinct identities. This was a radical departure from *The Book of Mormon* theology which had sought to at once restore the concept of one God in the American mindset. As a result of his introduction to Hebrew, Joseph began to use the epithets Elohim and Jehovah. With access to the original biblical text, Joseph resolved that there were distinct persons, or individuals, within the godhead. The relationship between the members of the godhead was not resolved in this time period. By the close of the Kirtland era, in 1839, the concept of one God was still believed in Mormon theology.[53]

With the publication of the *Book of Abraham,* in 1842, a new stream in Mormon thought emerged. This new thought stream would supersede the modalism of the *Book of Mormon*, and the binatarianism of the *Lectures of Faith*. Through the pages of the *Book of Abraham*, Mormons were introduced to the possibility that a plurality of Gods existed. Yet, the official doctrine of the Church, in the early 1840s, would still be the same as it was during the Kirtland period, a binatarian view of the divine.[54]

As problems began to surface and tension rose in the ranks of the Saints, questions regarding the prophetic calling of Smith began to circulate. Smith's individualism carried with it the inherent problem of personality clashes over points of secular and spiritual authority. Smith would vindicate his prophetic claim through academic arguments, and the introduction of new revelation, and with these two methods additional thought streams would make their way into the minds of the Saints. Joseph Smith, to vindicate his prophetic calling and in order to counter the growing dissent, would relay the story of his initial religious experience. This initial religious experience has come to be called the First (or 1st) Vision. While the First Vision was not an important part of early Latter-day Saint thought, by the later part of the 19th century it had become an important fundamental for the Church. As for Mormonism in the Kirtland period, it can be said that while the shifts in theology may have occurred, doctrinally Mormonism could still be considered a Christian sect. What James B. Allen has said of earliest Mormonism could also be applied to mid–1830s' Mormonism. That is:

> Mormonism's conception of God was not radically different from the majority of Christianity. The newly converted Saints probably did not have to change their image of God just because they had become Mormon.[55]

5. IN THE GRAND COUNCIL OF THE GODS

Redacting the Writings of Abraham

> And the Lord said, who shall I send, and one answered like unto the Son of man, here I am send me. And another answered and said, here I am send me. And the Lord said, I will send the first. And the second was angry and kept not his first estate, and, at that day, many followed after him. And the Lord said let us go down; and they went down at the beginning, and they organized and formed, (that is, the Gods,) the heavens and the earth. And the earth after it was formed, was empty and desolate; because they had not formed anything but the earth; and darkness reigned upon the face of the deep, and the spirit of the Gods was brooding upon the face of the water.
> And they said, the Gods, let there be light, and there was light. And they, the Gods, comprehended the light, for it was bright; and they divided the light, or caused it to be divided from the darkness and the Gods called light day, and the darkness they called night.
>
> *Book of Abraham*, 1842

On July 3, 1835, Michael Chandler arrived in Kirtland, Ohio. Chandler made a living by traveling through America with Egyptian artifacts, allowing rural America the opportunity to witness the greatness of ancient Egypt firsthand. Chandler's exhibition included four mummies and their accompanying burial texts recently excavated from Thebes in Egypt.[1] Chandler had chosen to come to Kirtland to meet with Joseph Smith. Joseph's reputation as a translator of ancient documents had spread throughout America, and it was for this reason that Chandler had sought out Smith.[2] In 1835, the world of ancient Egypt was still a mysterious place in time. Tomb robbing had brought many of Egypt's antiquities to museums and into the hands of many individuals in North America and Europe. In spite of the wide popularity of Egyptian antiquities, the mysterious meanings of the Egyptian hieroglyphics had not yet been deciphered. The key to deciphering the hieroglyphics, the Rosetta stone, had been discovered during Napoleon's campaign in Egypt in the early part of the century. The major task of deciphering the hieroglyphics had been begun by French scholar Jean-François Champollion. Champollion had published a précis of his preliminary work, in French, in 1823. Yet there is no evidence to suggest that the Mormon Prophet Joseph Smith would have had access to this précis. By 1835, when Chandler had come to Kirtland, the précis had not yet been translated into English. In the 1830s the mysteries of the Egyptian hieroglyphics were virtually unknown to the English-speaking people of America.

It was a quest for knowledge about the Egyptian artifacts that had initially brought Chandler to Kirtland. By the mid–1830s, Smith's reputation as a translator was widely known as a result of having translated the *Book of Mormon*.[3] Chandler had hoped that Joseph would be able to translate the texts and provide some insight into the identity of the mummies. J. Reuben Clark, counselor in the First Presidency under Prophet Joseph Fielding Smith, provides some background to the Chandler-Smith meeting.[4] Smith's history also records his first encounter with Chandler.[5] Smith states:

> On the third of July Michael H. Chandler came to Kirtland to exhibit some Egyptian mummies. There were four human figures, together with some two or more rolls of papyrus covered with hieroglyphic figures and devices. As Mr. Chandler had been told I could translate them, he brought me some of the characters, and I gave him the interpretation, and like a gentleman, he gave me the following certificate.
> "This is to make known to all who may be desirous concerning the knowledge of Mr. Joseph Smith Jun., in deciphering the ancient characters in my possession, which I have, in many eminent cities, showed to the most learned; and, from the information that I could ever learn, or meet with, I find that Mr. Joseph Smith Jun., to correspond in the most minute matters."
> Michael H. Chandler
Traveling with and proprietor
of Egyptian Mummies[6]

That Chandler had attempted to gain an insight into the contents of the Egyptian papyri is seen by the certificate he presented to Smith. While mainstream America may have seen the writings as mysterious, scholars who took an interest in the topic would have had gained access to Champollion's work, and thereby would have at least some clue as to the meaning of the characters. It appears that Chandler, in some of his earlier travels, had sought out other opinions with regards to the contents of the papyri.

Chandler, in presenting Smith with the certificate, stated that Smith's translation was accurate compared to the opinions of others to whom he had shown the papyri.

In retrospect it appears unlikely that either Smith or Chandler had any clue as to what the papyri actually contained. Given the process by which Smith had translated the golden plates containing the *Book of Mormon*, and the subsequent translation of the Egyptian papyri, it is doubtful that Smith was in possession of any language skills beyond English. Yet it is precisely this fact that is often pointed to as proof of Smith's divine call, and that both the *Book of Mormon* and the *Book of Abraham* are divine in origin. In assessing Smith's ability as a translator we do have several incidents that seem to cast doubt upon this ability. Taking into account that the golden plates from which Smith translated the *Book of Mormon* no longer exist, there are several historical comments regarding the translation, as well as copies of several of the original characters from the plates that still exist. As for the papyri that formed the basis of the *Book of Abraham*, the papyri still exist, and a facsimile of the actual text exists, so a comparative study could be undertaken.

The existence of several *Book of Mormon* characters date from early in Smith's career. In 1829, prior to the publication to the *Book of Mormon*, Martin Harris, a wealthy farmer and close acquaintance of Smith, had copied several of the *Book of Mormon* characters for closer examination. At the insistence of his wife, Martin took the characters to Charles Anthon, professor of oriental languages at Columbia University.[7] According to Harris, Anthon pronounced the characters to be genuine and the translation to be accurate. Satisfied, Harris mortgaged his farm and the *Book of Mormon* was published with the proceeds.

Smith's brief viewing of the ancient Egyptian texts convinced him that the texts were the writings of Abraham and Joseph during their tenure in Egypt.[8] The texts and mummies were purchased from Chandler for 2,400 dollars.

After acquiring the texts from Chandler, Joseph began to translate the papyrus. Joseph compiled an Egyptian dictionary, or grammar, to aid in the translation of the texts.[9] The grammar has survived to this day and is an extremely valuable research tool for scholars concerned with the *Book of Abraham*. The grammar is an item by item translation of the hieroglyphic symbols contained on the ancient texts and seems to have been the key Smith used to unlock the mysteries of the Egyptian papyrus. The grammar is important to our understanding of the *Book of Abraham*, as it provided the core materials from which the *Book of Abraham* was translated.

Background Sources of the Book of Abraham

Joseph's Egyptian grammar was to be the key through which the ancient texts could be translated. Smith meticulously copied the individual symbols of the hieroglyphics from the papyrus texts and attached a translation to them. The first chapters of the *Book of Abraham*, from 1:32–2:15, are included in the work. In the grammar there is no mention of a plurality, or a Council of Gods. Rather, a monotheistic concept of the divine is taught. In the work, God is defined as *Ah me os*, meaning having no beginning and no end. As well, Smith translates the symbol Aleph as meaning in the beginning with God, the Savior. The reference here is obviously to Jesus.

The grammar also gives additional information regarding Smith's thought at this time. The grammar, in giving rough translations of the Egyptian hieroglyphics, attaches different levels of meanings to each of the symbols. As an example, consider the translation of the term Kolob. In the version of the *Book of Abraham* found in *The Pearl of Great Price*, Kolob is designated as the star closest to where the throne of God is. In Joseph's grammar, Kolob is defined as being the farthest star in the heavens discovered by Abraham and Melchizedek. In another part of the work, Kolob is defined as being the eldest of the stars, the greatest body of the heavenly bodies that has been discovered by man. Joseph uses the term *E Beth Ka* to designate the heaven of heavens where God resides.[10]

The *Book of Abraham* is a cosmological tract. The work parallels both the biblical Genesis and Smith's *Book of Moses* accounts for the origin of the universe. Yet, it stands apart from these other works and is unique. The *Book of Abraham* mentions that many Gods were present at the creation. It is the first solid appearance in Mormon literature of what would become characteristic of Nauvoo thought, the plurality of Gods. Mormon apologist B. H. Roberts stated that in the *Book of Abraham* "we have the first unimpeachable reference to a plurality of Gods."[11]

The grammar contains Smith's first attempts at translating the papyrus which became the *Book of Abraham*. All of the material that provided the background text for the *Book of Abraham* is contained within the grammar. Yet, the grammar is silent on the concepts of a plurality of Gods, and that God was once a man.[12] If Smith discovered the plurality of Gods while reading the papyrus, it was not done so during the first several years of his acquiring the papyri texts.

Smith's grammar makes reference to a plurality of worlds and gives the location of the planet on which God dwells, but makes no mention of a plurality of Gods. While Smith's grammar contains all pertinent information that is unique to the *Book of Abraham*, one item is notably absent, the concept of a plurality of Gods. This leads us to theorize that the *Book of Abraham* was translated in two parts, and at two different times in Smith's history. The first two chapters were definitely translated while the Church was in Kirtland, prior to 1839. The grammar was compiled about 1835 to 1838. The remaining chapters of the *Book of Abraham* must have been translated after this.

The early chapters of the *Book of Abraham* are contained in the grammar, and teach monotheistic concepts of the divine. The polytheistic chapters of the *Book of Abraham* begin at Chapter Four. Smith must have translated from the Egyptian texts a second time. When this occurred is difficult to establish. Smith's diaries mention the papyrus often from 1835 to 1838.[13] The diaries are then silent with reference to the papyrus for the next several years. In 1842, Smith's diaries record that he has begun to work with the papyrus once again. Smith states that shortly before the publication of the translated papyrus in March of 1842 he started to translate again. The final result would be the final chapters of the *Book of Abraham*.

If the only concept contained in the *Book of Abraham* that is not present in the grammar is the concept of a plurality of Gods, it stands to reason that if Smith, as he claimed in his June 16, 1844, sermon, was introduced to the concept of a plurality of Gods while translating the Abraham papyrus, we would see this evidenced in the grammar. The concept of a plurality of Gods is, however, absent from the grammar. This does not mean that the origin of a plurality of Gods concept was not taken from the ancient papyrus, or for that matter that Smith did not come to the conclusion that a plurality of Gods existed while translating the papyri. Rather, two developments would have needed to take place in order for the sermon of June 1844 to be historically accurate. The developments would be: 1) Smith's introduction to Hebrew, and the meaning of Elohim; 2) Smith completing the translation of the papyrus at a later date.

Mormon apologist Hugh Nibley contends that the grammar was not used to translate the papyrus.[14] There are however too many similarities between the *Book of Abraham* and the grammar to dismiss the influence of the grammar on the *Book of Abraham*. Many of the meanings given to the symbols contained in the grammar reappear in the *Book of Abraham*. The contents of the first two chapters of the *Book of Abraham* are included in the grammar as well. These translated portions would date from the mid to late 1830s. Hebraist Louis Zucker also notes that several Hebraisms exist in the text of the grammar.[15] This can be accounted for by Joseph's learning of Hebrew in 1835-36.

Establishing a Provenance for the Book of Abraham

The current *Book of Abraham* shows that a distinct theological shift occurred while the book was being translated, or shortly before it was published. The first three chapters of the book consistently refer to God in a singular form. Beginning in the fourth chapter, a shift occurs and Gods is used consistently throughout the remainder of the work. A major theological shift appears to have occurred in Latter-day Saint thought between 1835, when the translation was begun, and 1842, when the completed translation appeared in the pages of the *Times and Seasons*.[16] (The completed translation of the papyrus was published in the *Times and Seasons* as the *Book of Abraham*. The completed translation appeared in the March 1, 15, and May 15 issues of the *Times and Seasons*.[17]) This shift, within the same document, can only be explained by the document being translated in separate stages.

A proper chronology and correct translation date for the *Book of Abraham* are important for any understanding to the development of the Mormon tradition. Students of the Latter-day Saint movement point to the *Book of Abraham* for the origin of the plurality of God's theology. If the entire work was translated during the 1830s, then a plurality of Gods concept would be represented in Mormon thought at least five years earlier than its first publication date. If, however, the portions of the work containing references to a plurality of Gods was translated just prior to the work's publication that would place the plurality of Gods concept at a later date in the Church's history.

Evidence is cited that Smith had completed the translation of the papyrus by November 2 of 1837.[18] The evidence supporting a two-stage translation theory of the *Book of Abraham* outweigh this claim.[19] The March 1 *Times and Seasons* published what was to become chapters 1:1–2:18. The earlier Egyptian grammar contained chapters 1:32–2:15 in a completely translated variant form. On March 8, 1842, Smith, in a statement recorded in the *History of the Church*, states, "I recommenced translating from the records for the tenth number of the Times and Seasons."[20] The tenth number was the March 15 issue of the paper which included the remainder of the *Book of Abraham* from 2:19–5:21. This would seem to support the two-stage translation theory.[21] This then would place the origin of the plurality of Gods concept in the 1840s, rather than the 1830s.

Another point that we should consider is the authority of the *Book of Abraham* and its influence upon the beliefs of the Mormon people. While there is no doubt that the *Book of Abraham* mentions a plurality of Gods, would this necessarily constitute its being considered as authoritative doctrine? Returning to B. H. Roberts' argument regarding the *Book of*

Abraham, that it is the first impeachable reference to a plurality of Gods, some comments are necessary. Roberts,[22] it appears, has fallen victim to the Mormon historical dilemma, interpreting past doctrinal teachings within present theological definitions. It is true that the *Book of Abraham* teaches a concept of a plurality of Gods. It is also true that it was published in 1842 and therefore became the first public literary record of that concept. In regards to this then the central question that needs to be addressed is: Did Mormonism believe in the concept of a plurality of Gods in the early 1840s? Available evidence would seem to suggest that Mormonism did not hold to a plurality of Gods concept, definitively, before 1844.

The earliest reference to the *Book of Abraham* papyrus is an editorial in the *Messenger and Advocate* in 1835.[23] The editorial stated that the papyrus was believed to be the writings of Abraham and Joseph while in Egypt. Between 1835 and 1842, there is little public mention of the papyrus until its publication in March of 1842.

The Mormon mindset in this period revolved around the translation of foreign documents. In the *Messenger and Advocate* editorial, the writer seems to suggest that this dispensation would see the return of many wonderful documents from past ages, explaining new truths of God. Of these soon to be revealed documents, the *Book of Mormon* had just been the first.

When the *Book of Abraham* appeared in the *Times and Seasons*, it was accompanied by a preface explaining that the document was taken from papyri "purporting to be the writings of Abraham" while he was in Egypt. The disclaimer, in the *Times and Seasons*, is similar to the introduction to the papyrus in the 1835 *Messenger and Advocate*. The preliminary release stated that the papyrus allegedly contained the writings of Abraham and Joseph while they resided in Egypt, and that the Saints should expect a translation in a short time.[24]

The teachings of the *Book of Abraham*, in order to be considered as official Mormon doctrine, would have had to have been canonized. In that event it would not have been considered Mormon doctrine until the 1880s. Yet we cannot assume that because a concept or document has not been canonized that it is not representative of the beliefs of the vast majority of an organization. Or even that because a document is not canonized, that it does not represent the official teachings of the organization. One only needs to look to the King Follett discourse of 1844 to realize that a problem exists between what is believed and what is canonized.

The publication of the *Book of Abraham* had far-reaching implications. The accepted doctrine of the 1840s would have been the concepts taught by a canonized document, the *Lectures of Faith*. The *Lectures of Faith* were accepted as official Church doctrine at the General Conference in the summer of 1835. In 1842, we have the introduction of a document teaching a nascent henotheism, the *Book of Abraham*. Yet, the *Book of Abraham* makes no claim to be authentic, rather it purports to be the writings of Abraham.[25]

This is not meant to imply that many Saints did not see the *Book of Abraham* as being a product of revelation or a work containing truth.[26] The older thought, represented by the *Lectures of Faith*, and the newer thought, expressed in the *Book of Abraham*, presented the Saints with at least two theological options to believe in. While the *Book of Abraham* gained in prominence, eventually becoming canonized in the 1880s, the *Lectures of Faith* became less representative of Mormon thought, and eventually were decanonized by 1921.

We should not imply by this argument that the plurality of Gods concept was not accepted as Mormon doctrine until the 1880s. Yet we can make the argument that the first unimpeachable public teaching, declaring the plurality of Gods concept to be eternal truth, was introduced to Mormonism with the King Follett discourse, and not through the *Book of Abraham*.[27]

Our reasons for arguing this are taken from two major sources. The first is the King Follett discourse, and the second is the *Nauvoo Expositor*. In the King Follett discourse, Joseph, in providing evidence to support his view for a Council of Gods existing, makes no reference to the *Book of Abraham*. His sole textual references are drawn from the biblical text of Genesis and its original Hebrew reading. The line of reasoning follows that if the *Book of Abraham* was a scriptural document that contained truth, Joseph would have referenced it in the King Follett discourse. Instead, he makes no mention of the *Book of Abraham*, but resorts to a midrashic exegesis of the Genesis account of the creation of the universe. While the King Follett discourse and the *Book of Abraham* deal with similar topics—the creation of the universe—Smith does not consider the *Book of Abraham* as a source text for the plurality of Gods concept. It is only after the dissent caused by the sermon itself, and the publication of the *Nauvoo Expositor* on June 7, 1844, that Smith cites the *Book of Abraham*. In Smith's defense of his prophetic calling, on June 16, 1844, he appeals to the *Book of Abraham* to prove that the plurality of Gods concept is of a divine source.[28]

William Law's *Nauvoo Expositor* claimed that Smith was a false prophet for teaching that a hierarchy of Gods and a plurality of Gods existed.[29] Smith addresses Law's criticisms in the sermon of June 16th. The sermon is the only reference to the *Book of Abraham* as an authoritative document.[30] Smith does not appeal to the *Book of Abraham* as scripture, he merely appeals to the central figure of the writing—Abraham. Smith's reference to the *Book of Abraham* in the June 16, 1844, discourse was an attempt to dispel dissension that had risen following the King Follett discourse's teachings. By formulating his argument to support a plurality of Gods concept from the *Book of Abraham*, his claims could go unchallenged in Nauvoo. Smith appeals to the "reasoning of Abraham," and as Smith had translated the *Book of Abraham*, who could dispute his interpretation of the papyrus of Abraham?

There is evidence to support the claim that Mormons in the early 1840s neither believed nor taught that a hierarchical Council of Gods, or a plurality of Gods, existed in the same sense as a post King Follett discourse Mormonism would hold. By examining the text it appears that the introduction of the *Book of Abraham* in 1842 was not seen as the introduction of new doctrine. If following the introduction of the *Book of Abraham* Smith would have elaborated on the plurality of Gods concept, or even referenced the newly translated work itself, then we could say that the belief was present in Mormonism. Yet we find little evidence to indicate that Smith taught the plurality of Gods concept between March 1842 and April 1844.[31]

It seems safe to say that to the majority of Latter-day Saints, in 1842, the *Book of Abraham* would have been seen as a peculiar work that had been translated by Smith. It is doubtful that it was seen as either authoritative or representative of Latter-day Saint belief in the early 1840s. It is only in light of the teachings introduced by the King Follett discourse that the work gained any importance at all. With the canonization of the *Book of Abraham* in 1880, we have the Church attempting to legitimize the teachings of the King Follett discourse by giving an earlier work, the *Book of Abraham*, scriptural status. We must conclude that through the teachings of the King Follett discourse, the plurality of Gods concept was introduced into Mormonism, rather than through the *Book of Abraham*.

The Hebrew Influence on the Cosmology of the Book of Abraham

How then does the *Book of Abraham* fit into the development of Mormon thought? What is its major role in the development of the Mormon concept of God? One thing is clear. The *Book of Abraham* teaches the concept of a plurality of Gods. While the *Book of Abraham* teaches that several Gods participated in the creation of the universe, it should not be taken as a work which contains the nascent concepts which by 1844 were fully developed into the cosmic henotheism of the King Follett discourse.

The teachings of the *Book of Abraham*[32] are fairly explicit with regards to the concept of a plurality of Gods. The work appears to be an expanded commentary of the origin of the cosmos. The first three chapters of the work definitely are an elaboration of material hinted at in the biblical Genesis creation account. The important passage, to our discussion, begins at the 24th verse of the third chapter. The majority of the first three chapters were translated by Smith in the middle to late 1830s. The first three chapters are translated in accordance with Smith's view of God at that time, a binatarian concept. This is seen in the following passage:

> And there stood one among them that was like unto God, and he said unto those who were with him: We will go down, for there is space there, and we will take of these materials, and we will make an earth whereon these may dwell.[33]

Beginning in Chapter Four, the text makes a drastic shift in its content and word use. Beginning with the first verse of Chapter Four the text introduces a plurality of Gods.

The text reads:

> And then the Lord said: Let us go down. And they went down at the beginning, and they, that is the Gods, organized and formed the heavens and the earth.

What makes the passages of the *Book of Abraham* distinct from his earlier works is Smith's conscious effort to translate the noun God (Elohim) as Gods. Smith does this on a consistent basis throughout the latter part of the Abraham text. Most likely this is the result of a literal rendition of the Genesis text conditioned by Smith's familiarity with biblical Hebrew.

While the belief in the plurality of Gods may represent Smith's personal theological reflections, it cannot be taken to represent the prevalent Mormon view of God in the early 1840s. It appears possible that the concepts outlined in the *Book of Abraham* are a byproduct of a greater intellectual undertaking, Joseph Smith's learning of Hebrew. His learning of Hebrew gave him the necessary language skills in order to use the Hebrew text of Genesis in 1844 to defend his King Follett discourse, and to translate the Hebrew noun Elohim in its plural form.

In June of 1844, to stem the dissent among the Mormon community caused by the King Follett discourse, Smith appealed primarily to the Hebrew text of Genesis for proof of a plurality of Gods. Smith would also appeal to the *Book of Abraham*, but only as a secondary argument. Using a translation of Genesis as his base text, Joseph would retranslate the English translation God as Gods. Transliterating from the English to the Hebrew, Smith concluded that the English translation must be inaccurate, and translated the Hebrew noun Elohim as Gods. In the creation account of the *Book of Abraham*, Smith replaces God with Gods. Joseph translated the Hebrew noun Elohim as a plural instead of its traditional singular reading. Smith's familiarity with Hebrew is evidenced throughout his translation of the *Book of Abraham*.

While Elohim is a plural form of the noun Eloah, traditionally it was always read as a singular construct. Yet where did Joseph acquire the language skills necessary to come to such a radical conclusion on his own? Joseph had his first introduction to Hebrew in 1835. The Prophet had acquired the services of Professor Joshua Seixas to instruct the School of the Prophets in biblical Hebrew. Seixas who was an able Hebrew scholar brought his newly published *Grammar* to use in instructing the class. Seixas' *Grammar* however follows traditional readings of the noun Elohim as a singular construct. On page 85 of the *Grammar*, Seixas states that Elohim is "a singular noun with a plural form."[34]

Proving that Joseph's introduction to Hebrew, under Seixas, influenced his translation of the *Book of Abraham* is not an easy task. That Smith was influenced by something during his learning of Hebrew can be proved. Louis Zucker points to several Hebrew influences contained in the Egyptian grammar and in the *Book of Abraham* as well.[35] As well, Joseph's study of Hebrew did coincide with the topics of translation in the *Book of Abraham*. Seixas had used parts of Genesis as the core text for his lessons. Yet Seixas' grammar shows that he was not responsible for the change in Joseph's theology. Perhaps, with Joseph's belief that the Bible had been mistranslated, he chose to translate Elohim in its plural form.

As late as 1840, we still have no clear public teaching of a plurality of Gods in Mormon literature. Parley P. Pratt, in an apologetical work from 1840, states that Mormons believe in the Father, Son, and Holy Ghost as one God. Pratt would add that the Father and the Holy Ghost are personages of spirit, and that the Son has a body of flesh and bone.[36] Unless Mormon writers believed and taught in private something contrary to what they published, we must conclude that the plurality of Gods theology is a product of the 1840s rather than the 1830s.

Whether the early Hebrew sessions under Seixas directly influenced Joseph's Nauvoo theology may never be determined. Some aspects of the Hebrew sessions however do appear to have contributed to a certain degree in expanding Smith's theology. Paralleling Joseph's learning of the Hebrew text, he began to use the Hebrew proper nouns Jehovah and Elohim with reference to God. If we look at a prayer written in 1842, we will be able to see this more clearly.

> O thou who seest and knowest the hearts of all men—thou eternal omnipotent, omniscient, and omnipresent Jehovah-God-Thou Elohim, that sittest,

as the psalmist enthroned in heaven, look down upon thy servant Joseph at this time, and let faith in the name of thy servant Jesus Christ, to a greater degree than thy servant has ever enjoyed.[37]

While Smith may have began using the proper nouns with reference to God, he never used them consistently. On occasions, Joseph would refer to the Father with the title of Elohim alone, rather than the double use of Jehovah—God as seen in the above prayer. There appears to be no set pattern for the use of Elohim or Jehovah within any specific context in Mormon literature of the time. The terms Elohim and Jehovah appear to have been used interchangeably to refer either to Jesus, or the Father, and even generically to denote God. Mormon writers during the 1830s usually used the term Jehovah when referring to the Father, and only occasionally used the name Elohim.[38] At times, Joseph Smith called the "god above Jehovah" Elohim.[39] Until 1915, Mormon writers, apostles, and prophets taught that Jehovah was the Father of Jesus. The controversy over who was Elohim and who was Jehovah was finally resolved in 1915 when the Father became Elohim and Jesus became Jehovah the God of the Old Testament.

Joseph's Kirtland theology was a progressive step towards his Nauvoo theology. Two factors contributed to the formation of the distinct Nauvoo theology: Joseph's introduction to Hebrew, and his emerging self-view as a Prophet of God. The latter, Joseph's prophetic calling, may have had a larger impact than Smith's introduction to Hebrew. Interpreting his calling as a call to restore true Christianity, rather than reform Christianity, allowed Smith to introduce new concepts, uninhibited. With the introduction of new theological concepts, based on an unconventional reading of the Hebrew text, Smith could vindicate his calling. As Louis Zucker has said of Smith during this time period:

> I simply do not think he cared to appear to the world as a meticulous Hebraist. He used Hebrew as he chose, as an artist, inside his frame of reference in accordance with his taste, according to the effect he wanted to produce, as a foundation for his theological innovations.[40]

Even though the Hebrew lessons under Seixas coincide with the translation of the *Book of Abraham*, there is no conclusive proof that a connection exists which would allow Joseph Smith to translate Elohim in its plural form. Perhaps we must look to Joseph's second attempt at learning Hebrew.

In 1841 Alexander Neibauer arrived in Nauvoo. Joseph Smith would again begin to study Hebrew under Neibauer. Along with his studies in Hebrew, Joseph would also study Greek, Latin, and German. Under

Neibauer's direction, Joseph would learn to read the four languages with a certain degree of competence.[41] Neibauer would meet with Joseph on a regular basis, instructing him in the various languages. Speculation does exist that Joseph's additional Hebrew sessions under Neibauer contributed to his Nauvoo understanding of the noun Elohim.[42]

Alexander Neibauer is an obscure figure in Mormon history.[43] Little is known of him, and despite his apparent contributions to the life of the Prophet, no biography has yet been undertaken. What little is known of him is gathered from various sources. Neibauer was born in the Alsace region of France. He was of Jewish ancestry, and had studied to become a rabbi. Apparently his focus changed, and he eventually became a dentist. Neibauer converted to the Church in Preston, England, in 1839. Neibauer holds the distinction of being the first Jewish convert to the Church. There is still a shroud of mystery surrounding Neibauer. In 1842, Neibauer contributed two edited articles published as "The Jews" to the *Times and Seasons*.[44] Of particular interest are his references from the *Zohar* in his articles. It appears that Neibauer, while perhaps not versed in its contents, at least was familiar with the work.

Smith's second attempt at Hebrew provides no additional information. If Neibauer, and his familiarity with mystical Judaism, influenced the translation of Elohim into its plural variant, the sources do not bear this out. Perhaps it is as Louis Zucker has concluded, that Smith used his knowledge of Hebrew, not as a translator, but as an artist, who took great liberties with the text.[45] This would seem plausible, given that Smith saw himself as a Prophet of God.

The Book of Abraham *in its Historical Context*

The prominence of the *Book of Abraham* in the development of Mormon thought is difficult to assess. As it appeared in 1842, it seems to be a transitional document between binatarian and henotheistic thought. There is no doubt that the *Book of Abraham* as it appears today is the product of two stages of translation. This is evidenced internally from the earlier modalistic chapters of the work, and the later polytheistic chapters. Additionally, Joseph's own words show that the book is the product of two stages of translation, and a final redaction.[46]

The problem then is not with what the work contains, or teaches, but rather can it be taken as being representative of Mormon thought in the early 1840s? The work may only have been representative of Smith's personal theology. Although they may have influenced the doctrines of the Church to a great degree, Smith's personal convictions did not constitute the beliefs of the Church's membership, and what it held to be true. The beliefs of the Church were decided by its membership, and this could only be done through a General Conference. The *Book of Abraham* was not presented to a General Conference of the Church for acceptance as doctrine until 1880. Yet one should not be so naive to believe that because a particular work has not been canonized, the church members would not adhere to that work as representative of their faith. The problem is compounded when a new work, one radically different in content, like the *Book of Abraham*, is introduced while an older set of beliefs, the *Lectures of Faith*, is still the official prevalent view. The problem would be easy to rectify if the *Book of Abraham* would have been introduced to the Mormons in Nauvoo through divine revelation, like the *Book of Mormon*, or a "thus saith the Lord," like the revelations of the *Doctrine and Covenants*. Yet the *Book of Abraham* received no such fanfare—only a small introduction in the *Times and Seasons* accompanied the text of the *Book of Abraham*.

How then are we to determine the importance of the *Book of Abraham* to the development of the Mormon concept of God? The answer lies in addressing the authority of the *Book of Abraham*. The problem of the authority of the *Book of Abraham* can be addressed in several ways. In order for the work to be considered authoritative, or expressive of the Mormon concept of God, and part of its belief system, it must be proved that the Church saw the document as such. Yet many preliminary questions would first need to be addressed. I believe that these questions are significant enough to cast doubt on the claim that the *Book of Abraham* is representative of Mormon thought in 1842.

If, in fact, the *Book of Abraham* is to be seen as authoritative, or rather a document of divine origin, why did Joseph Smith begin translating the papyri from which the *Book of Abraham* was taken, then cease, only to take up the translation again in 1842? It would seem probable, that if the papyrus contained important doctrine, or divine instructions, there would have been little time taken to translate and publish the document. If we contrast the time from the acquisition of the plates from which the *Book of Mormon* were translated until the publication of the work, a little over two years transpired. Given that there was also a considerable size difference between the two documents, one would have expected a quick translation and publication of the Abraham papyri. Yet, over six years passed between the commencement of the translation in 1835 and its final publication in 1842. When the work did make its appearance, it was only a partial translation of the entire Abraham material.[47]

Another problem is the way in which the *Book of Abraham* was published. The work was published in the Church-owned newspapers the *Times and Seasons* in America and *The Latter-day Saints Millennial Star* in

England. Unlike other important Latter-day Saint works, the *Book of Abraham* was published in the *Times and Seasons* in three successive editions of the paper. It is true that the Church-owned newspapers did publish material that was later republished in book form such as the revelations of the *Doctrine and Covenants*. While the *Book of Abraham* is smaller in size than the *Book of Mormon*, it was large enough to warrant a separate publication run, such as that which was published in the original edition of the *Pearl of Great Price* in 1851.

The argument can be made that the Church had set a precedent by publishing the revelations of Joseph Smith in Church-owned newspapers of the time. There is substance to the argument, considering that the majority of revelations that comprised the *Doctrine and Covenants* as well as the earlier *Book of Commandments*, were first published in Church periodicals. Both the *Times and Seasons* and the *Evening and Morning Star* carried the revelations that would eventually comprise the *Doctrine and Covenants*, and *Book of Commandments*. The two papers also carried revelations from the Prophet that would not be canonized. That the *Book of Abraham* first appeared in the *Times and Seasons* is then not that unusual. What is unusual is that the next publication date for the *Book of Abraham*, following its initial run in 1842, is in the first edition of the *Pearl of Great Price* in 1851.

The Pearl of Great Price was initially used as a missionary pamphlet in England. It was designed to introduce Mormonism to prospective converts. *The Pearl of Great Price*, including the *Book of Abraham*, was not introduced to North America until 1857, when a copy was secured and brought to Utah.

That there exist such wide gaps in publication dates for the document, and that it was not canonized until 1880, seems to indicate that it was not seen as an important doctrinal work by the Church. It was only after Mormons came to believe in the plurality of Gods that the work became important. This seems to follow the same pattern that emerged with the developing importance of the First Vision.[48]

As to the *Book of Abraham's* inclusion in the *Pearl of Great Price* in 1851? There exists the probability that with the concepts expressed clearly by the King Follett discourse, Mormons came to believe that a plurality of Gods existed. By pointing to the *Book of Abraham* they would have additional proof to substantiate that doctrine. The plurality of Gods concept as expressed by the *Book of Abraham* is subtle compared to the elaborate sermonizing of the King Follett discourse. If this argument is accurate, converts to the Church would have first been introduced to the existence of extrabiblical ancient sources, in order to substantiate the Mormon concept of a plurality of Gods.

Contemporary Sources, Mormon and Anti–Mormon

There are several anti–Mormon sources from the time period that may counter the argument that Mormons, generally, did not believe in or teach a plurality of Gods concept prior to 1844.[49] There are also additional Mormon sources from the same time period, 1838 to 1844, that do mention a belief in the existence of a plurality of Gods concept.[50] These references are all dated to the year 1843.[51] The only Mormon source that appears to predate the publication of the *Book of Abraham* in 1842 is found in *Doctrine and Covenants* Section 121: 28, 32.

The material contained in *Doctrine and Covenants* Section 121 was taken from a personal letter of Joseph Smith. The letter was written in 1839, while he was imprisoned in Liberty, Missouri. The letter was first published in the *Times and Seasons* in May of 1840.[52] The letter, as it appears in the present *Doctrine and Covenants*, contains references to a plurality of Gods which are lacking in the original published account in the *Times and Seasons*. In the present Section 121, verses 28 and 32 read almost as a prophecy of what is to be revealed. The passage reads: " And a time to come in which nothing shall be withheld, whether there be one God or many gods they shall be manifest." This passage is not contained in the original *Times and Seasons* publication. Verse 32 follows: "According to that which was ordained in the midst of the Council of the Eternal God of all other Gods before this world was...." The *Times and Seasons* account reads: "was ordained in the midst of the council of heaven in the presence of the Eternal God, before the world was."[53]

There exist several possibilities for this omission in the *Times and Seasons* account. Either an interpolation has taken place, between 1840 and the present edition of Section 121; or, the original letter contains the verses, but were omitted from the *Times and Seasons* account. The first publication of the Liberty Jail letter, in its present form, appeared in 1857 in the *Latter-day Saints Millennial Star*,[54] and was first included in the *Doctrine and Covenants* in 1876.[55]

There does seem to be some evidence to indicate that the original letter of Joseph Smith from Liberty Jail contained the two verses missing in the *Times and Seasons* account. If this is accurate, Smith would have edited the verses prior to their publication in the *Times and Seasons*.[56] The reasons for editing the verses is not known and any plausible explanation would lead to excessive speculation.

Using *Doctrine and Covenants* Section 121 to prove that a plurality of Gods was taught by Joseph Smith prior to the introduction of the *Book of Abraham* in 1842 cannot be done. The verses that could be used to substantiate a claim that Smith taught a Council of Gods exists are interpolations from a later time period. Even if the verses were included in the original letter by Smith, the omissions were not made public until 1857, after the introduction of the King Follett discourse. If the verses are contained in the original letter from Liberty Jail, we have no way of knowing what was intended by these statements, unless of course we interpret them in light of a post King Follett understanding. We lack contemporary sources which could illuminate the controversial statements in the letter from the Liberty Jail. I think it is fair to say that Smith could have considered the possibility that a plurality of Gods existed. However, to say that Mormons taught and believed that a Council of Gods existed in the early 1840s would do an injustice to the sources.

There exists a reference from Mormon sources in 1843 that could be seen as teaching a plurality of Gods concept. The reference is found in the *Times and Seasons* and is dated to March 1843. The reference mentions a plurality of Gods. The author of the brief reference is not known.[57] The reference adds no additional information to that already dealt with in the *Book of Abraham*. The appearance of the reference in the *Times and Seasons* constitutes its only appearance in Mormon literature.

The problem with the 1840s references is that they never received any additional attention from the Prophet. How then do we view these references? Are we to see them as expressions of Mormon doctrine, or personal revelations containing the same material as a previously published work? Are the revelations to be considered authoritative expressions of the Church's beliefs, or the personal beliefs of an individual? I would tend to hold to the latter.

The problem of finding authoritative statements by Smith to validate the plurality of Gods concept in the early 1840s is difficult. We have accounts that seem to indicate that individual Mormons in the early 1840s appear to have believed in the plurality of Gods. Whether this was the result of a misunderstanding of the teachings of Smith, or a belief that the individuals themselves came to believe from the information at hand is difficult to determine. At any rate the Church, officially, and the Mormons, generally, did not believe in a plurality of Gods, either before or immediately after the introduction of the *Book of Abraham*.

The anti–Mormon statements from the early 1840s are also difficult to assess. The 1840s anti–Mormon writers Henry Caswell and J. B. Turner followed a similar pattern to that set by anti–Mormon writers in the 1830s. They addressed the character of Smith, emotionalism, and the irrationality of the Church's membership, more so than its doctrines.[58] Caswell's tone in his first work, *The City of the Mormons*,[59] is subdued, compared to his second, *The Prophet of the Nineteenth Century*. Caswell's second work was based on J. B. Turner's *Mormonism in All Ages*.

Henry Caswell and J. B. Turner seem to indicate that the Mormons believed in a plurality of Gods concept in 1842. The Caswell reference is a response to Caswell asking a member of the Church whether Mormons believe in a Trinity. The unidentified Mormon responds that they believe that "the Father is God, the Son is God, and the Holy Ghost is God; that makes three at least who are God, and no doubt there are a great many more." Caswell goes on to quote the Mormon "that departed Saints become a portion of the Deity, and may be properly denominated Gods."[60]

J. B. Turner also records a statement that infers that the Mormons believed in a plurality of Gods prior to 1844. While not as direct a reference as Caswell's, Turner, responding to a work by Parley P. Pratt,[61] stated that: "He has declared that they are joint heirs with him." Turner offers an exegesis of the statement.

The Mormons mean:

> Why, truly nothing else than that the saints are all to become equal with God himself. In knowledge and power, and glory, equal to the Father. But this is not all.... Therefore they say, we shall create, uphold, redeem, save, and reign for ever, over still greater worlds than this which Christ governs.[62]

Caswell, in his second work, *The Prophet of the Nineteenth Century*, uses a strong polemical argument against the Mormons. Caswell quotes Turner extensively throughout his work. Drawing on, and expounding on, the Turner statement quoted above, Caswell adds: "Nor is this all. Every true Mormon is not only to be a God and a Christ hereafter, but in his own belief he has been a demigod, or at least an angel, from all eternity."[63]

The statement by Caswell is interesting. It alludes to several concepts presented in the *Book of Abraham*, such as the preexistence of the human spirit. There can be no doubt then that Caswell saw the *Book of Abraham* as an authentic Mormon document.

An assessment of the anti–Mormon writings of Caswell and Turner shows us several things. Caswell and Turner contend that the Mormons believed in a plurality of Gods. The writers draw their conclusions from what they perceive to be authoritative Mormon works. Yet the works from which they draw are not seen as being authoritative by the Mormons themselves. Turner's exegesis of Pratt's statement can be seen as a polemical tactic, given that we have no authoritative sources aside from the *Book of Abraham*, teaching a plurality of Gods concept at this time. Caswell's arguments, in *The Prophet of the Nineteenth Century*, rest upon Turner's exegesis of Pratt's statement. As for Caswell's encounter with the unidentified Mormon in Nauvoo, it is obvious that the individual believed in a plurality of Gods. Yet, can this be taken as the belief of the majority of Saints, or even as an official position? Given the limited authoritative Mormon sources to substantiate their claims, it seems that the anti–Mormon claims that the Mormons believed in a plurality of Gods was a polemical tactic.

The problems of the *Book of Abraham* may be caused by its attempt to reduce dissonance.[64] In this case this would mean while one particular concept is believed, a diametrically opposed concept is entertained or speculated upon. Edward Ashment contends that the *Book of Abraham* is an attempt to resolve conflicting doctrines prevalent in Mormonism at the time. These would include problems with the Elohist and Yahwist creation accounts of Genesis 1 and 3, and the Mormon's *Book of Moses*.[65]

It is impossible to ascertain if the *Book of Abraham* was perceived as a doctrinal work by most Mormons when it first appeared in 1842. The problems associated with the *Book of Abraham* bring us back to a greater problem, authority vs. canon.

The Authority of the Book of Abraham: *An Assessment*

In Mormonism documents are canonized because they teach currently held beliefs at the time of their canonization. Rather than canonize a document because the belief is held at the time of its introduction, Mormons canonize earlier documents because the belief has become entrenched in the belief system. The document that is to be canonized can contain doctrine believed by the Latter-day Saint populace for decades. An example of this is the revelation on plural marriage, which was not canonized until 1880, even though certain Saints had been practicing polygamy since the 1840s.

In canonizing a document, democratic procedures are used in the canonization process. What is accepted by the majority of individuals usually becomes official doctrine. The Church makes no secret of how its doctrine is formed. Each new revelation, translation, or doctrine is subjected to an entire vote of the Church. In order for a document to become part of the canon, it must receive unanimous consent of the membership. The Saints must believe that the document contains truth. The *Book of Abraham* is a classic example of this. When the work was canonized in 1880, the concepts it expressed (plurality of Gods) had already been believed for close to half a century. Yet the origin of the plurality of Gods concept does not come from the *Book of Abraham*, but rather from the King Follett discourse. The problem then is compounded. The canonization of the King Follett discourse would have complicated the logistics of the initial claim of Mormonism—it being a restoration of primitive Christianity. The King

Follett discourse makes no mention of any other work than the Hebrew reading of Genesis to support the plurality of Gods concept. While Smith's capabilities as a Hebraist could be questioned, his abilities as Prophet, Seer, and Revelator could not. No one then, within the Church, could question his translation of the *Book of Abraham.*

In canonizing the *Book of Abraham*, the claim can be made that the concept of a plurality of Gods is contained in a document that is as old as the biblical text itself. The concept as well was believed by Abraham and the patriarchs. This fits well into the overall Mormon hermeneutic that the Gospel is as old as Adam. The King Follett discourse, on the other hand, has its origins in April of 1844. While the Bible may have been incorrectly translated, the *Book of Abraham* was not.

If the King Follett discourse is the first clear expression in Mormonism that a plurality of Gods exists, the entire foundational claim of the Church runs into problems. If there is in existence a document as old as the biblical text itself, in this case the *Book of Abraham*, and it makes no mention of the concept of a plurality of Gods, then the foundational claim of Mormonism being a restoration of primitive Christianity and Joseph Smith as restorationist and Prophet of God falls. The Church then by failing to canonize the *Book of Abraham* would negate its own existence by using the criteria and self-definition it had established. It was therefore imperative that the *Book of Abraham* was canonized in order to give legitimization to the King Follett discourse and its concepts. By doing so, Mormonism was able to say that the concept of a plurality of Gods was known as early as Abraham, and that the concept had been removed from Christianity. Therefore, its claims to restoring the true Church were validated. Through canonizing a work that claimed to be ancient in origin, and containing similar doctrines to that already held by the Church, a stronger case for the restoration could be made. The absence of the plurality of Gods concept from Christianity could be seen as proof that the remainder of Christianity had become apostate. The absence of strong, authoritative statements about a plurality of Gods prior to 1844 would attack the claims of restoration. In this case, the need to place the teaching earlier into its history becomes paramount.

The fact that the *Book of Abraham* was not canonized until 1880 throws doubt upon the significance of the work in terms of Mormon doctrinal development. It seems that as the concept of the existence of a plurality of Gods gained dominance, following the introduction of the King Follett discourse, Mormons gradually came to regard it as true doctrine. As the concept became firmly entrenched in Mormon doctrine, the *Book of Abraham* gained greater significance as a doctrinal work. Yet, the significance that the *Book of Abraham* attained was solely based upon the impact of the

King Follett discourse on Mormon theology, and not as a result of the *Book of Abraham's* teaching.

The first appearance of the *Book of Abraham,* outside of its original publication in the *Times and Seasons* and the *Millennial Star,* was in the missionary pamphlet *The Pearl of Great Price* in 1851. By 1851, the plurality of Gods concept introduced by the King Follett discourse had had significant time to become part of the Latter-day Saint belief system. The inclusion of the *Book of Abraham,* in *The Pearl of Great Price,* as being representative of Mormon doctrine, was the result of the King Follett discourse's teachings, not the teachings of the *Book of Abraham.* Mormon groups that dismiss the particular teachings of the King Follett discourse (i.e., RLDS) also dismiss the *Book of Abraham* as being spurious. This causes one to speculate that if there had been no King Follett discourse, would the *Book of Abraham,* and the plurality of Gods, have become part of Mormon thought?

What we have been able to discern, in our discussion on the *Book of Abraham,* is that a shift occurred in Latter-day Saint thought. Yet, we cannot say that Mormon doctrine changed from monotheism to cosmic henotheism with the publication of the *Book of Abraham.* The *Book of Abraham* contains two distinct interpretations or views of the godhead. This is indicative of Joseph's theological exegesis, not a complete shift in Mormon theology. One should not necessarily call the use of the term Gods in the *Book of Abraham* a new theology, as the use of one term, Gods, does not constitute an entire theology. Arguably, the *Book of Abraham* was translated in two separate and distinct time periods. The translations would have been made between 1835 and 1842. This seems to be the case given that the word God is used in the translation of the first three chapters of the *Book of Abraham,* and the word Gods in Chapter Four onward. Joseph's grammar and diaries would also support the two-stage translation theory.

A conclusion can be reached from the *Book of Abraham,* namely that the work presented the possibility that a plurality of Gods existed. Whether Smith held to this view, or merely individual members of the Church, is also unclear. The problems surrounding the introduction of the work, its authenticity, and authority, and its acceptance by the general Church as doctrine are all left open to debate.

Several things are clear. First, the *Book of Abraham* teaches several concepts that would be incorporated into Mormonism at a later time. A plurality of Gods, preexistence, and a creation through the organization of matter are all taught in the *Book of Abraham.* Secondly, the *Book of Abraham* would become increasingly important after the King Follett discourse was given, as the document was used to substantiate the claim's of that sermon—namely, that a Council of Gods had existed at the organization of the cosmos.

6. IF ANY MAN LACK WISDOM

The First Vision and the Mormon Quest for Legitimization

> [B]y searching the scriptures I found that [mankind] did not come unto the Lord but that they had apostatized from the true and living faith and their [sic] was no society or denomination that built upon the gospel of Jesus Christ as recorded in the new testament and I felt to mourn for my own sins ... therefore I cried unto the Lord for mercy for there was none else to whom I could go [to] obtain mercy and the Lord heard my cry in the wilderness and while in [the] attitude of calling upon the Lord (in the 16th year of my age) a pillar of light above the brightness of the sun at noon day come down from above and rested upon me and I was filled with the spirit of God and the [Lord] opened the heavens upon me and I saw the Lord and he spoke unto me saying Joseph [my son] thy sins are forgiven thee. Go thy (way) walk in my statutes and keep my commandments behold I am the Lord of glory I was crucified for the world that all those who believe on my name may have Eternal life (behold) the world lieth in sin at this time and none doeth good no not one they have turned aside from the gospel and keep not [my] commandments they draw near to me with their lips while their hearts are far from me and mine anger is kindling against the inhabitants of the earth to visit them according to th[e]ir ungodliness and to bring to pass that which (hath) been spoken by the mouth of the prophets and Ap[o]stles behold and lo I come quickly as it [is] written of me in the cloud (clothed) in the glory of my Father.
> — Joseph Smith, 1832

On March 1, 1842, Joseph Smith revealed his story of his first heavenly vision to the American public. Details of the vision, which Smith had told to select persons in the past, were printed in the pages of the Church newspaper, the *Times and Seasons*. This initial religious experience of Joseph Smith has become known as the First Vision.[1] Joseph Smith had prepared the *Times and Seasons* account of his religious experience for John Wentworth, editor of the *Chicago Democrat*. Wentworth had requested the information from Smith for a friend of his, John Barstow, who was compiling a history of New Hampshire. Barstow did not use the material, and Smith had it published in the *Times and Seasons*.[2]

The brief account written by Joseph Smith answered several questions which Wentworth had concerning "the rise, progress, persecution, and faith of the Latter-day Saints." Besides the First Vision, Smith's letter to Wentworth included a brief history of his life and his role in the translation of the *Book of Mormon*. The letter to Wentworth would also include the Church's *Articles of Faith* and a history of the Church from its organization until the Mormons' arrival in Illinois.

Divergent Accounts of a Religious Experience

Various accounts of Joseph Smith's First Vision are found in private and public sources dated during his lifetime.[3] The earliest known account, a holograph account, dates from 1832. The first published account of the Vision was by Orson Pratt in Edinburgh. Pratt's account, published in 1840, was used primarily as a missionary tract in England.[4] The divergent accounts of the First Vision vary in their contents. Major details are either omitted, or altered, dependent on the audience or recorder.

The appearance of the material in the 1842 *Times and Seasons* was the first time many of the American Saints had heard of Joseph's initial visit from heavenly beings. The account of the First Vision, as recorded in the *Times and Seasons*, emphasized the presence of two beings who told Smith that there was a major work for him to do. The *Times and Seasons* account of Smith's Vision can be seen as an interpretation of the events surrounding his roles in the translation of the *Book of Mormon* and the founding of the Church. For modern Latter-day Saints the initial heavenly encounter and its account is seen as the basis for several important theological concepts. The concepts of the apostasy of Christianity, God having a body of flesh and bone, the existence of a plurality of Gods, and the divine call of Joseph Smith as Prophet all have their foundation in the First Vision story. In addition these concepts all find their support as divine revelations of God's truth in the First Vision account. To 20th-century Latter-day Saints the First Vision features prominently as part of the Church's proselytic program. The First Vision, to many, contains the essentials of the Church's beliefs in a condensed form.

Yet the important role attributed by modern Mormonism to the First Vision is a late development. It appears that its importance to the Mormon belief system has changed over the years and now occupies a lofty position with the tradition. As James B. Allen points out in an early article regarding the First Vision:

> This singular story has achieved a position of unique importance in the official doctrines of the Mormon Church. Belief in the Vision ... is second only to belief in the divinity of Jesus of Nazareth.[5]

The unique position attained by the 1st Vision in Mormon history is a development of the last half of the 19th century. It would be primarily through the post 1883 sermons of Apostle George Q. Cannon that the modern interpretation, and significance of the First Vision in Mormonism, began to take shape and gain its present significance.[6]

During the 1830s and early 1840s, little was mentioned of a heavenly vision or a theophany of any kind. Smith's visitation by the angel connected with the *Book of Mormon* was known by individuals both inside and outside of the Church during this early period.[7] The lack of any substantial primary sources surrounding the First Vision gave no indication that Joseph had been visited by additional beings earlier in his lifetime at all. Perhaps, Joseph saw no reason to reveal his personal religious experience. Yet, the fact that the initial vision is not mentioned in public discourses, or in private journals of the time, does raise a few questions surrounding the authenticity of the First Vision. Several of these questions have been addressed by Mormon historians Richard Bushman and James B. Allen.[8] As Allen states:

> The fact that none of the available contemporary writings about Joseph Smith in the 1830s, none of the Church publications in that decade and no contemporary journal or correspondence yet discovered mentions the story in convincing fashion.[9]

Allen goes on to say that not even the anti–Mormon literature mentioned the First Vision. As Allen states: "The earliest anti–Mormon literature attacked the *Book of Mormon* and the character of Joseph Smith but never mentions the First Vision."[10]

This lack of evidence from contemporary Mormon or anti–Mormon sources should not alarm us. Given the methods of recording the sermons of Joseph Smith, only about a fifth of the 250 known sermons of Joseph Smith were ever recorded. Many of these references survive as longhand accounts or reflective accounts written from memory. A large majority of these sources mention only the sermon topic.[11] Of the known sermons of Joseph Smith, only three of Smith's sermons were published before his death in 1844.

The nature in which the material associated with Smith has survived to this day creates problems. The majority of the Joseph Smith historical material survives as either holographic, dictated, or ghost-written manuscripts by Smith's scribes.[12] We do have minor sources which seem to indicate that the theophany was known by close associates of Smith in the mid–1830s. The similarity of words, contained in a sermon topic from 1835, and the First Vision may indicate that Smith had delivered a sermon on his First Vision. W. W. Phelps claims in his diary that he heard a sermon delivered in the Kirtland Temple by Smith entitled "This Is My Beloved Son, Hear Ye Him." Parley P. Pratt, writing to the Saints in Canada in late November of 1836, mentions what appears to be the same sermon.[13] Phelps and Pratt only mention the sermon topic, and do not give any details of the sermon.

Besides these two brief references by Phelps and Pratt there does not appear to be any additional contemporary sources mentioning Smith's sermon on the First Vision. Even if we take into account that the Phelps journal and Pratt's letter are referencing the First Vision and not the Moroni visits, the total sources mentioning the initial theophany, including Smith's account from 1835, are three. The documentary evidence seems to agree with Allen's conclusions; the First Vision did not play an important role in Mormonism during the 1830s.

D. Michael Quinn, in his *Early Mormonism and the Magic World View*, addresses the problem of not having any solid, contemporary evidence to support the First Vision. He points out that in early 19th-century America a theophany was a common occurrence and that Smith, in relating his heavenly visitation, would not have been seen as having a unique experience. Quinn continues that with time the Protestant churches generally began to regard such experiences as having occult origins, and they became less accepted by mainstream Christianity. It would only be after this shift had occurred within mainstream Christianity that relating a visionary experience was considered unique. Quinn notes that over time Joseph began to gain confidence in his calling, and when Joseph had reached a safe level of self-assurance, only then could the true story surrounding the origins of the Church be revealed.[14]

While Quinn's assessment may be accurate, it does not account for several major problems surrounding the First Vision. In an earlier chapter we have pointed out the foundational beliefs of the Mormon Church and the importance of the *Book of Mormon* to that foundation. The First Vision, as it appears in 1842, presents a partial reappraisal of the initial purpose of the Church. As was noted, the Mormon Church of the 1830s was not notably different in its beliefs from the rest of mainstream Christianity, rather it was an attempt to reduce the theological options of the age. With the introduction of the First Vision, we have a partial reevaluation of the Church's purpose and mission. The First Vision would appear to remove the initial emphasis of the Church. This initial emphasis was on an active God in the age of reason and a movement that restored long hidden truths of God to the world. These truths, the "fullness of the Gospel," were revealed through the *Book of Mormon* to the American public, and the world.

The First Vision in time would come to legitimize Joseph's changing and divergent theology by introducing a different origin for the Church and thereby reevaluating the Church's original purpose and mission. The First Vision, itself the result of speculative theology, would give legitimization to the new thought that was emerging in Nauvoo, and place that thought into an earlier time period—namely the foundational period of the Church. In doing this, Smith could counter detractors to the new thought by claiming that they were not new concepts, but that they had been revealed to him at his initial religious experience.

Smith's self-perception over the years had been altered, moving from servant of God to Prophet of the last dispensation.[15] By claiming to have received revelations from God, Smith could do little else but continue on the road on which he had begun. Subsequently, a prophet without new revelations from God is not a prophet. Chronologically, the introduction of the First Vision in Mormon history followed the publication of the *Book of Abraham*. As we have noted earlier, the *Book of Abraham* introduced Mormons to the possibility that a plurality of Gods could exist.[16] Could Smith have introduced the First Vision to lend additional support to concepts expressed in the *Book of Abraham*? In light of the current monotheistic theology, evidenced in Mormon publications during that time, the concepts expressed in the *Book of Abraham* would not have been received as eternal truth.

The late introduction of the First Vision story and no previous mention of an initial theophany creates some additional problems, particularly with regards to the timing of its introduction in 1842. The lack of publicity surrounding the First Vision, for most of the Church's early history, may be seen by detractors of the Church as an admission that the First Vision was fabricated. While the essential details of the events may be called into question, that some form of religious experience was had by Smith cannot.

Throughout early Latter-day Saint history, we have Joseph making references to an experience, or an encounter with divine beings. That is not disputed. The details of the experiences varied, according to the time and to whom they were related. Three versions of this initial experience were related to scribes during Joseph's life, during the years 1832, 1835, and 1839. While the details of the experiences are different from each other, there are similarities.

When comparing the various versions of the First Vision[17] with the official version,[18] key points of difference become apparent. There is a common point in which they agree. The common point is that a heavenly being visited Joseph. The nature of the message, whether it was a response to a personal question or a greater call to restore Christianity, varied throughout the years. In addition, the nature of the beings that visited Joseph Smith changed. Smith's first account, an account dating from 1832, records that one being, that appears to have been Jesus, appeared to him. In spite of its lack of detail, much can be made of this, considering the fact that at this time Smith believed that the Father and the Son were the same person.[19]

Other accounts record that it was an angel that had appeared to Joseph in his initial encounter. Again, it is difficult to assess if the writer of the account was referring to the Moroni visits or the First Vision. In later versions of the Vision, the Father and Jesus both appeared, with the angel being relegated to a secondary role.

What appears to be a recurring theme throughout the various versions is the interpretation of the original event, in light of the current theology. That is to say, as Joseph's theological interpretations shifted from modalism to cosmic henotheism, the details of the vision expanded in the same direction. In a nutshell, this can be seen as: while Joseph still held to basic modalistic concepts, there appeared only one heavenly visitor. During Joseph's binatarian stage, 1835, 1839, 1842, two persons appeared in the details of the vision. We see that as Joseph's theology expanded, so did his understanding and his interpretation of the events surrounding what he saw as his prophetic call.

The First Vision Accounts as Expressions of Contemporary Theology

The first recorded version of the First Vision is in Smith's own handwriting. Smith entered the account at the beginning of his 1832 diary.[20] In this early account, Joseph makes no mention of any prophetic call. There is however a mention of a recurring theme that seems to be consistent in all of the vision accounts, that pertinent questions motivated his prayers to God. In the 1832 account the only major details that are given the reader is that a voice, given the context Jesus, tells Joseph that his sins are forgiven. No direct mention is made of any additional beings present in this earliest account. The 1832 account differs from later accounts in that it does not mention that two or more beings were present at this initial visitation.

This 1832 account seems to be in perfect accordance with Joseph's theology in this time period. Drawing our evidences from other external Mormon sources of the period, it is safe to say that Joseph Smith would have still believed in a modalist concept of God at this time. From Smith's theological perspective, the Father and the Son would have been the same person, as the *Book of Mormon*, the *Book of Moses,* and the *Joseph Smith Translation* would all show.

The second account of the Vision dated 1835 contains additional details in contrast to the 1832 account.[21] The additional details can be accounted for by the shift that occurred from modalism to binatarianism. By 1835, primarily through the learning of Hebrew, Joseph had expanded his theological perspective on God and had made a distinction between the Father and the Son. In the 1835 account written by Warren Parish,[22] Joseph states that:

> a personage appeared in the midst of this pillar of flame, which was spread all around and yet nothing consumed. Another personage soon appeared like unto the first and he said unto me; "thy sins are forgiven thee."

The imagery conveyed in this version of Smith's theophany is reminiscent of the appearance of Yahweh to Moses and the calling of Moses as prophet of Yahweh. Perhaps these additional details, lacking in the first account of 1832, were a direct result of Joseph becoming progressively aware of his calling and his place in history.[23] While still not sure of his place in it, he is beginning to interpret history in light of his self-understanding and the historical events that surround him. If we look at the history of Joseph, we see a figure in the process of becoming acutely aware of his destiny but, at the same time, grappling with it on the basis of insecurities.

As historical events surrounding Smith began to unfold, he acquired a greater understanding of his place in history. Smith may have reinterpreted his formative religious experience in light of his then present understanding. As time progressed, Joseph would come to realize his place in the unfolding history of the world. Once realizing his destiny, he made every attempt to show this superior status to his followers and the surrounding secular society. That Joseph, by his death in 1844, knew his place in history cannot be denied. In a sermon delivered shortly before his death, Joseph Smith makes an attempt to prove to his followers that, despite his inadequacies and failures, he is a prophet of God on the same level as Moses, Elijah, Peter and Paul.[24] Yet, in light of these claims, in his followers' understanding, their interpretation of the mission and the character of the biblical figures and that of Joseph paled by comparison. This, in turn, was evidenced by the tension throughout the Church's history, eventually resulting in his death in 1844.[25]

This sacred view of the biblical figures, their mission and character, is based upon the validity of the biblical text, and a supposition that all that can be known of the biblical figures is contained in the biblical text. In Joseph's case, we have additional knowledge of a prophetic figure which would seem to remove him from the realm of the sacred, and cause his followers to view him as fully human with no aspect of the sacred contained within his mission and character.

This view of Joseph, and the dichotomization of either wholly sacred or wholly profaned rather than a syncretization of the two, is based upon an understanding and interpretation of events, and the validity of the reports surrounding that interpretation. As well, an understanding of the mission and character of the biblical figures, and the imposition of that model upon Joseph, by his followers all come into play. Examples of this dichotomy and imposition are still evidenced today. Mormon fundamentalist groups, primarily those that lean towards an earlier interpretation of Mormonism, all believe Joseph Smith to be the Holy Ghost. They believe Joseph Smith to be the Testator, or Second Witness, that Jesus spoke about in the Gospel of John. This view was fostered by the mission and character of Joseph as Prophet of the Restoration, and by the *Book of Mormon* as a second witness to Christ, plus Joseph's role in bringing this message to the world. These groups view Joseph as divine or wholly sacred.

On the other pole exist evangelical Christians who deny the authenticity of Smith's message on several grounds. They deny the theophany, because no man has seen God. They deny the *Book of Mormon*, because whoever adds to the Bible is cursed of God. Finally they deny Smith's mission as Prophet of God, because he dabbled in treasure seeking, the occult, and practiced polygamy, which are all contrary to evangelical Christian interpretations of the biblical text.

For the evangelical Christian community, the mission and character of Joseph Smith are contrary to their understanding and interpretation of the mission and character of Moses, Elijah, Peter, and Paul. From the evangelical perspective, the mission and character of Smith fails compared to the biblical figures. By comparing what is known about Smith's mission and character to what is known about the biblical figures' mission and character Smith does not make the grade as a servant of God. Evangelical Christians compare Joseph Smith, a man about whom much is known, against established and accepted servants of God, men about whom little is known. This is based upon their understanding that all that was known, can be known, or will be known about the biblical figures is contained within the biblical text.

For example, we know where Joseph Smith was born, where he lived, what he ate, where he died, and how he died. These points are all verifiable.

Of any of the biblical figures, is as much known about them as about Joseph Smith? For some of the biblical figures more is known about them than others. We still have no concrete information about the birth of Peter or Paul, how long they lived, and when they died. We have traditions that have been passed down within the Christian Church that answer these questions to a degree. What we do know about the biblical figures is what they taught and the impact of that teaching upon the audience and upon subsequent generations that held to those teachings.

With regard to their teachings, we are able to draw some form of character analysis that will give us a glimpse of what the individual figures may have been like. It is doubtful that this problem can be resolved by comparing Joseph Smith, an individual about whom much is known, to individuals of whom little is known.

In returning to our original topic, the First Vision account of 1835, we are able to draw several key points of information from it. The theological precepts alluded to in the 1835 Vision are in perfect congruence with the thought of Joseph Smith at the time. This can be seen in documents such as the *Lectures of Faith* and the 1837 *Book of Mormon*. The two documents reflect a slight shift from the original strict modalism of the early Kirtland period to a binatarian theology. The First Vision account of 1835 is similar to the theology of the *Lectures of Faith*. The Vision can be chronologically placed between the *Lectures of Faith*, and the revision of the *Book of Mormon* in 1837. The *Lectures of Faith*, while prepared during the winter of 1834-35, were not available for sale until after August 17, 1835.[26] The *Doctrine and Covenants*, which contained the *Lectures of Faith*, was accepted as part of the canon at the August conference of 1835. The date Smith recorded the Vision was November 9, 1835. The 1835 Vision presented a more detailed explanation of Smith's heavenly encounter, mentioning that two beings had appeared to him. Smith would add that one of the beings, an angel Smith said, had stated that "Jesus Christ is the Son of God."[27]

In the 1835 Vision account a distinction is made between the two beings present. The versions of the vision that followed this shift are even more pronounced. By 1838, as a result of Smith's introduction to the Hebrew language, the Father and the Son were often identified as Elohim and Jehovah. This had created a clear distinction between the members of the godhead. As Smith moved closer to a henotheistic concept of the divine, the persons in the godhead would be seen as separate and distinct beings. In the 1839 account of the First Vision, the Father and the Son both appear and give instructions to Joseph Smith.[28]

The 1839 account is significant to our understanding of the First Vision.[29] It is this version that has become the official account of Smith's initial theophany. The 1839 account is the earliest recorded account we have of who the individuals that appeared to Smith were. Aside from Smith's interview with *Pittsburgh Gazette* editor David White in 1843,[30] no other reference to the theophany mentions who the individual beings were. The story of the theophany was relayed eight times during Smith's life, with each account varying in its details.[31]

Between the years 1837 and 1840, there appeared to have been little speculation on the godhead. Perhaps the social conditions of the time, the failure of the banking and land speculation venture in Ohio, and the Mormons' eventual expulsion from Missouri did not allow for theological speculation.[32] If the view of Apostle Parley P. Pratt is indicative of Mormonism in the early 1840s, no major theological changes have occurred. As Parley P. Pratt would say in 1840: "Whoever reads our books, or hears us preach, knows that we believe in the Father, Son, and Holy Ghost as one God."[33]

The Use of the First Vision to Legitimate the Prophetic Call

The last few years of the Church's Kirtland tenure produced little in the way of doctrinal development. As I have alluded to earlier, the time appears to have been marked by social upheaval. Fawn Brodie in her biography of the Prophet, *No Man Knows My History*, states that as a result of the failures in the secular realm in both economic and social experiments (i.e., Kirtland Anti-Banking Society, United Order, expulsion from Missouri, apostasy) claims that the Prophet had fallen were beginning to circulate.[34] This pattern emerged again later, when social conditions rose in Nauvoo that were not favorable to the Saints.[35]

It appears that at critical times in the Prophet's history, when questions begin to circulate regarding his leadership abilities and particularly his calling as the Prophet, his most innovative theological statements are made. This can be seen from later dates, especially in 1844, through the introduction of the King Follett discourse and the sermon of June 16. By 1839 the Saints had endured failure in Ohio and expulsion from Missouri. Having endured hardship the Saints were set on carving a new kingdom for God on the banks of the Mississippi, at a place they were to call Nauvoo. It is perhaps to quell the rising dissent and to restore confidence in his ability to lead the Church of the last dispensation that Smith chose this time to reveal his most personal religious experience, the First Vision.

There is, however, a major difference in the social conditions between 1839 and 1844. The King Follett discourse and the June 16 sermon were public discourses aimed directly at quieting opposition to himself.[36] It should be remembered that the dissenters had gone public in 1844 with their allegations against the prophet. The Vision on the other hand was not made public, but was related to select individuals. There is no doubt that the 1839 account of the theophany was seen as an important item, by Smith. Smith had prepared the account for an official history, a history that was to be made public.[37] The Vision played an important part in how Smith wanted the Saints and the world to remember him, his call, his mission, and the role he played in the history of the world.[38]

Joseph Smith responded to the discontented Saints by assuring them that he was the Prophet of God. It is precisely following the failure of expectations in Ohio and Missouri that Joseph affirms his calling by preparing the 1839 First Vision account. The difference between this version and the earlier versions is the content of the message. In the 1839 account, Smith is called by the Father and the Son, making clear to all who questioned that despite the secular failures that he was still a Prophet of God. In this light, the First Vision story can be seen as an attempt to resolve inner conflict arising from what must have been seen as an abandonment by God of his people and to restore faith among the Saints. Through the relating of the Vision Smith can be seen as reasserting his position as head of the Church. Through his divine call, the social upheaval facing the Saints could be resolved. In a way it may have been Smith's way of assuring his followers that God had not abandoned them and things would turn out for the best. Joseph Smith needed followers with faith in his calling. He was sustained as the Prophet of the Church and kept in that position through a democratic process, rather than as a divine right. (Interestingly this democratic process is evident in the greater cosmological scheme of Mormonism as God rules the universe through cooperation with his council, comprised of lesser Gods and angels.)

If a historical model can be drawn with the information pertaining to the First Vision it appears that at specific times Joseph Smith used his religious experience strategically to reaffirm his position as head of the Church. This can be evidenced in several places throughout Mormon history. In 1832, problems among the Saints had brought doubt to the minds of the Saints regarding Smith's ability to lead the Church.[39] Coincidentally, this marked his first affirmation of having received a vision from God. When Smith gives the particulars of his vision, it is in terms of his own theological understanding of the time, modalism. The 1832 Vision makes no mention of either member of the godhead appearing to him, only that a personage of light appeared.

The 1835 Vision mentions that both the Father and the Son appeared to Joseph Smith. The variances in the particulars of the 1832 and 1835 visions can be explained. In 1832 Smith still held to a Judeo-Christian concept that no man has seen God. As well, his strict modalism would only allow for one being as God. By 1835, Smith perhaps had become aware that several individuals had made claims to having theophanies. Men such as Emmanuel Swedenborg, Charles Finney, and others all claimed to have seen God. With this in mind Smith began to reinterpret his initial religious experience in terms of an encounter with the divine. Smith had come to make a distinction between the Father and the Son after 1833, and the personages of the First Vision became the Father and the Son.

Despite all of the above we have not yet touched upon a question that seems central to our discussion. If Smith had not made the First Vision part of the public record, how would the people be assured of Smith's calling, if they were not aware of the theophany in the first place? The answer can be that while Smith made no public proclamation surrounding the First Vision, several key members of the Church, W. W. Phelps, Parley P. Pratt, Oliver Cowdery, all did have knowledge of the theophany. In what may be a speculative leap Smith's selection of key leaders within the Mormon community to whom he would reveal his theophany would in fact strengthen his claim to possessing a divine call. While rank and file members of the church may have questioned the leadership of Joseph Smith, and may even have resigned from the church as a result, without a strong, respected core of individuals surrounding him, Smith would have faced a mass exodus of those same rank and file members. Choosing key individuals whom he could trust would provide several avenues and voices. This eventually disseminated the story of the Vision to the remainder of the Church. In contrast to the 1844 apostasy it was precisely the opposition from key members of the inner core that resulted in Smith's death. While a public affirmation of his calling would have been quicker in resolving the conflicts in Kirtland, we have no solid historical evidence aside from the Phelps journal entry and the Pratt letter to support the notion that Smith revealed his theophany to the Saints publicly.

Another plausible answer can be that Smith was not really attempting to gain public approval of his calling as much as he was attempting to alleviate the doubt that existed in his own mind surrounding his calling.

If we look at this problem in this light, Joseph Smith was aware that he had had a religious experience and had been called as a servant of God. As to the particulars of this calling, and to how this calling was to manifest itself, he was not aware. In fact, it appears that he was not even aware of who exactly had called him. Was it a messenger of God, God himself, or Jesus that had called him to do a major work? As events began to unfold before him he saw the hand of God, per se, in the unfolding of the events which were beyond his control. Smith then began to interpret these events in light of his self-definition and calling. The appearance of, and the telling of, the theophany at critical times can be seen as a method of self-assurance that he was called of God. Smith would then see the chaos that was present as part of a greater plan, which in God's eyes was perfectly structured, but from mankind's reductionist viewpoint seemed chaotic. The relaying of the First Vision was a source for the renewal of his own faith in his calling and in God, and that while the temporary conditions seemed chaotic, God was still in control and had not abandoned Joseph Smith or the Saints in general.

The telling of the First Vision to select individuals would confront the social conflict on two sides. Initially, it was a personal affirmation for Smith that he was still the Prophet, and secondly, to the Saints at large, it reaffirmed this prophetic call in the eyes of the people. The social problems that had existed in Kirtland and Missouri would be resolved and Smith's prophetic calling then could no longer be questioned. In essence it may have been Smith's way of saying that God was still in control in spite of the failures and hardships that the Saints had endured.

The significance of the First Vision in Mormon history can take on many definitions. The telling of the First Vision had both immediate and future implications. On a personal level, it was psychological success. It gave Smith's work meaning and him a sense of destiny. On an institutional level the Church was reaffirmed that someone beyond the man, Joseph Smith, was in control of the situation, and that the conditions that existed were all part of the greater plan of God.

In a greater societal context the First Vision story takes on another dimension. Originally the appearance of heavenly beings in an early 19th-century setting was not uncommon. As North American society began to move away from a mythological to a scientific interpretation of its worldview, the First Vision became increasingly important. This interpretation would seem to follow the historical evidence surrounding the expanding role of the First Vision. As Allen has so aptly pointed out, the First Vision did not figure prominently in any evangelistic endeavors by the Church until the 1880s.[40] Allen, while presenting historical evidence, fails to offer a plausible explanation for this occurrence. Could it be that the early converts, while believing the *Book of Mormon* and practicing the gifts of the spirit (tongues, prophecy, healings), plus having a common New England background, would not interpret Smith's theophany as being that significant or unique from any other early 19th-century person with a religious experience?[41] Over time, in the shadow of the enlightenment, a belief in theophanies and a theology more reminiscent of an earlier mythological view were gradually being abandoned. It would follow then that the emergence of the First Vision in Mormon history, as a public document, could have been used to convince the Latter-day Saint that God had appeared to Joseph Smith and had called him to do a major work, to restore apostate Christianity.

This may account for the First Vision being used as parts of missionary pamphlets by Orson Pratt in 1840[42] and by Orson Hyde in 1842[43] during their missions in Europe. Seeking converts from mainline denominations, the Saints in Europe never achieved major missionary success outside England. It may be of interest to note that the greatest missionary field in Europe, England, was the home to Methodism, which concentrated upon the experiential over and against a logical approach to religion. Orson Hyde's first missionary tour of Germany produced few converts. The German mission, including Switzerland, Austria, and Germany, has fewer converts today than Canada, a country with about a third of the population.

The emergence of the First Vision as an important arm of the Church's proselytic program in the 1880s can be seen as a faith promoting tool designed to reform a Church that had become stagnant by years of isolation in Utah. Seeing the renewal of faith brought on within the Church by the introduction of the First Vision, it took on a new meaning and gained precedence as a missionary tool in America. Transitions in American religious society by the 1880s had brought us into the fundamentalist-modernist era. The advances of biblical criticism in the 1840s, 1850s, and 1860s had crossed the oceans from Germany to America.[44] In the 19th century, American theology had become demythologized. As it had been used earlier in Europe during the 1840s, the First Vision began to take on its new meaning. God had once again spoken. The *Book of Mormon*, and the establishment of the Church in the 1830s, had hoped to show an active God in the age of reason. The First Vision would attempt to show that God had not forsaken the world, but had spoken, and continued to speak as God had done in the past.

Joseph Smith, and the Mormon Church to a greater extent, had come use the First Vision to legitimate the claims as the only true Church on earth. This legitimization was once carried out by the *Book of Mormon*, and the gifts of the Holy Spirit (tongues, prophecy, healings). With time, the *Book of Mormon* began to play a minor part in Mormon theology as new revelations began to take precedence. Through the emergence of the First Vision as an important part of Mormon theology, Joseph Smith and the Church had legitimized their roles as Prophet of God and true Church.

As Mormon thought developed, we see a dialectic emerging as newer progressive thoughts compete for dominance over older views. As new interpretations of older thoughts are given, there is a reluctance to completely discard the old concepts. This creates a series of theological options for the members of the Church. Yet, at certain times, the Church has completely discarded the older thoughts by reinterpreting them. The Church also changed by allowing new thought to attain precedence over old thought in an unchallenged fashion.

These aspects of development within the Mormon tradition are seen through the removal of documents such as the *Lectures of Faith*, which once were part of the Mormon canon but have now become obsolete. The *Lectures*, which had played only a minor role in Mormon doctrinal development, proved to be dispensable. On the other hand, other canonized works could not so easily be removed, even though they also had become obsolete. The *Book of Mormon* and the *Book of Moses* are prime examples of this. Their modalism represents a theological perspective further removed from the cosmic henotheism of today than the *Lectures of Faith* were. The modalism of the *Book of Mormon* and the *Book of Moses* present a theological view that is no longer prevalent in the Church, nor has it been for over 100 years. Yet, to remove these two works would require a major reinterpretation of Mormon doctrinal history.

There have been attempts at reconciling the divergent theological opinions in the Church over the past 100 years. If an attempt has been made it has usually taken on two facets, removal or reinterpretation. The divergent material is either removed, as with the *Lectures of Faith*, or denied, as with the Adam-God doctrine. The second facet involves a reinterpretation of older material, whereby earlier concepts are reinterpreted by definitions worked out in a later time period. In this sense when the *Book of Mormon* teaches the belief in one God, it is read as "one in purpose," rather than within its original modalist context.

The Mormon quest for legitimization of its foundational purpose has produced a Church that has within its theological framework the tools with which to reconcile its past doctrinal inconsistencies (i.e., progressive revelation or the concept of modern prophecy superseding past prophecy), yet it is reluctant to use it. Throughout its history, instead of appealing to modern prophecy and the argument of line upon line or progressive revelation to deal with obsolete or inconsistent concepts, it has appealed to reinterpretation and alignment of past concepts with present concepts. The emergence of the First Vision is a syncretic approach to deal with past doctrinal inconsistencies on a broad scale. What it attempts to do is, in one giant sweep, gather all of the doctrinal inconsistencies, such as a plurality of Gods, God being an exalted man, the purpose of the Church, and the calling of Joseph Smith, and place it into an earlier time frame. The First Vision becomes an attempt to deal with 50 years of doctrinal development, and reinterpret this development as insignificant, or as something that never occurred.

This quest for legitimization is something that need not have been done. The validity of the Church, by self-definition, was based upon the ability to remain progressive and changing throughout history. This is something of which the Church never took complete advantage. Instead, when stagnation occurred, a new origin myth was introduced, and from it, the Church took on a new self-definition which it carved from societal expectations, as the need for legitimization took precedence over the earlier self-definition.

The Mormon Church, despite its claims to progressive revelation, became stagnant in its thought. It reached a certain point of development and from that point it did not progress. Rather, the Church reinterpreted its foundational purpose and mission. By placing the First Vision into its historical context, as the origin myth of the Mormon Church, we can see that the First Vision, as commonly believed by most Latter-day Saints, is a product of a theologically stagnant church. The First Vision replaced the *Book of Mormon* as the central piece of theology that legitimized and validated the Latter-day Saint Church's existence.

As the *Book of Mormon* had once answered the questions of its time period, so too would the First Vision answer the questions of late 19th century. While the *Book of Mormon* dealt with the Jacksonian American questions, Christology, free will, democratic process, predestination, and infant baptism, the First Vision dealt with greater questions that had emerged, namely, the theory of evolution, and the evolution of humans to Gods. As an origin myth for the Mormons, the First Vision looks historically out of place. It answers the questions of a later generation rather than the questions of an earlier generation to which it is allegedly seeking to address. Only in the shadow of evolutionary progression and the rise of science can the First Vision make sense. Evolution had established a culture of anthropocentrism. The questions arising from this would naturally be how far can man develop. In a Western based linear view of history, the only result can be to become a God.

The First Vision would legitimize the claims of the Church in light of new scientific evidence and discovery. That the Church saw things in this light is evidenced by the backlash against science by leaders of the Church in the 20th century.[45]

The First Vision replaced the *Book of Mormon* as the key to Mormon self-definition and understanding. It redefined the Church's mission and legitimized the existence and purpose of the Church. The First Vision gradually came to validate the Church's claims to being God's true Church. It attempted to make sense out of an ever-changing world, and attempted to bring a message of hope to an American public that was rapidly becoming prosperous and enlightened. The First Vision attempted to harmonize new scientific theory with a belief in God. By placing the First Vision back into its own history, the Church would give itself an added advantage by stating that God was progressive, and that God revealed to humankind his plan in terms of humankind's own understanding. As humankind came to new heights of understanding, new areas of theology could be opened. The Church could add to its claims that they had insights into the new scientific theories long before others, proving to a doubting public that God was not dead, and that the Mormon Church was true.[46]

7. AND YE SHALL BE GODS

Placing the King Follett Discourse in Its Historical Perspective

> Inasmuch as we have for years borne with the individual follies and iniquities of Joseph Smith and many other official characters in the Church of Jesus Christ, (conceiving it a duty incumbent upon us so to bear,) and having labored with them repeatedly with all Christian love, meekness and humility, yet to no effect, feel as if forbearance has ceased to be a virtue, and hope of reformation vain; and inasmuch as they have introduced false and damnable doctrines into the Church, such as a plurality of Gods above the God of this universe, and his liability to fall with all his creations; the plurality of wives, for time and eternity; the doctrine of unconditional sealing up to eternal life, against all crimes except that of shedding innocent blood....
>
> [W]e call upon the honest in heart, in the Church, and throughout the world, to vindicate the pure doctrines of Jesus Christ, whether set forth in the Bible, Book of Mormon, or Book of Covenants; and hereby withdraw the hand of fellowship from all those who practice or teach doctrines contrary to the above, until they cease so to do, and show works meet for repentance.
>
> *Nauvoo Expositor*, 1844

At the General Church Conference of April 1844, the Latter-day Saints had gathered at Nauvoo, Illinois, to hear what would prove to be the Prophet Joseph Smith's greatest sermon. The sermon is now commonly called the King Follett discourse. Strong public reaction to the teachings of the sermon would ignite a chain of events that would lead to the death of the Mormon Prophet Joseph Smith.

Parts of this chapter have appeared in an earlier article titled "Turbulence in Early Mormonism and the Death of Joseph Smith: The Nauvoo Expositor *(1844),"* North American Religion, Vol. 2 *(1993): 135–201.*

Throughout its first 14-year history, many members of the Church had expressed discontentment with some of the teachings and the practices of the Church. Yet earlier parties of dissent had not included such high-profile individuals as Second Counselor in the First Presidency, William Law, Nauvoo Circuit Court Judge, Robert D. Foster, or Nauvoo Stake High Council President, Charles Ivins. The teachings of the King Follett discourse provided additional fuel to an already existing ember as the dissenters sought to put an end to the alleged abuses of the Prophet Joseph Smith.

For many of the faithful Latter-day Saints the teachings of the King Follett discourse were all part of what the Lord had revealed, and a glimpse of what would be revealed at a future time. The dissenters however were only willing to follow Joseph Smith so far. If in April this limit was not known, by June 7, 1844, the entire city of Nauvoo would know the limits, as the dissenters' allegations against the Prophet would become public knowledge.

Dissent in Nauvoo: The Nauvoo Expositor

On June 7, 1844, the first and only edition of the *Nauvoo Expositor* was published. It is estimated that one thousand copies were printed.[1] Of these five hundred were to be distributed outside of Nauvoo. The *Expositor* was intended to be the official organ of the new Church established in Nauvoo by the dissenters.[2] The *Expositor* was to be a weekly feature in Nauvoo intended to rival the Church's *Times and Seasons*, and the secular *Nauvoo Neighbor*, giving a new voice to marginalized Mormons in Nauvoo.

Among the key allegations made against Smith in the pages of the *Expositor* were those of teaching false doctrines. The perceived false doctrines were the very concepts that Smith had introduced in April of that year, that a hierarchy of gods exist and that humans could become gods.[3] Polygamy, a concept introduced to key members of the Church a year earlier, also proved to be a point of controversy.

Yet the controversy between Smith and the dissenting members that erupted in Nauvoo on June 7, 1844, had earlier roots. Between the April conference and the first edition of the *Expositor*, Smith had made several attempts at reconciling the differences between the dissenters and himself. Several meetings took place between Smith and the key figures of the dissenting party, Robert Foster and William Law.[4] By May of 1844, it appeared that no reconciliation between Smith and the dissenters could be made and they were individually excommunicated from the Church. Believing that

Smith was a fallen Prophet, William Law had begun his own Church in Nauvoo with approximately 200 to 300 members.[5] Law's Church believed in the doctrines taught by Smith before 1839, prior to the introduction of the distinctive Nauvoo theology.[6]

The rift between Law and Smith had begun shortly after the introduction of polygamy in 1843. While polygamy and Smith's alleged seduction of William's wife Jane were key issues of dissent between the two, there also seems to have been some contention over the sale of properties to new Mormon immigrants.[7] It appears that Law had held title to several properties in central locations near the temple. Smith, using his authority as trustee in trust of the Church, required that new Mormon immigrants purchase poorer quality lands near the river. Law saw Smith's economic dealings as unjust and an infringement on Christian faith and free will.

William Law had been called to the First Presidency by revelation, and was sustained by the general Church membership annually from 1841 until his excommunication in 1844.[8] In spite of their differences, Smith had to abide by the general Church's decision and accept Law's position, as Second Counselor and as Prophet, Seer and Revelator. Law could only be removed by legitimate means, and only a unanimous vote by the general Church body could remove Law from his position of power. As the tension between Law and Smith grew, Smith came to regard Law as a thorn in his side. In December 1843, while addressing the Saints in Nauvoo, Smith had referred to Law as a Judas.[9] Soon stories began circulating in Nauvoo that Law was plotting to take the Prophet's life. As a man who wielded economic power, William Law was determined to set the Church back on the right path, and if Joseph Smith fell as a result of that, so be it. Smith saw Law as a real threat to his power, and undertook every available opportunity to bring Law back to the fold. When the "Prospectus" for the *Nauvoo Expositor* appeared in the *Times and Seasons*, Smith sent Sidney Rigdon to negotiate the terms of peace with Law.[10] That sought-after peace with Law never came.

In the past Smith had removed opposition to his authority by excommunicating the dissenting parties. This action soon restored calmness to the Mormon community. In spite of the recent excommunications, Smith's attempts at reconciling the differences had not succeeded in bringing about the desired peace. This time, instead of the expected calm, the Mormon community of Nauvoo would plunge into chaos.

The dissenters had charged Joseph with the crimes of adultery (over the polygamy issue), and of perjury, for falsely accusing a visitor to Nauvoo for the crime of murder. Smith, in an attempt to counter the charges, had secretly gone to the county seat at Carthage, Illinois, to be tried for these allegations. The court session was held over until October, and Smith returned to Nauvoo with his hopes of bringing a quick end to his troubles unrealized.[11] Smith had attempted to absolve himself of the alleged crimes with which he had been charged by using the power of the Nauvoo municipal court.[12] The Nauvoo Charter had granted the city of Nauvoo special privileges, and Smith used these privileges to issue a writ of habeas corpus for the adultery and perjury allegations. This allowed Smith to be tried before the Nauvoo municipal court.[13]

On June 7, 1844, the storm broke, as William Law and the other dissenters went public with their allegations against the Prophet in the pages of the *Nauvoo Expositor*. The Church-owned *Times and Seasons* and the *Nauvoo Neighbor* had carried the "Prospectus" for the new paper in their latest editions. The *Expositor's* "Prospectus" claimed that it would provide "general knowledge."[14] While keeping to its original prospectus, it is not hard to see that the chief motivation for the publication of the paper was to put an end to Smith's power structure and bring reform to the Church.

With the publication of the *Expositor* the dissent in Nauvoo began to grow. Smith took quick action to stop it. On June 8, a special meeting of the Nauvoo city council was convened. Smith citing legal precedent petitioned the council to have the press of the *Nauvoo Expositor* destroyed. The council also called for the impeachment of non–Mormon councilman Sylvester Emmons for his part in editing the *Expositor*.[15] On June 10, 1844, Smith, by order of mayor and city council of Nauvoo, declared the *Nauvoo Expositor* to be a public nuisance, and had the press and all remaining papers destroyed.[16] Judging from the reaction of the council, the publication of the *Expositor* was a serious threat to Smith's power and authority.

Approximately one hundred members of the city militia, the Nauvoo Legion,[17] took part in the destruction of the *Nauvoo Expositor*. The action against the *Expositor* had resulted in the press, undistributed copies of the paper, and the type, set for the second edition of the *Expositor*, being destroyed. While there was a legal precedent allowing a city council to destroy libelous materials, the Nauvoo council had destroyed the presses. This action was in violation of the U.S. Constitution.[18] Prior to the publication of the *Nauvoo Expositor*, no libel law had existed in the Nauvoo city ordinances. One of the first tasks of the June 8 city council meeting was to draft an antilibel ordinance with broad, sweeping powers. The proscribed method for the passage of legislation as law mandated that the new law had to be made public knowledge before any charges could be laid.[19] From the drafting of the antilibel law to its execution only several hours had transpired. Mayor and council had hurried the process to suppress the *Expositor* and silence William Law.[20] Following the destruction of the press William Law fled to Carthage and filed a formal complaint against Smith for instigating a riot.

On June 12, 1844, Sheriff David Bettisworth arrived in Nauvoo to arrest Joseph Smith. Smith agreed to stand trial, but only in Nauvoo.[21] Virtually assured of the final verdict, Joseph was tried before the Nauvoo municipal court and acquitted of the charges. The municipal court of Nauvoo had been empowered to investigate allegations and to hold preliminary hearings, but had not been empowered to process a final verdict.[22] Smith had used his authority, and position of power, to avoid due legal process for his part in the destruction of the *Nauvoo Expositor*.

The destruction of the press, and the subsequent acquittal of Smith, had brought the entire state of Illinois to the brink of civil war. Newspapers throughout Missouri, Iowa, and Illinois urged the citizens of the respective counties to rise to arms and lay siege to the city of Nauvoo and to take Joseph Smith by force. Amid rumors that citizens from the surrounding states were making their way to Nauvoo, Joseph Smith called the Nauvoo Legion to arms.

Like a Lamb to the Slaughter: The Death of a Prophet

On June 18, 1844, the Mormon Prophet Joseph Smith placed the city of Nauvoo under martial law. For calling the Nauvoo Legion to arms, and for utilizing state ammunition and arms against the citizens of Nauvoo, Joseph Smith would be charged with treason against the State of Illinois.[23] For declaring martial law in Nauvoo, Joseph Smith would be arrested and forced to stand trial in Carthage, Illinois. The trial date was set for June 29, 1844. The Prophet Joseph Smith never made it to trial.

The events surrounding the destruction of the *Nauvoo Expositor* had escalated beyond Smith's expectations. In order to bring peace to Nauvoo, Smith had invited Governor Thomas Ford to investigate the events leading up to the destruction of the *Expositor's* presses. On June 21, 1844, Governor Ford arrived in Nauvoo with the state militia. Ford made a brief investigation of the events surrounding the destruction of the *Nauvoo Expositor*. Ford concluded that Smith had violated the individual rights of U.S. citizens, and that he had abused his civil and judicial privileges under state law and the Nauvoo Charter. Ford maintained that Smith had violated the Constitution of the United States on four major points, and that these acts had brought the State of Illinois to the brink of civil war. The assessment by Ford of Smith's actions showed that Smith had violated several central points of entrenched civil liberties. The violated liberties were: 1) freedom of the press; 2) unreasonable search and seizure; 3) no distinction made between civil and judiciary branches. In addition, Ford charged that

Smith had used privileges granted under the Nauvoo Charter to exclude himself from due legal process for his role in the *Expositor* affair.

The Nauvoo Charter had granted the Mormons special privileges and powers. In 1840 the Mormons had petitioned the Illinois state legislature for the Charter in order to avoid the types of problems that had occurred in Missouri. Of particular importance to the *Expositor* incident were Sections 11 and 16 of the Nauvoo Charter.[24] Section 11 of the Charter gave the mayor and council the rights in principle to carry out the destruction of the presses. The section is as follows:

> The City Council shall have power and authority to make, ordain, establish and execute, all such ordinances, not repugnant to the Constitution of the United States or this State, as they may deem necessary for the peace, benefit, good order, regulation, convenience, and cleanliness of said city.[25]

Section 16 provided the often abused judicial powers for the Nauvoo courts, granting that:

> The Mayor and Aldermen shall be conservators of the peace within the limits of said City, and shall have all the powers of Justices of the Peace therein, both in civil and criminal cases, arising under the laws of the State: they shall as justices of the Peace, within the limits of said City, perform the same duties, be governed by the same laws, give the same bonds and Security as other Justices of the Peace, and be commissioned as Justices of the Peace in and for said City by the Governor.[26]

It was under the sanction of Section 16 that Smith had moved his trial from the circuit court of Hancock County to the municipal court of Nauvoo. Smith had used this same provision a year earlier for his benefit. Lucy Mack Smith records in her biography of the Prophet that Smith had faced charges of treason against the State of Missouri.[27] The earlier trial of June 30, 1843, appears to have been transferred to the Nauvoo Municipal Court, where Smith had control of the judicial powers. The Lucy Mack Smith citation has Smith's brother Hyrum making a defense of Smith and the Mormons for their role in the Missouri troubles before the municipal court at Nauvoo.

The escalation of the events at Nauvoo had forced the hand of Governor Ford. Ford told Joseph Smith that in order to avoid civil war and the complete destruction of Nauvoo, that he should surrender to the authorities and stand trial on the criminal charges.[28] In an attempt to absolve himself of all wrongdoing in the destruction of the *Nauvoo Expositor*, Smith appealed to Governor Ford. In his letter dated June 22, 1844, Smith argues that he had followed legal precedent on the matter, and that if he had erred in his judgment for having the *Nauvoo Expositor* destroyed, he would allow due legal process to take place, and provide reparations to the publishers of the paper.[29]

Smith's offer of reparations for the press' destruction is reminiscent of earlier troubles in Missouri. Perhaps this earlier incident, in Missouri, had given Smith assurance from prosecution by making an offer for reparations to the *Expositor's* editors. An offer for reparation had been extended to the Mormons in Missouri, after the destruction of the *Evening and Morning Star* press. In June of 1833, about 400 citizens of Independence appointed a committee to deal with the Mormon problem. The committee, composed of leading citizens, presented five resolutions to the Mormons. The third resolution requested that the presses of the *Star* cease printing. The resolution threatened repercussions to the Mormons if they failed to comply with the demands. The resolution stated: "That those who fail to comply with the above requisitions, be referred to those brethren who have the gift of tongues, to inform them of the lot that awaits them."[30] The committee carried out its threat, and the building housing the *Evening and Morning Star* was razed to the ground and the presses and type confiscated. On June 23, 1833, a committee of 17 informed the editor of the *Evening and Morning Star* that as soon as he was ready to leave Independence, the citizens would repay him for any losses incurred in the destruction of the *Star*.[31]

While the events in Missouri and Nauvoo were similar, eleven years had passed since the *Star* incident, and the Saints were now in Illinois, not Missouri. Ford's response to Smith was that the destruction of the *Expositor's* presses had created complicated problems, and that they could not be as easily dismissed as a simple error in judgment by Smith and the Nauvoo city council. Ford dismissed Smith's solution to the problem. Ford concluded that the conflict could not be resolved by making monetary reparations to the publishers of the paper.[32] Ford was convinced that the only way in which the conflict in Nauvoo could be resolved would be for Smith to go to Carthage and to stand trial on the charges.

Smith seemed to recognize that the end was near, and standing trial in Carthage was an event that Smith would rather not face. In an attempt to avoid the trial, Smith set out towards the west, across the Mississippi. Through the urging of several of his close companions, Smith returned to Nauvoo and began to make preparations to go to Carthage and to stand trial. On June 27, 1844, Joseph Smith, the Mormon Prophet, while being held in custody for trial, was shot to death. Smith's hasty action in destroying the presses of the *Nauvoo Expositor* and its remaining copies had brought him to his death.

The King Follett Discourse in Historical Perspective

The *Nauvoo Expositor* outlines several key areas of tension in the social structure of the Latter-day Saints community in Nauvoo. Unlike earlier dissenters, who quietly withdrew from the Church, the publishers of the paper were high ranking Church officials and prominent businessmen in Nauvoo. Earlier dissent had often been relegated to personality conflicts between Smith and the other individuals involved. Such were the cases with Ezra Booth, Oliver Cowdery, John C. Bennett, and David Whitmer.[33] Earlier dissent as well had not coalesced around a strong central figure, like William Law. The nature of previous dissent had allowed Smith the privilege of dismissing the apostates' claims as irrelevant, and allowed Smith to maintain control of the Church.

The tension that was evident in Nauvoo in June of 1844 was not the cry of a bitter individual. Between 200 and 300 people had united their voices against what they saw as gross injustices done in the name of God and the Church of Jesus Christ of Latter-day Saints. Perhaps, for the first time in the Prophet Joseph Smith's life, he had encountered a group that had both the methods and the means to publicly confront his teachings, his power, and his authority, and his claim of Prophet of God. The outcome of this confrontation proved fatal for Smith, and for the Church at Nauvoo. Within two years the majority of the Mormon community at Nauvoo would move westward and begin a new kingdom on the shores of the Great Salt Lake. The events surrounding the publication and destruction of the *Nauvoo Expositor* become critical to our understanding of the final months preceding the death of Joseph Smith. The publication of the paper, and the way in which the *Expositor* affair was handled by Smith, directly contributed to the death of the Prophet.

From a historian's perspective, the *Expositor* provides us with the historical setting surrounding the events that led to the death of one of America's great religious leaders. The arguments, and charges, that the editors of the *Expositor* level against Smith are not purely theological, but social and economic as well. The Nauvoo dissenters concentrated their arguments into five main points: 1) Smith's total defiance of state laws; 2) The uniting of church and state and using his ecclesiastical authority to manipulate state and federal politicians; 3) Ignoring established Church judicial practices by excommunicating William Law; 4) Controlling the financial affairs of the Church through ecclesiastical authority; 5) Teaching false doctrine, primarily the plurality of Gods, and practicing polygamy.[34]

It is with the fifth allegation that we will concern ourselves in this chapter. This last point speaks volumes and is critical to establishing a proper chronology for the development of the Mormon concept of God. In past chapters we have dealt indirectly with the contents of the King Follett discourse. We shall now turn our attention to the central themes expressed in the King Follett discourse.

The contents of the King Follett discourse are integral to our overall understanding of Mormon doctrinal development. The King Follett discourse is also essential to our understanding of doctrinal development during the Nauvoo period, as well as the next 80 years of speculative theology. The King Follett discourse provides a point, to which all previous doctrinal statements are correlated. The discourse also provides the base for all future Mormon theology. It is in the contents of the three-hour sermon that Mormon doctrine would move from a binatarian concept of the divine to a henotheistic concept. If a belief in a plurality of Gods was held by the Saints before 1844, it was not widely held or as clearly defined as the concept expressed in the King Follett discourse.

It is particularly the two sermons delivered by Smith, prior to his death, that solidified the concept of a plurality of Gods in Latter-day Saint thought. In this section we will examine the details of the King Follett discourse and Smith's final public sermon of June 16, 1844.

In the early part of 1844, dissent and apostasy were evidenced in Nauvoo. The failure of economic ventures and a steady stream of new immigrants to Nauvoo had produced an unstable environment. Smith, in an attempt to stabilize conditions, had carried his spiritual authority into the temporal realm. This action by Smith had caused several of Nauvoo's key business leaders to question the Prophet's legitimacy to lead the Church. In the past Smith had always dealt with dissent effectively, either through excommunication of the dissenting factions, or through the introduction of new thought to solidify his claim to having revelations from God. The result had always been that any major dissent was dispelled. In this light the King Follett discourse was an attempt to dispel dissent.

The dissent in Nauvoo had been growing since the revelation on polygamy in 1843. Those that had followed the Prophet since the founding of the Church had seen him become increasingly more conscious of his call in life. As time progressed, Joseph began to interpret the events surrounding himself and his people within an enlarged paradigm. Over time he gradually came to interpret all events within an almost cosmic millenarian time frame. He seemed to possess an uncanny sense of destiny, a belief that he had been called of God to usher in a new age. While this confidence is lacking in the early Smith, it reaches an apex preceding his death at Carthage.[35]

The economic and social events preceding the April Church Conference had again cast doubt upon Smith's claim of being the Prophet. When

Smith took to the podium, at the April Conference, he was vindicating his calling in the eyes of his followers, and attempting to quiet the dissent among the inner circle. It was precisely this message that came out loud and clear in the words of Joseph Smith.

The Conference convened on April 24th. That the state of affairs and rumors circulating in Nauvoo were of primary importance at the Conference is seen in the address of Sidney Rigdon. Rigdon took the stand first, choosing for a sermon text "Behold the Church of God of the Last Days." Rigdon spoke of his conversion to the Church and of the troubles that the Saints had endured in the past 14 years. The reference to 14 years would resurface throughout Rigdon's speech, as well as the following day in Smith's sermon. Underlying Rigdon's sermon is a strong apologetic tone. Rigdon is attempting to legitimize the new teachings, while at the same time attempting to silence the dissenters in Nauvoo who had made allegations of revealing new doctrines in secret.

Rigdon makes reference to the early Latter-day Saint beliefs. Rigdon states that:

> many things were taught, believed, and preached then, which have since come to pass. We knew the whole world would laugh at us; so we concealed ourselves, and there was much excitement about our secret meetings, charging us with designs against the Government, and with laying plans to get money, &c.

Rigdon continues:

> The time has come to tell why we had secret meetings. We were maturing plans fourteen years ago which we can now tell. Were we maturing plans to corrupt the world, to destroy the peace of society? No. Let fourteen years' experience of the Church tell the story. The Church would never have been here if we had not done as we did in secret. The cry of "False prophet and impostor!" rolled upon us. I do not know that anything has taken place in the history of this Church which we did not then believe. It was written upon our hearts and never could be taken away. It was indelibly engraved; no power beneath yonder heavens could obliterate it. This was the period when God laid the foundation of the Church, and He laid it firmly, truly, and upon eternal truth... We do not care who sinks or swims, or opposes, but we know here is the Church of God, and I have authority before God for saying so ... I know God. I have gazed upon the glory of God, the throne, visions and glories of God ... if even now we should tell the glories and privileges of the Saints of God to you and to the world? We should be ridiculed. No wonder we shut it up in secret. If we were to tell you when Jehovah is looked upon, lo it is beauty, it is heaven, it is felicity to look upon Jehovah. I should marvel otherwise. If a man tells you one glory or one message, he

is learning another at the same time. Do not be astonished, then if we even yet have secret meetings, asking God for things for your benefit.[36]

Sidney Rigdon's speech was a defense of the prophetic calling of Joseph Smith. Rigdon seemed to say that God had revealed many things to him and Smith in the early days. These revelations they had kept secret from the majority of the Saints, because they were not ready to receive the great truths of God. But now the time had come and the day had arrived when the Saints were ready to receive the revelations, the eternal plan of God that Smith and Rigdon and selected others had known for years. Sidney Rigdon's speech of April 6 set the stage for the Prophet Joseph Smith on the following day. On April 7, 1844, through the words of the King Follett discourse, Smith would reveal to the Saints the true nature and character of God.

The sermon addressed several key points relating to the nature of God. The sermon, delivered to an estimated 10,000 to 20,000[37] Saints, was as much a legitimization for Smith's calling, as it was a theological treatise. Amid social upheaval and a legitimate fear for his life, Smith would stand before his people with one last triumphant appeal. Smith does not use a written text for the sermon. As Moses had stood before Israel, Joseph Smith stood before the Saints. Smith claims that the Holy Spirit is speaking through him. It is precisely this claim that Smith uses to legitimize his claim as Prophet of God.

The sermon was recorded, in part, by several individuals. The present copy of the sermon is a redaction of existing accounts of the sermon. Smith's personal scribes, Willard Richards, Thomas Bullock, and William Clayton, all recorded accounts of the sermon. Others present, such as Joseph Fielding and Wilford Woodruff, added additional accounts of the sermon.[38]

Smith begins the sermon by indicating that all past teachings regarding God have been based on false teachings. Smith states:

> There are but a few beings in the world who understand rightly the character of God. The great majority do not comprehend anything, either that which is past, or that which is to come, as it respects their relationship to God. They do not know, neither do they understand the nature of that relationship; and consequently they know but little above the brute beast, or more than to eat, drink and sleep. This is all man knows about God or his existence, unless it is given by inspiration of the Almighty.[39]

Smith provides evidence for his claim to be the Prophet of God by downplaying the significance of the charge of false teacher made against him. Smith argues that if he can reveal the true character of God, then his claim to be a prophet of God would be a legitimate one. He argues that he has been honest and not pretentious or presumptuous in his claims to have received revelations from God. To strengthen this claim, Smith argues that if he is a false teacher, the Spirit of God would reveal it to the people. Smith charges that being a false teacher is no reason to be put to death. He cites the American constitutional privilege of religious freedom as proof that every individual has the right to be a false teacher. It is up to each individual, prompted by the Spirit of God, to decide truth from error. Smith argues that if false teaching were reason enough to be put to death, then he would be obligated to kill 99 out of 100 ministers.

Having established his preliminary arguments, Smith would expound upon a series of speculative theological statements having no true parallel in Latter-day Saint theology before April of 1844. It appears that the underlying reason for the sermon was to give a fresh new revelation of God to the people, to quiet their allegations that he was a fallen prophet. It is for that reason that the statements made by Smith in the King Follett discourse are important. Smith introduced the new thought to maintain his primacy as the Prophet of God, by revealing that he alone knew the character and nature of God. In formulating his sermon, Smith appeals to two main arguments, the inspiration of the Holy Spirit, and the Bible by using his knowledge of Hebrew and other languages.

Contemporary accounts of the King Follett discourse, from private journals, seem to indicate that the teachings of April of 1844 were new.[40] It seems that Smith deliberately introduced new concepts to strengthen his arguments against the dissenters, their allegations of teaching false doctrine, and of teaching doctrines in secret. Smith would legitimate his claim to being a Prophet of God through the words of the King Follett discourse.

The contents of the King Follett discourse touched upon several theological concepts. Aside from the major topic, the nature of God, Smith touched upon baptism, repentance, and the unpardonable sin. The majority of the sermon dealt with a topic which has become known as the "Doctrine of Eternal Progression." This concept can be reduced into its four main components. These four are: 1) That God is an exalted man, having progressed through the ages; 2) Man's spirit is co-equal with God and he can become a God; 3) That innumerable Gods exist in the universe that are progressing in knowledge; 4) That there exists a council or a plurality of Gods. It is these four points that Smith seeks to elaborate upon and use as a defense against his detractors.

In Smith's words:

> I will prove that the world is wrong, by showing what God is. I am going to enquire after God; for I want you all to know him, and be familiar with him; and if I am bringing you to a knowledge of him, all persecutions against me ought to cease. You will then know that I am his servant; for I speak as one having authority.

As Smith begins to talk about the nature and character of God, his new concept of God is introduced to the Saints. Smith states:

> I will go back to the beginning before the world was, to show what kind of being God is. What kind of being was God in the beginning? Open your ears and hear, all ye ends of the earth, for I am going to prove it to you by the Bible, and tell you the designs of God in relation to the human race and why He interferes with the affairs of man.
> God himself was once as we are now, and is an exalted man, and sits enthroned in yonder heavens! That is the great secret.

Smith turns to the Bible to support his doctrine of God being an exalted man. The sermon continues:

> I am going to tell you how God came to be God.... It is the first principle of the Gospel to know for a certainty the Character of God, and to know that we may converse with him as one man converses with another, and that he was once a man like us; yea, that God himself, the Father of us all, dwelt on an earth, the same as Jesus Christ himself did; and I will show it from the Bible....What did Jesus say? (Mark it Elder Rigdon!) The Scriptures inform us that Jesus said, as the Father hath power in Himself, even so hath the Son power—to do what? Why what the Father did. The answer is obvious—in a manner to lay down His body and take it up again.
> Here then, is eternal life—to know the only wise and true God; and you have got to learn how to be Gods yourselves, and to be kings and priests to God, the same as all Gods have done before you, namely, by going from one small degree to another, and from a small capacity to a great one, from grace to grace, from exaltation to exaltation, until you attain to the resurrection of the dead, and are able to dwell in everlasting burnings, and to sit in glory, as do those who sit enthroned in everlasting power.... These are the first principles of consolation... [T]o know that, although the earthly tabernacle is laid down and dissolved, they shall rise again to dwell in everlasting burnings in immortal glory, not to sorrow, suffer, or die any more; but they shall be heirs of God and joint heirs with Jesus Christ. What is it? To inherit the same power, the same glory and the same exaltation, until you arrive at the station of a God, and ascend the throne of eternal power, the same as those who have gone before. What did Jesus do? Why; I do the things that I saw my Father do when worlds came rolling into existence.[41]

Appealing to the biblical text once again, Smith would begin to speak on the creation of the cosmos. Again Smith points out that he is not teaching anything that the biblical text does not already teach. While admitting that what they are about to hear may be new, the existence of a plurality of Gods, it is not contrary to the biblical text. Smith, using his knowledge of Hebrew and the first chapter of Genesis as his proof text, introduces the plurality of Gods concept into Mormon theology:

> I suppose I am not allowed to go into an investigation of anything that is not contained in the Bible. If I do, I think there are so many over-wise men here, that they would cry "treason" and put me to death. So I will go to the old Bible and turn commentator today.
> I shall comment on the very first Hebrew word in the Bible; I will make a comment on the very first sentence of the history of creation in the Bible— *Berosheit*. I want to analyze the word *Baith*—in, by, through, and everything else, *Rosh*—the head, *Sheit*—grammatical termination... I will transpose and simplify it in the English language... In the beginning, the head of the Gods called a council of the Gods; and they came together and concocted a plan to create the world and people it. When we begin to learn this way, we begin to learn the only true God.[42]

William Law and the others took exception to Smith's interpretation of the first chapter of Genesis. They believed that Smith's teaching on the plurality of Gods was proof positive that he was a fallen Prophet. On this day Smith made no claim to special revelation in revealing the true nature of God. Rather he resorted to the Hebrew text of Genesis to substantiate his arguments. Those that had learned Hebrew with Smith in Kirtland's School of the Prophets would have been able to come to the same conclusions from the text.

In his defense against the criticisms levied by Law through the pages of the *Nauvoo Expositor*, Smith would continue with this theology in another sermon on June 16, 1844.

> I have always and in all congregations when I have preached on the subject of deity it has been the plurality of Gods. It has been preached by the Elders for fifteen years. I have always declared God to be a distinct personage. Jesus Christ separate from God the Father and the Holy Ghost was a distinct personage and a spirit, and these three constitute three Gods if this is in accordance with the New Testament lo and behold we have three Gods anyhow and they are plural; and who can contradict it.[43]

With the sermons of April and June of 1844, the Mormon concept of God would move to a henotheistic position. It was the events surrounding the two sermons that has given them the weight they carry in Mormon theology. The death of Smith on June 27, 1844, sealed the words of his mouth. Smith's death was proof that the sermons were of God. To many Mormons, Smith's last public addresses could not be seen in any other light than the final words of a lamb going to the slaughter. The sermons became the final words of the great Prophet of God who sacrificed his life for his people.

Vindicating the Prophet: Establishing a Provenance for Cosmic Henotheism

Speculation exists that Smith had not introduced any new concepts in the King Follett discourse, and so the reaction to the sermon, on doctrinal grounds, is unfounded.[44] Early statements do exist that hint at several of the concepts expressed in the King Follett discourse. Yet these statements lack the authority given the King Follett discourse. Statements relating to a plurality of Gods and that men can become Gods would fall into this category.[45] Upon close examination, these earlier references, when seen in the context of the current theology, do not teach the concepts attributed to them. The King Follett discourse would give the earlier statements a new meaning and present them as eternal truth. The relationship of the earlier statements, made by Smith, to similar statements made in the King Follett discourse is not based upon progressive theology, or a line upon line concept. Rather, the earlier statements are merely seen as teaching similar concepts to the King Follett discourse, based upon epistemological reasonings and a line upon line, or progressive, theological paradigm. It is the King Follett discourse that gives the earlier statements any life and meaning, and not vice versa.

Of the four concepts, comprising the Mormon apotheotic belief, one has not been dealt with to any great extent, the concept that God was once a man.[46] Current Mormon syllogistic arguments for this concept run as such. Jesus did nothing that he did not see the Father do. Jesus had a physical body, died, and rose with a resurrected body, therefore the Father must have as well.

The earliest statement we have with regards to this concept is given by Joseph Smith at the opening of the Nauvoo Lyceum. The reference is dated January 5, 1841. The statement, as recorded by William Clayton and William McIntire, infers Smith's sermon text was John 5:26. Smith, making observations on the sectarian God, states: "that which is without body or parts is nothing. There is no other God in heaven but that God who has flesh and bone."[47] What Smith seemed to say is that God, with a body of flesh and bone, was a resurrected man. The text also adds a reference to the Council of Spirits and how important it would be to take on bodies and become human.

The concept of God having a material body was taught two years later. On April 2, 1843, at Ramus, Illinois, the Prophet would mention that the Father had a body of flesh and bone. The statement, recorded by Willard Richards, who was not present at Ramus,[48] mentions that God had a body of flesh and bone. William Clayton, who was present at Ramus, makes no reference to God having a body of flesh and bone. Instead, Clayton mentions that the Holy Spirit is a person and so cannot dwell in an individual's heart.[49] The sermon, given at Ramus, was first published in 1856 and included as Section 130, in the 1876 *Doctrine and Covenants*.[50]

The canonized version of the sermon is taken from the Joseph Smith diary kept by Willard Richards. Its publication in 1856 would have been the first time many Saints would have had access to the sermon. Given the available evidence we have no knowledge as to the extent this teaching impacted the Saints at the time it was given in 1842. The absence of the concept, in Clayton's account, is either an omission on his part, or the statement was not made by Joseph Smith on that date.

William Clayton and Willard Richards both mention Smith describing the indwelling of the Holy Ghost as a sectarian notion. It is within the context of speaking of the Holy Ghost, as a personage, that Richards' reference to God having a tangible body is made. There is no evidence to indicate that Richards' statement is an interpolation from a later time period. Yet, the statement occurs only once, and judging from the reaction to the concept in 1844, it is safe to assume that the belief that the Father has a material body was not widely held, and would have been seen as a foreign concept when taught in the King Follett discourse.

Smith would deliver his third sermon with reference to God being a resurrected man on June 11, 1843.[51] Several individuals recorded the sermon. Willard Richards and Wilford Woodruff provide the most detailed accounts of the sermon, and are the only ones that mention that Smith preached on the topic that God had a body of flesh and bone. In the sermon, Smith would again deliver a polemic against the sectarian notion of God. Smith used polemical arguments to describe the Christian concept of God as "Father, Son, and Holy Ghost, all stuffed into one person." Smith would contend that that was absurd, and pointed to several biblical texts where the three individuals were independent of each other. Smith uses this to bring home the point "that the Son doeth what He hath seen the Father do." This would become integral to his argument that God was a resurrected man. Smith continued on the topic of the resurrection and stated: "Gods have an ascendancy over angels, angels remain angels, some are resurrected to become god."[52] The sermon would also contend that a plurality of Gods exists. Smith uses the biblical text to support his argument that the Father, Son, and Holy Ghost are separate individuals.

Upon examination of the sermon accounts, it becomes clear that Smith is arguing two major points. Smith's main emphasis is in motivating the Saints to complete the temple, so that washing and anointings may be performed. It is with that topic in mind that Smith begins and ends the sermon. That the members of the godhead are separate individuals, and that the Father has a material body, appear as secondary topics. In all six accounts of the sermon, temple work was the primary message of the sermon. Only two accounts make reference to the godhead. This can lead to several assessments. Either the concept was so well known among the Saints that referencing it would seem trivial, or it was not considered to be of importance by the hearers.

The statements made earlier by Smith, in 1841 and 1842, on the resurrection of God the Father were given in small group settings. It is doubtful then that many would have been extremely familiar with the concept. Only singular accounts of the sermon topic exist. This appears also to have happened with the revelation on polygamy in 1843. It could also be possible that the audience did not consider the resurrection of God the Father to be an extremely important point. Judging from the reaction to these very concepts in 1844, it is doubtful that many would have believed in the resurrection of God the Father before the King Follett discourse.

It is difficult to assess what Smith had in mind when he made the comments on June 11, 1843. It is also difficult to assess the number of people that heard the sermon. Given however that it was given in Nauvoo, a large number of Saints probably heard the sermon. Of the sources, only two of the six make mention that God the Father was a resurrected being. The interesting part is that there is no reaction to the sermon. Smith does not defend his theological position in a subsequent sermon. This is in sharp contrast to the King Follett discourse when the entire city explodes.

While dependent on extremely scarce sources, there is some evidence to support the claim that Joseph Smith taught that God the Father was a resurrected being on at least three occasions: January 5, 1841, April 2, 1843, and June 11, 1843. His arguments to support this teaching came mostly from the biblical text, and not from any revelation. The statements often appear as secondary references to a larger topic. In two of the cases, January 5, 1841, and June 11, 1843, Joseph makes the statements as a joking response to what sectarians believe. It stands to reason that if Joseph Smith did teach that God the Father was a resurrected being, many that followed him had no idea what was meant by the teaching, or its implications.

It is only in this light that the reaction to the King Follett discourse and the events leading to the death of Joseph Smith should be seen. Granted, there may have existed social problems in Nauvoo which added to the dissent in the summer of 1844. Yet, it is not social problems that Joseph Smith addresses in his last public address. The sermon of June 16 does not address the other four points of contention brought out in the *Nauvoo Expositor*. No, Smith addresses the concept of a council comprised of a plurality of Gods and that men can become Gods, because Jesus and the Father were once men.

In the King Follett discourse, Smith, as he had done earlier, would appeal to the biblical text to defend his position. As he had also done earlier, Smith appealed to the Hebrew text to support his views.[53] In his final sermon of June 16, 1844, Smith would appeal to many sources to support his arguments. In addition to the biblical text, Smith would appeal to revelation by the Holy Spirit, using this as evidence to which only he would be privy, to support his teachings.

Through the King Follett discourse, Smith had attempted to quiet the dissent in Nauvoo by restoring the faith of the people in his prophetic call. He miscalculated. His teachings were not received as great truths. Rather, the Nauvoo dissenters used the sermon as insurmountable evidence that Smith was a fallen Prophet. The reaction to Smith's April sermon was broad and swift. This can be seen from Smith's sermon, given on May 2, 1844. The sermon would be delivered a full eight days before the "Prospectus" of the *Nauvoo Expositor* would be published. The sermon would be Smith's first post King Follett discourse appeal to the Saints, in defense of his prophetic call. Smith, appealing to the broad spectrum of Saints in Nauvoo, claims that what he has taught for the last 14 years is supportable. Using the biblical text for his evidence, Smith claims that many translations would agree with his exposition of the scriptures, including the German, Latin, Greek, and Hebrew. In response to his detractors, Smith would respond:

> It has always been my province to dig up hidden mysteries—new things— for my hearers. Just at the time when some men think that I have no right to the keys of the Priesthood—just at that time I have the greatest right... My enemies say that I have been a true prophet. Why I had rather be a fallen true prophet than a false prophet. When a man goes about prophesying, and commands men to obey his teachings, he must either be a true or false prophet. False prophets always arise to oppose the true prophets and they will prophesy so very near the truth that they will deceive almost the very chosen ones.[54]

On May 26, Smith would preach again to the Saints in Nauvoo. Judging from the sermon, Smith was well aware of the dissenters' accusations.

The "Prospectus" of the *Nauvoo Expositor* had been published on May 10, 1844, and had clearly stated its purpose. Smith, in an effort to stem the growing dissent in Nauvoo, resorted to personal attacks upon the leaders of the dissenting faction, William Law and Robert Foster. Smith's sermon of May 26, 1844, is an attempt to rescue his character from the attacks to which it had been subject. In the sermon Joseph Smith would reveal to the Saints at Nauvoo how he saw himself in the history of the world.

Smith would state:

> God is in the still small voice. In all these affidavits, indictments, it is all of the devil—all corruption. Come on! ye prosecutors! ye false swearers! All hell, boil over! Ye burning mountains, roll down your lava! for I will come out on top at last. I have more to boast of than ever any man had. I am the only man that has ever been able to keep a whole church together since the days of Adam. A large majority of the whole have stood by me. Neither Paul, John, Peter nor Jesus ever did it. I boast that no man ever did such a work as I. The followers of Jesus ran away from Him, but the Latter-day Saints never ran away from me yet.[55]

The sermon did little to stem the dissent, as the dissenters published their views in the *Nauvoo Expositor*, on June 7, 1844. Smith would make a final appeal to the Saints on June 16, 1844. In his final sermon, Smith would reiterate the concepts of the King Follett discourse and make one final attempt to prove that his teachings were not the rambling of a fallen Prophet, but rather eternal truths. The attempt failed. By June 18, the city of Nauvoo was under martial law. By the night of June 27, 1844, Joseph Smith the American Prophet lay dead in Carthage, Illinois.

Joseph Smith's two sermons in April and June of 1844 would set the stage for the next phase of Mormon doctrinal development. The sermon that had contributed to his death, the King Follett discourse, would be published in the August 15, 1844, edition of the *Times and Seasons*.[56] With the death of Joseph Smith in 1844, the concepts that became representative of the Mormon concept of God, that a hierarchical Council of Gods exist and that men may become Gods, moved from speculation to eternal truth. Having seen Smith give his life for his teachings, Joseph Smith's successors would take his teachings to a new level.

8. ADAM OUR FATHER AND OUR GOD

Doctrinal Development During the Early Utah Period

> Now hear it, O inhabitants of the earth, Jew and Gentile, Saint and sinner! When our Father Adam came into the Garden of Eden, he came into it with a celestial body, and brought Eve, one of his wives, with him. He helped to make and organize this world. He is MICHAEL, the Archangel, the Ancient of Days! about whom holy men have written and spoken—HE is our FATHER and our GOD, and the only God with whom WE have to do.
>
> Brigham Young, April 9, 1852

With the death of the Prophet Joseph Smith in 1844, a new chapter in Mormon history would begin. Smith's unexpected death had caused a controversy to arise over who would lead the Church.[1] Members of the Quorum of the Twelve Apostles,[2] longtime Church members, and recent converts vied for the leadership position of the Church.

In the end the question of who would succeed the Prophet Joseph Smith proved to be a complicated matter. The problems with succession were rooted in a revelation given by Joseph Smith in 1835. As a result of this revelation, which had stated that all councils within the church were equal within the hierarchy, many individuals in the Church saw themselves as having as equal a claim to the leadership as the Twelve Apostles. With Smith dead, Second Counselor William Law in apostasy, the remaining member of the First Presidency, Sidney Rigdon, as well as the Presiding Bishopric, all laid claim as the rightful successor to Smith. The Prophet's brother, William, then Patriarch of the Church, also contended for the leadership of the Church against Brigham Young, the remaining Twelve

Apostles, and all other contenders. In his 1845 pamphlet, *A Proclamation*,[3] directed against Brigham Young, apostle William Smith made his case for being the rightful heir to the fallen Joseph Smith. First Counselor Sidney Rigdon also laid claim to the Church's leadership.[4] Rigdon failed to achieve his goal and was excommunicated along with the other claimants to the leadership.

When the controversy surrounding the succession was resolved, Senior Apostle Brigham Young became the second leader of the Mormons.[5] Under Brigham Young's leadership, the Saints would cross the great plains and establish a new kingdom on the shores of the Great Salt Lake.

None of Joseph Smith's immediate family left Nauvoo for the Salt Lake Valley. Smith's widow, Emma, married Major Lewis Bidamon. Smith's eldest son, Joseph Smith III, became leader of the Reorganized Church of Jesus Christ of Latter Day Saints on April 6, 1860.[6] The Reorganized Church, or RLDS, was formed from a collection of minor Mormon groups which came into existence after the death of Smith. The RLDS believe in the doctrines of the Church, as taught by Joseph Smith before 1839. The RLDS hold a monotheistic theological position, and deny that Joseph Smith ever taught that a plurality of Gods existed.[7]

The large western portion of the North American continent had recently been seceded to the United States from Mexico. It would be in the heart of the Rocky Mountains, to the former Mexican territory, that the Saints would migrate. The valley of the Great Salt Lake was a desolate, isolated parcel of land when the Saints arrived there in 1847.[8] Within 50 years new towns and cities would be built from Cardston, Alberta, in the north, to San Bernardino, California, in the south. An attempt to establish an independent Mormon theocracy, called Deseret, taking in most of what is now California, Nevada, and Utah, as well as parts of Wyoming, Arizona, and Idaho,[9] was also undertaken.

It would be in the valley of the Great Salt Lake that the Mormons would establish their new headquarters, and practice their faith free of social and political influence. The Wasatch Mountains would provide a refuge, to which Saints from around the world could gather and hear the oracles of God. This brief period of freedom under their second Prophet Brigham Young would cause the Mormon doctrine of God to take a new direction. Previous topics, alluded to by Joseph Smith, would be expanded on by Brigham Young, Orson Pratt, George Q. Cannon, and several others. The theological concepts surrounding the nature and character of God which emerged in the early Salt Lake period were based squarely on the teachings of the King Follett discourse, Smith's greatest sermon. Building upon Joseph's greatest sermon, several individuals would expand upon the primary focus of that discourse, the origin, nature, and character of God.

The emerging thought would take on several facets as varying hermeneutics and philosophical approaches would clash. By the turn of the 20th-century, Mormon theology would culminate not as a codified belief system, but rather as a collection of varied theological options.

During the early Salt Lake period several major theological developments occurred within Mormonism. It would be in this time period that concepts, initially introduced in the 1840s, would acquire a new status, a new interpretation, and be eventually canonized in the 1880s. Yet while these concepts may not have been part of the official corpus of Mormon literature, several of the concepts taught by Joseph Smith during the Nauvoo period were accepted by the Saints as truth, or authoritative and binding, before their canonization. In the years between 1844 and 1880, we see the introduction of additional theological concepts into Mormonism. These concepts were rooted in the Nauvoo discourses of Joseph Smith, primarily his King Follett discourse. These new concepts were attempts at clarifying earlier speculative or unclear concepts, and were compared to additional sermons given by Smith during his life. In effect, with Smith no longer alive, an attempt had to be made to preserve and clarify the varied teachings of the Prophet of the last dispensation.

During the early Salt Lake period two competing concepts of God were promoted by leaders of the Church. The concepts were based in principle upon several premises established by the teachings of the King Follett discourse. The central premise on which the emerging theology was based was that God was once a man who had progressed over time to become God. During the next half century following the death of Joseph Smith, Mormon leaders attempted to explain how man could become God, and also to answer the primary question of how God had become God.

Smith's King Follett discourse had established a central point; man could progress to Godhood. Smith did not take this concept to its fullest possibilities before his death. The King Follett discourse taught that man and God possessed the same essence. Smith's death in June of 1844 prevented any further clarification on this topic. Hence, with only a single sermon from which to start, the Mormon leadership would need to expand upon that and provide a clear exposition on the nature and character of God. It would be during the early Salt Lake period that the origin and destiny of God, and therefore man, would be dealt with.

In the King Follett discourse Smith claimed that the core essence of God and man was co-equal. The equality of God and man was based on a belief that they consisted of the same substance. Smith claimed that this shared substance was intelligence or spirit. In Smith's theology the spirit of man was eternal and had existed with God in the beginning. It was this eternal spirit that progressed to Godhood.[10] With a materialistic concept of the divine firmly established at the close of the Nauvoo period, several new questions needed to be addressed. The questions that Mormon leaders sought to answer were attempts at clarifying how God had become God, and the nature and character of this being called God. Yet answering this central question relating to the origin and nature of God was not as clearcut as many would believe. Having scanty sources from which to reach their conclusions, the task proved difficult to resolve. Nowhere is the difficulty of resolving the question of the origin and nature of God seen than in the sermons and writings of President Brigham Young and Apostle Orson Pratt. The concepts expressed through the teachings and writings of Orson Pratt and Brigham Young would dominate the theological development of the early Salt Lake period.

Brigham Young and the Adam-God Theology

In the early 1850s a peculiar doctrine emerged in the teachings of President Brigham Young. Popularly known as Adam-God, this concept was one of the primary Mormon doctrines of God taught during the early Salt Lake period. Brigham Young and other adherents of the doctrine claimed that the concept had its origins in the teachings of the Prophet Joseph Smith.[11] If this is the case, the Adam-God doctrine is not based on any clear doctrinal statement made by Smith, but rather upon several vague references made by him. With the introduction of henotheistic thought in the spring of 1844, Brigham Young would use the earlier vague statements by Smith, and attempt to harmonize these statements with the teachings of the King Follett discourse.[12]

Young held firmly to his calling as Prophet, and the process of continuing revelation. Young believed that his teachings were not limited by canon or precedent but that the words of the current prophet would supersede any past revelation. In his mind the foundation of the Church rested upon the process of continued revelation. While many differed with Young on this point, no strong opposition emerged except for Orson Pratt.[13]

During the life of Joseph Smith, many of the Apostles were serving missions in the United States, Europe, and Canada. Being preoccupied with missionary work, they were not collectively present to hear the Prophet's discourses and would come by their information secondhand. Upon Smith's death, the Apostles assumed control of the Church. It would be their understanding of Smith's doctrines that would define Mormonism during the latter 19th century. While some of the Apostles were present to hear a particular sermon, others were not. The Apostles' absence from

Nauvoo was not predetermined. Apostles who had heard Smith deliver a particular sermon may have occupied lower positions in the hierarchy than those who were absent from Nauvoo. Positioning in the hierarchy was not determined by either the Apostles' absence from Nauvoo or their presence in Nauvoo. Positioning in the hierarchy was based on seniority in the Quorum of the Twelve. The right and privilege to teach doctrine was based on this hierarchy. Under Brigham Young's tenure, the words of a present prophet were to be held in favor over a past prophet. The problems this caused is seen in the Orson Pratt–Brigham Young debates over Brigham's concept of Adam-God.[14]

The doctrine of Adam-God teaches that when the council of the Gods (the Elohim) met to decide the fate of the recently created earth they chose one of their number, Michael, to bring one of his wives to earth and provide mortal bodies for the spirits in Heaven. Michael then became an Adam and one of his wives an Eve. This meant that the person, Michael-Adam, was the father of the spirits in Heaven, as well as the father of their mortal bodies. Michael-Adam was the father of Jesus or Jehovah and had participated in the creation of this world and the peopling of it.

Michael was a lesser God in the Council of Gods and was chosen by the Council to populate this earth. Michael through natural or sexual relations with his wives produced the spirit offspring in the preexistence. These spirits included Jehovah and Lucifer. Michael was then sent to earth to provide mortal bodies so that each spirit could attain exaltation, or Godhood. When Michael came to Earth he took on a mortal body, discarding his exalted body, and became Adam the Father of the human race.

Grasping the logistics of the Adam-God doctrine can be difficult. The doctrine is not explained clearly in either theological or philosophical terms. Rather, when one examines what is being taught by the doctrine, new questions arise rather than having old ones answered. The Adam-God doctrine appears to have been the dominant Mormon theological position on the godhead during the latter half of the 19th century.

It is difficult to conclude when the Adam-God doctrine became part of Mormon theology. The earliest record of the doctrine of Adam-God being taught publicly is in 1852 by Brigham Young. The sermon was first published in the *Millennial Star*. The sermon states:

> Now hear it, O inhabitants of the earth, Jew and Gentile, Saint and sinner! When our Father Adam came into the Garden of Eden, he came into it with a celestial body, and brought Eve, one of his wives, with him. He helped to make and organize this world. He is MICHAEL, the Archangel, the Ancient of Days! about whom holy men have written and spoken—HE is our FATHER and our GOD, and the only God with whom WE have to do.[15]

Young, and other leaders in the Mormon Church would teach the concept over the next several decades.[16] There was some disagreement and some disbelief over Young's teaching of Adam-God within the Mormon Church. On June 8, 1873, 21 years after his first public proclamation of the concept, Young would chastise the Saints for their unbelief in the doctrine:

> How much unbelief exists in the minds of the Latter-day Saints, with a particular doctrine that I revealed to them, that God revealed to me, that Adam is our Father, and our God, and the only God with whom we have to do.[17]

The Adam-God teaching appeared in Mormon books, sermons, and periodicals for most of the late 19th century. Adam-God is a speculative teaching on the nature and character of God. The concept was not based upon any clear canonical or scriptural tradition. Rather, it appears to be rooted in vague theological expressions of Joseph Smith, and Brigham Young's personal revelation.

Given these speculative ideas and the lack of clear theological positions, the ground was ripe for contending concepts to emerge within Mormonism. The concepts introduced during Young's tenure, as President of the Mormon Church, while having their roots in the vague theological speculation of Joseph Smith, acquired new and significant meanings. The importance of Adam-God to Mormon theology is best seen in its inclusion in the early temple ritual.

The source for the Adam-God doctrine as being part of the temple ritual comes from the first written account of the ritual dating from 1877.[18] Before this date, the ritual appears to have been transmitted orally. In a part of the temple ritual called the "Lecture Before the Veil," the Adam-God concept formed part of a cosmological lesson. The "Lecture Before the Veil" was an elaboration of several concepts that Young had expressed in public sermons dating back to 1852. The 1877 lecture appears to be a later version of the concept. Its late date had allowed the concept the time to fully develop. It was this concept of God that was taught to select members in the temple ritual. For select Mormons, the concept of knowing the true character of God was paramount to receiving exaltation to the highest glory. Knowledge of the character of God meant that they were aware that "Adam is our Father and our God."

Brigham's "Lecture Before the Veil" held that Michael, along with Elohim and Jehovah, had created this world. When the world had been created, Michael took on a mortal body and became Adam. Adam descended to earth with one of his wives who became Eve. The pair had been the parents of spirit offspring born in the preexistence. Now the pair would provide mortal bodies, so that their spirit children would be able to begin their progression to Godhood. In order to become mortal, the pair ate of the tree of knowledge which transformed them from exalted immortal beings to mortal beings.

Key points are brought out in the narrative of the temple ritual. Michael, or a member of the Council of Gods, is sent to populate the earth. He brings one of his wives with him and they begin the human race. Michael also had a hand in the creation of the earth, and is the same individual who fathered the spirit children currently in heaven. Michael is Adam as well as God the Father.

Brigham believed and taught that Adam was God, the father of the spirits as well as the mortal bodies. In Brigham's teachings Adam was seen as God the Father, the literal Father of Jehovah, or Jesus.

Brigham's concept of Adam-God added to the material already in existence on the godhead. Earlier documents had established at least several contending views on the godhead. Questions surrounding Elohim and Jehovah, the creation of the world, and the plan of exaltation had not yet been resolved of their inherent difficulties. Brigham added to the confusion present in Mormon doctrine following the death of Joseph Smith.

While Adam-God did appear in official Church periodicals, and in the Church's rituals, it was never accepted as authoritative and binding by the general Church and made part of its canon. Opposition to the concept was not tolerated, regardless of positioning in the Church hierarchy. In the 1850s to 1860s, Mormon Apostle Orson Pratt and Brigham Young would engage in several discussions over their respective views on the origin and nature of God. While not successful in persuading Young, Pratt's concept of God provided a widely held alternative to Brigham Young's theory for many of the Mormon faithful.

Orson Pratt: There Was a Time When There Was No God

While many within the Church may have come to believe in the view of God as taught by Brigham Young, a strong dissenting voice appeared. This voice belonged to Apostle Orson Pratt. Pratt's dissent to Brigham's teaching was not rooted in a malice towards Young. Rather, Pratt, by his own claims, believed that his view on God did not differ from Young's at all. Yet Young did not see the matter in the same light as Pratt. Throughout the 1850s and 1860s President Brigham Young would take Orson Pratt to task for teaching what Young perceived as false doctrine. Young saw problems in Pratt's teachings on the origin and nature of God. The problems between Pratt and Young would culminate with a partial censure of Pratt's writings in 1860, and finally several years later with a complete censure of his writings. Young went so far as to even have the Saints remove Pratt's writings from bound volumes.[19] The latter act came as a result of Young touring the northern Cache Valley and finding that the vast majority of Saints had failed to act upon an 1860 presidential declaration against Pratt's writings.[20]

Censuring Orson Pratt proved to be difficult. Orson Pratt, like Brigham Young, was one of the original Twelve Apostles and had been present when Smith delivered many of his sermons. Pratt contended that he had never taught any new doctrines but only repeated what he had heard Joseph Smith teach.[21] Further, Pratt added, the President's views did not necessarily represent the views of the membership, nor were those views binding upon the Church if not accompanied by revelation. In essence Pratt was saying that unless a clear revelation is given regarding a particular doctrine, the President's views are no more binding than anyone else's views on the topic.[22]

The self-educated Orson Pratt had come to be known as a staunch defender of Mormon doctrine, and many within the Church had come to view his teachings as official Church doctrine.[23] As one of Mormonism's foremost apologists Pratt had written extensively on a variety of topics in an attempt to prove the validity of Mormonism rationally. His main audience was the non–Mormon public. Through periodicals such as *The Seer*, as well as numerous books and pamphlets, Pratt would explain Mormon doctrine to the world and provide a solid defense of its teachings in light of history and reason. Philosophically, Orson Pratt was a materialist drawing heavily from Scottish philosophy. Pratt's desire to reconcile doctrinal divergency, and maintain logical doctrinal integrity, motivated much of his writings. Orson Pratt, like his successor B. H. Roberts, based his apologetical approach on the principle that all truth was God's truth. In addition Pratt firmly believed that any new revelation must coincide with revealed doctrine. It was his preoccupation with maintaining doctrinal integrity that caused the majority of problems with Brigham Young.

Orson Pratt's disagreements with Brigham Young were the result of Pratt's stricter hermeneutic, rather than of any direct insubordination. Having been heavily influenced by philosophy and history, Pratt demanded physical proof as a basis for truth. As a result Orson Pratt would rely heavily on scriptural authority as his basis in the formulation of his theology. In turn Young, while not completely adverse to using a text as an instrument for doctrinal teachings, relied on revelation to come to many doctrinal conclusions.²⁴ While using the text as a starting point, Young was not bound by a systematic methodology in reaching conclusions. This lack of systematic interpretation often led to varied interpretations and a high degree of doctrinal inconsistency.

Orson Pratt's tenure in Scotland, during the 1840s, had introduced him to philosophy. It is little wonder then that Pratt would use the materialist philosophy of David Hume, Adam Smith, and others as the ground work for his own. Reconciling science with religion figured very prominently in Orson Pratt's writings.²⁵ With the advent of new social and scientific theories brought about by the work of Charles Darwin, Herbert Spencer, and others, Orson Pratt would attempt to reconcile the Church's doctrines with new scientific knowledge.

The dual concepts of a material God which progressed and cosmic pluralism had emerged as part of Mormonism's eternal truth following the King Follett discourse in 1844. Earlier Mormon works had had an impact on Mormon cosmology and theology, but not to the extent that the King Follett discourse had.

In the first half of the 19th century Christianity in Europe was undergoing a drastic reinterpretation through the works of David Strauss, F. C. Bauer, and Friederich Schleiermacher. The discipline of philology was now being applied to the biblical text. In America several groups of individuals, largely through the works of deist writers, had come to see the biblical text as any other ancient text. Thomas Paine's *The Age of Reason* had popularized the deist beliefs. J. Barton Stone, Alexander Campbell, Ralph Waldo Emerson, and William Ellery Channing would all proclaim a new Christianity in light of a new understanding.

Within Mormonism we see early attempts in its history to proclaim truth and remove perceived difficulties. In an attempt to harmonize the two creation accounts of Genesis 1 and 2, the 1830 *Book of Moses* stated that all things were created spiritually before being created materially. By 1844 many Mormons had come to believe that the creation of the universe was an organization of existing matter, rather than a creation ex nihilo.²⁶ The *Book of Moses* cosmology proved integral to Pratt's overall theology. Pratt would use the creation narrative as the foundation for his concept of God, and the origin of the universe. Naturally Pratt's materialistic leanings would not allow for a creation ex nihilo. Something cannot come into existence from nothing. Something must therefore exist before. The concepts of materialism and immaterialism were foundational to Orson Pratt's theology, as he began to formulate his ideas on the nature of God and the origin of the cosmos.

Building on the theology of Joseph Smith, Orson Pratt set out to clarify and harmonize the difficult parts of Smith's sermons with the more refined concepts and the Mormon scriptures.[27] In an early work on the nature of God, Orson Pratt had attempted to reconcile Joseph Smith's plurality of Gods concept with the Church's entrenched monotheistic beliefs.[28] Orson Pratt would explain in his *The Seer*, of February 1853, that:

> All these Gods are equal in power, in glory, in dominion, and in the possession of all things; each possesses a fullness of truth, of knowledge, of wisdom, of light, of intelligence; each governs himself in all things by his own attributes, and is filled with love, goodness, mercy, and justice towards all. The fullness of all these attributes is what constitutes God.... The Gods are one in the qualities and attributes. Truth is not a plurality of truths, because it dwells in a plurality of persons.... Each person is called God not because of his substance, neither because of the shape and size of the substance, but because of the qualities which dwell in the substance. Persons are only tabernacles or temples, and TRUTH is the God, that dwells in them all.... Therefore in all our future statements and reasonings, when we speak of a plurality of Gods, let it be distinctly understood, that we have reference alone to the plurality of temples wherein the same truth or God dwells. And also when we speak of only one God, and state that He is eternal, without beginning or end ... that we have no reference to any particular person or substance, but to *truth* dwelling in a variety of substances.[29]

In another writing Orson Pratt addressed how these minute God particles were formed, or organized, into a being in the following: "When, therefore, the infant spirit is first born in the heavenly world, that is not a commencement of its capacities. Each particle eternally existed prior to this organization."[30] Pratt contended that prior to the organization of the individual particles into being, each existed independently, with consciousness, emotion, and knowledge. Under proscribed universal laws, the independent particles would cease to act independently, and become one in thought, purpose, and action. It would be this organization of God particles, or infant spirit, that would be placed in the celestial female, and result in the birth of a spirit child.[31]

Orson Pratt had characterized the progression of God, and man for that matter, as beginning as an independent particle, or self-existing intelligence, progressing to organized being in the celestial womb, to spirit offspring, to mortal man, to resurrected being, to exalted man, finally resulting in Godhood.[32] In the theology of Orson Pratt, while the being God had a beginning, the divine essence of God, intelligence, did not.[33] In Pratt's view of the nature of God, there existed no continual eternal progression. Once individuals had achieved Godhood, they became in possession of all truth. The exalted being then possessed all attributes of God to their fullest measure.[34] This countered Brigham Young's view, which saw God as an eternally progressing being attaining new levels in knowledge and power. Pratt's absolutist views would be taken up following his death, in 1881, by Charles Penrose and still later by B. H. Roberts.

Using Varying Approaches to Explain the Divine

In their attempts to define the nature, character, and origin of the Gods, Orson Pratt and Brigham Young began to clarify the related Mormon concept of the preexistence. The idea of a preexistence for humankind figures prominently in Mormon soteriology. The concept of a preexistence is the foundational concept for the doctrine of eternal progression. The doctrine of the preexistence deals with the organization, begetting, or creation of the human spirit, and how individuals become Gods. Present Mormon theology holds that a spirit is born in a natural way, the same way material children are born. The spirit child is the natural child of two exalted beings or Gods. The spirit children reside in heaven awaiting mortal bodies through which they can begin their progression to divinity.[35] The notion that spirits are born is based on parts of Brigham's theology.

The modern position on the preexistence was not always held. In the 1850s and 1860s two varying concepts competed for primacy. Orson Pratt and Brigham Young took varying approaches to the question of the origin and nature of God. Pratt used logic and reason, based upon canonical material, in his attempt to answer the questions surrounding the origin and nature of God. In turn, Brigham Young resorted to revelation, or speculation, on unclear theological statements made earlier by Smith. The concepts that emerged from the speculative exercises added to the already existing confusion surrounding the godhead. The concepts of Pratt and Young also laid a foundation for continued speculative exercises by others.

Brigham Young's teachings concerning God centered on Adam-God. In addition to this, Brigham also taught that God had come to this planet from an already existing planetary system bringing with him wives, plants, and animals to become Adam, the first man.[36] It is clear that Brigham Young saw God the Father as begotten, or born, that there had always been Gods, and that the Gods will eternally progress in knowledge and power. Brigham claimed that God was a personal being who was to be worshiped as God. A personal God, who had a Father, had been alluded to by Joseph Smith. The concept appears to have gained prominence through a poem written by Eliza R. Snow.

Eliza R. Snow, the plural wife of Joseph Smith, claimed that the Prophet Joseph Smith had told her that there existed a mother in Heaven. Brigham Young's concept of Adam-God had adapted parts of the God with a consort idea of Snow. Snow's mother in Heaven concept comes from a poem which appeared in the *Times and Seasons*.[37] The poem intimated that spirit children have both a mother and a father. The spirit children are born to the parents in Heaven, in the same way natural children are born. Brigham Young's concept of the divine would follow the line popularized by Eliza R. Snow, that spirit children are born as beings not organized from organic particles, or from intelligences.

Apostle Orson Pratt believed in an alternate concept for the origin of the Gods. Orson Pratt taught that there was a time when there was no being called God.[38] Orson Pratt contended that the Gods consisted of small indivisible particles with an unspecified degree of intelligence and divine attributes. While these intelligences progressed through different phases of existence, the attributes that made God were eternal. The attributes of God permeated all things through the Holy Ghost in varying degrees.[39]

Orson Pratt and Brigham Young appear far apart on the essentials of their beliefs. Both, however, saw God as a resurrected being that had his origin in another part of the universe. Brigham Young, as well, saw all planets as having an Adam and an Eve. The views of Orson Pratt and Brigham Young differed only philosophically. Orson Pratt saw the attributes of God, and the fundamental intelligences, as that which made God God. Orson Pratt's position was fundamentally pantheistic. Pratt believed that Adam, a being distinct from God the Father, could not be the Father of the spirits of the human family, as spirits were organized and not begotten. Brigham Young defined the nature of God in more personalistic terms. Young saw God as an exalted material being, possessed of divinity, and it was the being, God, who was to be worshiped, not his attributes.

The positions taken by Brigham Young and Orson Pratt were varying approaches to the same question, the nature of God. Orson Pratt saw his position as what the scriptures restored by Joseph Smith taught.[40] Orson Pratt's defense was based upon a belief that a present prophet should not contradict a past prophet's teaching or the scriptures. Equating Adam with the Father of our spirits, as Young had taught, was a violation of this principle. Pratt, despite his standing, was censured by Young and the Church's leaders. In 1860, and again in 1865, the Church issued official declarations against the speculative views of Orson Pratt.[41] Young's views would prevail as the dominant teaching of the Church, but with some reservations being held by several within the Quorums, until his death.

The concept of Adam-God was difficult for Orson Pratt to grasp. For his efforts Orson Pratt was censured for not believing Brigham's Adam-God concept. The fundamental division between Brigham Young and Orson Pratt was not directly related to the Adam-God concept per se. Rather, the division while rooted in a hermeneutical understanding was theologically centered on the origin and nature of man, and subsequently the Gods. Young followed a line based on the poem by Eliza R. Snow, that spirit children are begotten as beings which progressed eternally. Orson Pratt countered this concept. Pratt maintained that all material things are comprised of minute particles. These minute eternal particles, intelligences, or spirit, were organized to become a being. It was the intelligences, in Pratt's views, that contained the divine essence and nature, and not the being called God.[42]

The Orson Pratt–Brigham Young debates are an interesting series of discussions over theological positions. Brigham Young, in an attempt to validate his teaching of Adam-God claimed that the concept had been revealed to him by God through Joseph Smith. The apparent revelation is now part of the *Doctrine and Covenants* Section 64.[43] Orson Pratt, in reading this section, did not come to the same conclusions that Young had drawn. Eventually, Orson Pratt was brought into line and began to teach the doctrine of God as held by Brigham Young.[44]

While much of Young's Adam-God concept faded into obscurity with his death, Orson Pratt's evolutionary pantheism, in a refined state, would become the basis for the primary Mormon concept of God in the 20th century.[45] The views of Pratt and Young would continue to be taught by Mormon leaders until the whole question surrounding the origin and nature of God was finally resolved in 1915.

The theological concepts of the early Salt Lake period, while having roots in Nauvoo and Joseph Smith's theology, were expanded on by Brigham Young, Orson Pratt, and others. It is primarily because of their refinement, by Young and Pratt, that they have gained the significance that they hold today in Mormon thought.

Summary

During the early Salt Lake period, nascent Nauvoo concepts evolved into significant doctrines. We have shown that while these concepts have their origins in the thought of Joseph Smith, they were expanded on and given a place of significance in the concept of eternal progression by Brigham Young and Orson Pratt. Through their enhancement, the concepts moved from speculative thought to core parts of Latter-day Saints soteriology.

When we view the King Follett discourse as the watershed in Latter-day Saints theology, we see that its concepts would become of great significance. Following the discourse, the teachings would acquire a deeper meaning, and became essential to an individual's eternal progression. In the King Follett discourse Joseph set out to teach the Saints about the nature of God. This nature of God was interpreted by Smith's successors in finitist and absolutist terms.

Under Brigham Young's tenure, Latter-day Saints theology illuminated several unclear statements made by Joseph Smith. Several of the ideas expressed in the King Follett discourse had been refined before 1844. The concept of spirit had been clarified to mean pure refined matter in 1843. In 1842 "create" had come to mean "organize." Prior to this date it meant creation ex nihilo.[46] The enhancements on the nature, origin, and character of God made by Brigham Young and Orson Pratt were based squarely on the King Follett discourse. As the starting point for all Mormon theology postdating it, the King Follett discourse has become the most important theological document originating in 19th-century Mormonism.[47]

With the death of Orson Pratt, in 1881, the last of the original Twelve Apostles passed away. Orson Pratt's influence in the development of Mormon theology would continue long after his death. The concepts taught by Orson Pratt would resurface in the teachings of several apostles during the latter 19th century. The first 40 years, following the death of Joseph Smith, had seen the Church address several topics alluded to by the Prophet Joseph Smith. Both Brigham Young and Orson Pratt had attempted to resolve the difficulties in the theological heritage left to them by Joseph Smith.

Using divergent hermeneutical approaches, Brigham Young and Orson Pratt had sought to continue the work begun by Joseph Smith. Using the King Follett discourse as their starting point, Orson Pratt and Brigham Young had attempted to explain to the Saints how God came to be God. The King Follett discourse had focused on knowledge of the divine as central to the plan of exaltation.[48] As the emphasis shifted, a knowledge concerning the nature, character, and origin of God became important to an individual's exaltation. With the shift, Pratt and Young's work became extremely important to the Saints. Yet, the close of the early Salt Lake period had not resolved many of the doctrinal conflicts that had emerged from the Nauvoo theology of Joseph Smith. The first 14 years of the Church's history had left a vast system of unresolved theological conflicts. It was in its first 14 years that the Church had moved from a strict modalist theological movement, to a cosmic henotheistic sect. In the years following Smith's death, continued theological speculation only added to the already existing doctrinal concepts.

While clarification had been accomplished on certain theological points, others had remained untouched. If anything, the work undertaken by Orson Pratt and Brigham Young merely added to the theological options available to the Saints. Mormonism in the latter 19th century consisted of a core of generally accepted theological beliefs, primarily centered on the teachings of the King Follett discourse and a large body of speculative statements. The teachings of the discourse had made older theological concepts obsolete.[49] With the King Follett discourse as the starting point for the next 70 years of theological speculation, Mormon leaders attempted to incorporate the Church's first 14 years of theology into their conclusions. They, however, failed to recognize the irreconcilability of some of these earlier statements with the newer speculative statements.

The attempted harmonization of early Mormon theology (variant forms of monotheism) with the teachings of the King Follett discourse's henotheism proved to be a difficult task. While some concepts became refined or reinterpreted, others received little or no attention, and remain as speculative strands of early Mormon thought. Several major theological concepts still have not been addressed, such as the concept of the Holy Ghost.[50] The theological options present within late 19th-century Mormonism provided a basis for discord among the Mormon leaders, and members of the general Church as well. During the next fifty years, beginning in 1880, Mormon leaders would make strong efforts to reconcile the divergent views that had emerged within the Church's belief system.

As in earlier periods, such as the Kirtland and Nauvoo periods, late 19th-century doctrinal harmonization occurred as the result of internal and external conditions rather than as a conscious effort by the Church at doctrinal harmonization.[51] It would be primarily the works of Mormon intellectuals B. H. Roberts, John A. Widstoe, and James E. Talmage—works addressing 19th-century intellectual questions, especially evolution—that would contribute to the harmonization of past doctrines. What had not been of a primary concern to earlier Mormon leaders, the reconciliation of science with religion, became paramount to late 19th- and early 20th-century Mormon leaders. Since its early days, Mormonism had seen all truth as having its origin in the same source, God. Therefore, whether that truth came from science, or religion, mattered little. The Church was strongly rooted in an intellectual heritage since the School of the Prophets in Kirtland.[52]

Under Brigham Young, the Church had come to favor revelation over intellectual logic and reason. In addressing new scientific questions of the 19th century, the Church recognized that it had no clear doctrinal statements to counter the new theories emerging in the secular world, or from within its own theological heritage. The search for a clear doctrinal position became important, as many conservative members within the hierarchy perceived the new theories as a threat to the Church's existence itself. The past 70 years of doctrinal speculation had provided numerous options for the Latter-day Saints to believe in. This caused tension between the educated members of the hierarchy, who formulated their arguments based upon intellectual reason, and those within the hierarchy, who formulated their arguments around revelation.

The mid 19th century saw the emphasis of the Church return to that of its early years, where the concentration was on the charismatic gifts, such as revelation or prophecy. By the 20th century, this had caused a unique paradox to emerge. The Church, while rooted in revelation,[53] had, since the mid 1830s, laid a heavier emphasis on intellectualism. These two forces would collide as the Church sought to reconcile its doctrinal past based upon two separate but clearly defined sets of values and premises. These premises were that all truth was God's truth, and that science and religion would never be at odds. Yet, at the same time, revelation could override anything written, or spoken of, in the past. The hierarchy of the Church and the Prophet, who were privy to the counsel of God, declared what was truth.[54]

Late 19th-century Mormonism had become a collection of competing doctrines, methodologies, approaches, and hermeneutics. Several individuals sought to reconcile past doctrinal inconsistencies within the greater Mormon paradigm that all truth was God's truth. Individuals who attempted to use intellectual means, logic and reason, supplemented by scriptural arguments to reconcile doctrinal inconsistencies, incurred the censure of members of a dogmatic hierarchy that held to revelation as the source of all truth. At last a minor reconciliation was attempted, and it proved to be successful.

9. Unity from Diversity

Apostle James E. Talmage and the Birth of Mormonism

> We claim scriptural authority for the assertion that Jesus Christ was and is God the Creator, the God who revealed Himself to Adam, Enoch, and all the antidiluvial [sic] patriarchs and prophets down to Noah; and the God of Abraham, Isaac, and Jacob; the God of Israel as a united people, and the God of Ephraim and Judah after the disruption of the Hebrew nation; the God of the Old Testament record; and the God of the Nephites. We affirm that Jesus Christ was and is Jehovah, the Eternal One.
> James E. Talmage, *Jesus the Christ*, 1915

The Mormon concept of God had developed during the 19th century within a series of stages, conditioned by several forces. By the early 20th century the modalism evidenced in the early Church was no longer the dominant view of official Mormonism. While the Mormon canon reflected the earlier predominantly modalistic view of God, the introduction of new thought streams had clouded the Mormon view of God. Official Mormon doctrine that believed and taught by the Saint's hierarchy, and that which was to believed by the Church at large, was not modalistic. Early 20th-century Mormonism consisted of a series of inharmonious, speculative theories, or theological options, that centered around a henotheistic concept of the divine. It followed then that the beliefs of the Church at large would also reflect the same inconsistency that existed in the teachings of the Church's leadership.

In the Church's early years, when the *Book of Mormon* and the Bible were the primary sources for revealed truth, there had existed a form of doctrinal cohesiveness. This cohesiveness drew its strength from the matrix in which Mormonism began and the stabilizing influence of the early converts. As the Prophet Joseph Smith began to exercise his calling as Prophet of God, new concepts would be introduced to the Church's belief system. When the revelations began to decline by the mid–1830s, intellectual speculation replaced revelation as the primary source for truth. This in turn led to the introduction of speculative theories, and newer paradigms emerged rooted in an attempt to reconcile the existing body of oral and written revelation.

During the tenure of Brigham Young, key points found in Joseph's theology were added to or expanded on. This in turn produced a loosely knit collection of theories, speculative reasonings, and revelations rather than any cohesive Mormon theology.

With no systematic theology in place, the doctrines of the Church were left open to private interpretation by the membership. In spite of sanctions by the Church hierarchy, various views were still believed by the Church at large, and taught by influential members of the Church's hierarchy. The problem proved difficult to resolve even though the bureaucracy that had emerged within the last half of the 19th century had a clearly defined power structure. It would be primarily through the works of B. H. Roberts, John A. Widstoe, and James E. Talmage that the existing divergent streams of Mormon doctrine would attain some harmony with the existing official theological sentiments of the Church hierarchy. John A. Widstoe and James Talmage would attempt to resolve the major theological difficulties, thereby giving birth to a new Mormonism.

During the late Salt Lake period, Mormon doctrinal development had been conditioned by several events. These events challenged the Church's foundational claims. In an attempt to meet the challenges, two significant works, John Widstoe's *A Rational Theology*[1] and James E. Talmage's *Jesus the Christ*[2] would be produced. A third development during this time would involve the removal of an earlier theological document from the Church's canon, the *Lectures of Faith* in 1921. In the 20th century Mormon leaders would make attempts to reconcile its divergent views on God and present a harmonious theology to its membership and the world.

In the following pages we will place the birth of the Mormon concept of God within its proper time frame, the 20th century, and show the events surrounding the church's decision to harmonize the divergent teachings of its past.

Discord Among the Lords Anointed

Among the many teachings that emerged from the theological speculation begun by Joseph Smith's King Follett discourse was the concept of a material God. What had begun in the 1840s would eventually culminate

9. UNITY FROM DIVERSITY 145

in a series of debates throughout the later 19th and early 20th century. Following the groundwork established by Smith, leaders of the Church would seek to rectify the problems caused by the introduction of a material God. Among the earliest individuals to address the materialism of God were Orson Pratt and John Taylor in 1845.[3]

Through much of the 1840s Mormon works dealing with the nature of God centered upon the teachings of the King Follett discourse.[4] The theological conclusions reached by Taylor and Pratt were based upon the accuracy of the sermon, as recorded by William Clayton and Thomas Bullock. The original publication of the King Follett discourse contained several key concepts that were deleted from subsequent redactions of the sermon.

The first publication of the King Follett discourse had taught that man was co-equal with God. The 1844 text had also used mind, spirit, and intelligence interchangeably. The 1855 Grimshaw redaction of the King Follett discourse had changed the text to read that the mind or intelligence was part of the spirit.[5] While this may seem insignificant, it was an important change. Post 1844 Mormon writers like Orson Pratt did not make the distinction between intelligence and spirit, but remained true to the 1844 text of the discourse, and to what were apparently Smith's original teachings. Following the 1857[6] publication of the discourse, writers used the 1857 discourse to state that the spirit was comprised of intelligences. Depending on which version of the King Follett discourse was used would determine how an individual would address the origin and nature of God.

The speculative theology, enhanced by Mormon leaders after 1844, reached a critical point in the early 1880s. In 1884, Elder Charles W. Penrose delivered a sermon on the nature and characteristics of God.[7] In his sermon, Penrose reintroduced some fundamental principles that had first emerged with Orson Pratt in 1853. Following a speculative line, first introduced by Joseph Smith and elaborated upon by Orson Pratt, Penrose would resurrect the debate over the nature of God. Penrose proposed once again the possibility that God progressed throughout eternity from an initial stage as an intelligence. Penrose had awakened Orson Pratt's doctrine of God from its sleep.[8] In his discourse, Penrose stated that all things were organized from self-existing particles called spirit or intelligences. These particles existed prior to the person of God. Penrose's view of God held that God had a beginning, but the intelligences did not; they were eternal. Penrose's argument was however in direct opposition to the line of theology that had been developed by Brigham Young as well as the official declarations of 1860 and 1865.

In the discourse Penrose stated:

> But if God is an individual Spirit and dwells in a body, the question will arise "Is He the Eternal Father? Yes, He is the Eternal Father." Is it a fact that He never had a beginning? In the elementary particles of His organism, He did not. But if He is an organized Being, there must have been a time when that being was organized. This some one will say, would infer that there must have been a time when that being was organized. This some one will say, would infer that God had a beginning.[9]

Penrose continues his argument by inferring that the minute particles from which God originated, or the point at which He began, not the being that is called God, was eternal. God, Penrose states, progressed through degrees of glory becoming God. God is eternal then, in the sense that his essence, or intelligence, is eternal. In Penrose's words:

> This spirit which pervades all things, which is the light and life of all things, by which our heavenly Father operates, by which He is omnipotent, never had a beginning and never will have an end ... Intelligence or the light of truth never was created, neither indeed can be.

Penrose's discourse was true to the teachings of Joseph Smith. Smith had stated that he would reveal that God was not God from all eternity. Penrose's discourse did little to solidify the concept of God in Mormonism. In spite of two official declarations in the 1860s, the Church was again forced to deal with the speculation regarding the origin and nature of God. In 1892 the same controversial topic that had produced the Orson Pratt–Brigham Young debates was again before the Church's leaders.[10] First Counselor George Q. Cannon addressed the controversy. Once again, the Church promoted the view established in 1865 that it was the being God that was an object of worship and not the combined, organized intelligences that contained the essence of divinity that were to be worshiped.[11]

In spite of official declarations of 1860 and 1865, the controversy over a finite or absolute concept of God continued in Mormonism. Charles W. Penrose would eventually become a member of the First Presidency. In that capacity, Penrose would exert an influence over the direction Mormon doctrine would take. The very concepts that President Young had found so offensive in the thought of Orson Pratt were emerging once again. Penrose's ideology proved detrimental to both B. H. Roberts and John A. Widstoe, who favored a finite concept of God.

B. H. Roberts and the Mormon Doctrine of Deity

The years 1900 to 1930 proved to be important decades in Mormon doctrinal development. In the first three decades of the 20th century,

Mormonism would reconcile several troublesome areas. It would also be in the early 20th century that Mormonism would finally deal, conclusively, with the controversy regarding the origin, nature, and role of God.[12]

In 1910, B. H. Roberts was preparing a manual to be used in the Seventies Course in Theology.[13] Roberts had intended the ideas in the manual to be an expansion of his earlier *New Witnesses for God*. Roberts held that intelligences were self-existent before they entered into spirit bodies, and then naturally progressed to material bodies. These intelligences were autonomous and self-conscious prior to their incarnation. The intelligences were neither begotten nor born, but had always existed. Roberts explained that the reason Jesus was considered the "firstborn" was that Jesus had taken on a spirit body before all of the other intelligences.[14]

The Church hierarchy, primarily Charles W. Penrose and Anthon Lund, objected to Roberts' speculation. Penrose and Lund reasoned that if what was eternal was self-existing autonomous intelligences, and if man was capable of progressing, there must have been a time when all intelligences were at the same point on the progressive scale. This, they concluded, caused two fundamental problems: that there was a time when there was nothing called God, and that man could be viewed as being equal to God.[15]

The speculative principles of Roberts were problematic for several members of the Council of the Twelve, especially Charles W. Penrose. The First Presidency's major disagreement with Roberts was over Roberts' theological speculation that intelligences were self-existing, conscious, autonomous beings, not minute particles of matter. The disagreement appears rooted in a discrepancy over whether intelligences were part of the spirit, or whether they were to be equated with the spirit itself. Both positions could be supported by the two existing accounts of the King Follett discourse. The discrepancy could have been resolved with a standard King Follett discourse text.

B. H. Roberts and Charles Penrose would continue their debate in the following year. In 1912 Roberts had prepared the original manuscript for the *History of the Church*. In Roberts' absence, Penrose had removed the King Follett discourse from the *History of the Church*, stating that the discourse had been incorrectly reported.[16] Upon Roberts' return, he had 25,000 copies of the discourse printed and sent to all ward and stake leaders.[17]

Evidence seems to indicate that Roberts, in formulating his views, had attempted to reconcile the pre–Nauvoo use of the terms intelligence and spirit with their acquired Nauvoo meanings.[18] As well, Roberts had based his theology on the 1857 version of the King Follett discourse which had said that intelligence was only part of the spirit, not the identical substance. This would allow Roberts to see an eternal intelligence which eventually became part of the spirit.[19] B. H. Roberts would make a final attempt to present his views in a work entitled *The Truth, the Way, and the Life*. The work never met with official approval and was not published during his lifetime.[20]

Roberts' reasonings had brought Mormon theology to a point that it was not willing to admit to: a finite God. The Church, however, was not prepared to endorse an absolutist concept of God either. Despite several attempts, Roberts was never able to convince the Church hierarchy to accept his views.

Yet Roberts' views on intelligences and the nature of God would emerge in the writings of Apostles John A. Widstoe and James E. Talmage. Talmage and Widstoe had greater success in their attempts at presenting their views than Roberts had. John Widstoe's *A Rational Theology* would initially receive the same opposition as Roberts' work had earlier. In Widstoe's work, the speculative statements were toned down, but allowed to remain in the work.

John A. Widstoe: The Origin of God Through Cosmic Evolution

For a church with a strong emphasis on secular education, the Mormon Church has had few intellectuals in positions of power. John A. Widstoe therefore occupied a unique position in Mormon history. Along with Orson Pratt, Sidney Rigdon, James Talmage, B. H. Roberts, and a few others, John A. Widstoe should be considered one of the great theological minds of the Church.

John A. Widstoe had been educated at two of the finest universities in the world, Harvard and Göttingen. Widstoe had received his Ph.D. in chemistry, and not in theology. His scientific background helped Widstoe to become one of the primary apologists and theologians for the Church in the 20th century.[21] Through his major work, *A Rational Theology*, as well as the monthly articles appearing in the *Improvement Era's* "Evidences and Reconciliations," Widstoe would leave his mark on Mormon theology.[22]

John Widstoe's *A Rational Theology* was originally intended to be used as an instruction manual for the Church's priesthood quorums. Seeing it in its initial draft stages, several of the Church hierarchy began to question the suitability of the work for general use. While the work was in pre-publication stages, it had received special editorial attention by President Joseph F. Smith. Smith thought the work too speculative on certain points of the godhead, and instructed Widstoe to make revisions to the manuscript. Smith ordered Widstoe to stop working on the book until he had had a chance to review its entire contents.[23]

The First Presidency, especially Anthon Lund, had objected to Widstoe's assertion that man and God were co-eternal.[24] Widstoe had followed B. H. Roberts in asserting that intelligences existed as individuals prior to becoming spirits. Widstoe had reasoned, if God had not created man, then man must be co-eternal with God. For Widstoe, God was God because he had progressed and operated on a different level of advancement.[25] President Smith thought that Widstoe had gone too far, and ordered a revision of the manuscript of *A Rational Theology*.

Widstoe's assertion that God had evolved from a superior intelligence (a being superior to the others) to become God, was problematic for the Church's leaders. Widstoe defended his position. He saw the divine plan as a plan for the advancement of personal eternal beings, or intelligences. These beings, Widstoe explained, were intelligences that had always existed. By using the will, and with the aid of the other intelligences, a person's progression could be accelerated. God was God because God possessed the greatest amount of knowledge and had the most perfected will. As a result of his knowledge, the sum of all other intelligences, God was able to recognize the laws of the universe and use them to His benefit.[26]

In the First Presidency's eyes, this meant that there was a time when there was not a God.[27] It also meant that God was God because of God's ability to maintain the allegiance of the other intelligences and not because God possessed some inherent substance or nature. The whole concept of cosmic evolution, and a primary collection of co-equal, co-eternal intelligences, did not appeal to President Smith. Smith challenged Widstoe to defend his ideas from a scriptural position. Nothing was officially resolved in the discussion and Widstoe's *A Rational Theology* went to print as a toned down version of the original manuscript.[28]

In spite of its editing, Widstoe's *A Rational Theology* still contains a cosmic evolutionary theory on the origin of God.[29] John A. Widstoe had approached the problem from a perspective that all truth was able to be harmonized. He had attempted to incorporate late 19th-century scientific theories into his work.[30] Widstoe had incorporated Herbert Spencer's evolutionary argument, that organisms increased in complexity, in the formulation of his theology.[31]

Despite the controversy with the First Presidency, Widstoe would continue to be a spokesman for Mormon doctrine. Through his *Evidences and Reconciliations*,[32] doctrinal questions would receive theological answers on a monthly basis. As a regular feature appearing in the official Church organ *The Improvement Era*, Widstoe's quasi-scientific, rational theology would influence an entire generation of the Saints.

After the Penrose-Roberts and the Widstoe-Smith controversies, it became apparent that a more definitive statement regarding the godhead was necessary. Apostle James Talmage would provide that statement.[33]

James E. Talmage: A Doctrinal Exposition on the Father and the Son

Apostle James Talmage stands out among the many individuals who have made significant contributions to the Mormon doctrine of God in the 20th century. Talmage, a trained geologist, had a history of controversy with other general authorities. The controversies of the past had centered around the growing influence of biblical criticism and evolution among Mormon intellectuals.[34]

As a result of the growing number of speculative theories believed and taught by some General Authorities, the Church saw that a comprehensive treatment on the nature of the godhead was in order. By the first decade of the 20th century, Mormonism had become a religious movement governed by an open canon and oral scripture. These two central tenets had allowed a number of theories on the godhead to simultaneously coexist in Mormonism. With such divergency in thought even among the General Authorities, the general membership of the Church had many theological options, all which had a ring of the truth to them.

Intellectuals within the Church had sought to form logical cohesive doctrinal positions based upon the scriptures and the discourses of the Prophet Joseph Smith. Revelation and reason had clashed often in 19th-century Mormonism. In the Church's struggle to resolve divergent teachings, reason would eventually triumph. This was accomplished through the work of James Talmage.

James Talmage wrote three pieces of literature that made significant contributions to the development of the Mormon doctrine of God. James Talmage's work *The Articles of Faith*[35] had originally been given as a series of lectures in the early 1890s. In the fall of 1898, the First Presidency had asked Talmage to rewrite the lectures and present them for approval. The First Presidency had intended to present the finished work as an official exposition of the doctrines of the Church.[36] In his *The Articles of Faith* first published in 1899, Talmage dealt briefly with the person and work of the Holy Ghost.[37] Talmage asserted that the three persons of the godhead exist in a unity of "attributes, powers and purpose."[38] Talmage made an attempt to reconcile the Church's early theological position, modalism, with the current plurality of Gods concept. Talmage would contend that the oneness spoken of in the scriptures "cannot rationally be construed to mean the Father, Son, and the Holy Ghost are one in substance, and in person, nor that the names represent the same individuals under different names."[39] Rather, Talmage expressed:

This unity is a type of completeness; the mind of any one member of the Trinity is the mind of the others... The one-ness of the Godhead, to which the scriptures so abundantly testify, implies no mystical union of substance, nor any unnatural and therefore impossible blending of personality. Father, Son, and Holy Ghost are as distinct in their persons and individualities as are any three personages in mortality.[40]

Talmage's book made official the prevailing Church sentiment on the godhead and also declared the Holy Ghost to be a person.[41]

The problems that had existed in Mormon theology prior to the publication of the *Articles of Faith* are seen in many of the Church's official works. The disparity between the Church's canon and the discourses of the Church's prophets had caused confusion in the minds of many Latter-day Saints. The ambiguity of past statements had left many questions surrounding the unity of the godhead, the role of Jesus as the Father, and the roles of the Father and the Son in the creation unanswered. Talmage's second work sought to resolve many of these conflicting statements.

In the years 1904 to 1906, James Talmage delivered a series of lectures titled "Jesus the Christ." The primary purpose of the lectures was to educate the Latter-day Saints on the person and work of Jesus.[42] It is doubtful that Talmage had any idea that his lectures would provide the basis for a rebirth in Latter-day Saint theology. Perhaps, if not for the Widstoe-Smith affair, the need for a work like *Jesus the Christ* would not have existed. In the early part of 1914, the First Presidency asked Talmage to prepare his lectures for a book.

By September 14, 1914, Church officials were becoming anxious that the work be prepared as soon as possible. Church officials summoned Talmage to the temple, where he was to sit and write until the work was completed. The call to Talmage was in the wake of the Widstoe-Smith affair, which had happened in June of 1914. On April 19, 1915, James Talmage completed the volume. By May 4, 1915, the book was in the hands of the First Presidency and prepared for publication.[43] Talmage's *Jesus the Christ* was an expansion of some of the views expressed in his *Articles of Faith*.[44]

Talmage, in *Jesus the Christ*, would clear up the controversy surrounding the role of Jesus. Talmage would write:

> We claim scriptural authority for the assertion that Jesus Christ was and is God the Creator, the God who revealed Himself to Adam, Enoch, and all the antidiluvial [sic] patriarchs and prophets down to Noah; and the God of Abraham, Isaac, and Jacob; the God of Israel as a united people, and the God of Ephraim and Judah after the disruption of the Hebrew nation; the God of the Old Testament record; and the God of the Nephites. We affirm that Jesus Christ was and is Jehovah, the Eternal One.[45]

Elohim, Talmage would write, was the name of the "Eternal Father, whose first born son in the spirit is Jehovah—the only begotten in the flesh Jesus Christ."[46]

Talmage's work had finally resolved the conflict over the roles of the Father and the Son, and designated Elohim as the Father, and Jehovah as the preincarnate Jesus. This had resolved a doctrinal problem that had existed since the early 1830s.

Several *Book of Mormon* passages also presented problems for Church leaders in the 20th century. Following the publication of *Jesus the Christ* in 1915, the Church was inundated by letters from members regarding the new views.[47] In 1916, the Church issued an official doctrinal statement, attempting to reconcile contradictory *Book of Mormon* passages with the new views on the godhead.[48] The doctrinal statement prepared by James Talmage attempted to explain how Jesus could be called the Father. In spite of the attempts to harmonize the doctrines of the past, several problems still existed following the issuance of the 1916 statement.

The doctrinal statement explained 1830 modalist *Book of Mormon* theology against the background of 1915 Mormonism.[49] Talmage would explain, in detail, how Jesus could be called the Father. Talmage explained that Jesus is called the Father because he participated in the creation,[50] he is the Father of those who abide in the Gospel,[51] and through divine investure of authority.[52] It is doubtful that the author of the modalist passages of the *Book of Mormon* had Talmage's explanations in mind when he wrote them.

Talmage was to redefine Mormon concepts and terms, and then use this newly redefined entity, to explain the past doctrinal statements of its leaders. By taking the apparently contradictory statements contained within the *Book of Mormon* and other discourses, and reinterpreting them in light of present doctrinal understanding, Talmage gave the impression that Mormonism had never held a modalistic Christological position.

Several explanations can account for Mormonism's reinterpretation of its past doctrinal teachings. First, it must be said that a mechanism is present within Mormonism that would allow for doctrinal changes to be implemented without need of explanation or redefining, the ninth *Article of Faith*.[53] What does seem likely is that a stronger and older hermeneutic tradition overrides the Church's ninth *Article of Faith*. The Latter-day Saint belief that the entire Gospel is as old as Adam,[54] and was known by men of God throughout history, stands in the way of a line upon line, doctrinal development schema. The concept has its origin in the early 1830s, and is found in both the *Book of Moses* and the *Joseph Smith Translation*. This hermeneutic is used early in the history of Mormon thought. This is evident from Joseph Smith's sermon of June 16, 1844. In the sermon Smith maintains that he has taught a plurality of Gods since the early days of the Church, whereas the evidence does not support this claim.

The hermeneutic employed by the Church's leaders resulted in the decanonization of a major document. During the process of producing a new *Doctrine and Covenants*, the Church recognized that it could not harmonize the *Lectures of Faith* with the Church's current doctrinal position.

With the publication of Talmage's *Jesus the Christ*, a newly defined Mormonism had emerged. Yet, there existed a major problem. There was a canonized work that clearly taught an earlier concept of God, the *Lectures of Faith*. Something needed to be done with the *Lectures*. Talmage, again, would play a role in the decision of what to do with the *Lectures*.

In November of 1917, a council was conveyed to discuss the question of what to do with the *Lectures of Faith*.[55] The council appointed a committee consisting of George F. Richards, Anthony Ivins, Melvin J. Ballard, and Talmage to consider the options that were available to the Church concerning the *Lectures of Faith*. The questions surrounding what to do with the *Lectures of Faith* had surfaced in the wake of the doctrinal statements of 1915 and 1916, and the decision of the Church to issue a new edition of the *Doctrine and Covenants*. The central mandate given to the committee was whether or not to include the *Lectures of Faith* in the new edition of the *Doctrine and Covenants*.

The committee focused on several questions, such as authorship and the acceptance of the *Lectures of Faith* as part of the canon in 1835.[56] The committee resolved that the *Lectures* should not be included as several problems surrounding the origin of the *Lectures of Faith* had not yet been resolved. The committee felt that the original intent of the *Lectures of Faith* was that they were to be aids in instruction and, therefore, were never intended to be part of the canon.[57]

The committee's decision seems strange, given that the *Lectures* were accepted by the General Conference of 1835 as part of the original *Doctrine and Covenants*.[58] In fact, they were included in the previous three editions, two of which appeared during the lifetime of the Prophet Joseph Smith. Another point, as well, was that the section in which the *Lectures of Faith* appear is titled "Lecture First on the Doctrine of the Church of the Latter Day Saints." The revelations, which now comprise the entire *Doctrine and Covenants*, were prefaced by the title "The Covenants and Commandments of the Lord to His Servants of the Church of the Latter Day Saints." It is clear that the *Lectures of Faith* were seen as the doctrines of the Church, as taught by Joseph Smith in 1835.[59]

The committee's decision to remove the *Lectures of Faith* was based not on the reasons they gave, but rather that the *Lectures of Faith* could not be reconciled with the new Mormonism. Under the influence of

B. H. Roberts, John A. Widstoe, and James Talmage, Mormonism was making great attempts to tie together loose theological concepts. The *Lectures of Faith*, rather than aid in creating a harmonious theology, contributed to preserving a historic theology that was no longer believed. That the *Lectures of Faith* were singled out for decanonization is strange. The *Book of Mormon* and the *Book of Moses* also reflect the modalism of early Mormonism. Whereas the vague modalism of the *Book of Mormon* and the *Book of Moses* could be reinterpreted, the clear statements of the lectures could not.

Today, the concepts that emerged from Talmage's work are accepted as official Mormon doctrine. The work of Roberts, Widstoe, and Talmage played heavily in the decision to remove the *Lectures of Faith*.[60] While the ambiguous statements of the Prophet could be harmonized, it appears that the clear doctrinal teachings of the *Lectures of Faith* could not and were therefore removed.

Summary

In this chapter we have pointed, briefly, to three events that changed the shape of Mormonism. It is the nature and impact of these events which I believe show just cause for saying that the Mormon doctrine of God is a product of the 20th century with roots in 19th century.

While Talmage and Widstoe built on the teachings of past Latter-day Saints leaders, they also redefined what these leaders had originally intended. Both Talmage and Widstoe reshaped Mormonism in as dramatic a fashion as the King Follett discourse had done in 1844. In effect, the two dates of 1844 and 1915, the dates that the King Follett discourse and *Jesus the Christ* appeared, can be seen as watersheds in Latter-day Saints doctrinal history.

In the King Follett discourse we see a synthesis of speculative doctrines. It appears that Smith, in attempt to quiet the dissent in Nauvoo, introduces a major theological treatise. Between 1835 and 1844, Smith had given few revelations. In addition the failures in Kirtland and Missouri, and the beginning of dissent in Nauvoo, had been problematic for Smith. This had caused many to question his prophetic call. The King Follett discourse was Joseph Smith's attempt to regain authority among his people. The democratic nature of early Mormonism proved detrimental for Smith. In any democracy, dissent is inevitable. While individual dissent could be removed, Smith lacked the authority to quiet any large dissenting factions.

The teachings of the sermon were an effort by Smith to regain his primacy among his followers. In this light, the teachings of the King Follett discourse could be seen as new doctrines. The concepts introduced in the summer of 1844 were speculative theological concepts, they were not refined theological positions. The doctrines introduced by the King Follett discourse drastically changed the face of Mormon theology. The distinctive theology that arose in Nauvoo would provide the base for the next 50 years of Mormon theology. Many of the concepts expressed by Smith in the King Follett discourse were unclear. Yet the King Follet discourse was the clearest expression of theology that the early Saints had. Those that followed in Smith's footsteps made attempts to clarify the various theological statements made by him. Individuals such as Orson Pratt sought to harmonize the speculative statements of Smith with the Church's canon. This proved to be a difficult task. The outcome of the exercise was a plethora of theological options.

In the latter half of the 19th century several individuals, conditioned by the influx of science, sought to reconcile Mormon thought with scientific knowledge. The result of this exercise provided some doctrinal synthesis. James Talmage's *Jesus the Christ* synthesized speculative doctrines that had emerged from the King Follett discourse. Building upon the King Follett discourse, James Talmage would bring together the loose theological ends, and produce a new Mormon theology. In J*esus the Christ*, many of Mormonism's past doctrinal teachings and speculative theories coalesced, and were given an official sanction by the Church. The Church by sanctioning Talmage's *Jesus the Christ* had made it the official Mormon statement on theological topics.

Adam-God, the nature of God, the plurality of Gods, Elohim and Jehovah, each concept in turn was redefined and given its proper place in Mormon theology. The importance of Talmage's *Jesus the Christ* cannot be underestimated. Through it the past 80 years of theological speculation were given either a vote of confidence or removed. This was done despite the Latter-day Saints' claim to possess oral scripture.

James Talmage's work, in effect, gave birth to a new Mormonism. The new Mormonism was one that on the surface appeared less speculative and prone to change. The effects of *Jesus the Christ*, and the "Doctrinal Exposition on the Father and the Son," were solid attempts at reducing the diversity in Mormon doctrine. The two works provided a frame against which all new revelations and teachings would be correlated. As well, the works provided the paradigm through which all past doctrinal teachings would be interpreted. The two works would be seen as the official standard by which all speculative theology, past, present, and future, would have to harmonize.

The Mormon experiment with an open canon and oral scripture proved to be detrimental rather than helpful. The two concepts had created a

Church where speculative theories and official preferred dogma were competing for validity in the hearts and minds of the Saints. After the publication of *Jesus the Christ*, all new theological concepts would have to be brought in line, not with the established canon, but rather with *Jesus the Christ*. The established canon, with its divergent beliefs, contributed to the theological options evidenced in late 19th-century Latter-day Saints' theology. Talmage's work, in effect, redefined most of Joseph Smith's teachings and gave them a proper place and context within historic Mormon theology.

Some Parting Words

In essence the modern Mormon concept of God is the product of B. H. Roberts, John A. Widstoe, and James Talmage rather than of Joseph Smith and Brigham Young. While Joseph Smith and Brigham Young provided the core for future Mormon beliefs, Roberts, Widstoe, and Talmage redefined and gave new meanings to this core. While the modern Mormon Church's teachings have roots in the Church founded by Joseph Smith, it would be primarily John A. Widstoe and James Talmage who would clarify and attempt to synthesize the speculative teachings of the previous century.

The Latter-day Saints have claimed since 1830 that Joseph Smith restored primitive Christianity to the earth. What this meant, and continues to mean, is that the original teachings and practices of Christianity were restored. Yet if one compares modern Mormonism to its 1830s counterpart, there appears to be no consistency in the Mormon doctrine of God. Yet these inconsistencies should not alarm the members of the Church or the student of Mormonism. Within the construct of Mormonism, the Church has a mechanism in place that would allow it to introduce new thought into its belief system. This mechanism is outlined in the ninth *Article of Faith*. The ninth *Article of Faith* states: "we believe all that the Lord has revealed and will yet reveal many great and glorious truths pertaining to the kingdom."

With such a belief as part of its official statement of faith, we can then expect to see changes within the doctrines of the Church. Yet, would these changes necessarily have to be as drastic as those evidenced within Mormonism? Mormonism shifted from modalistic monotheism to cosmic henotheism within a period of 14 years. As well, Joseph Smith throughout his life attempted to legitimize the introduction of new thought. The new teachings appear to have been delivered in times of tension, when his prophetic calling was in doubt.

The myth that Joseph Smith was early in possession of the concept of a plurality of Gods cannot be supported by the evidence. Only by placing later teachings earlier into Church history can the myth of doctrinal consistency be passed off as accurate history.

A more objective view would see Mormon doctrinal development as a result of Joseph's attempt to come to grasps with surrounding events, and the interpretation of his religious experience, in terms of his surrounding environment.

There is no doubt Mormonism has developed, or progressed, from modalism to cosmic henotheism. Yet Mormon leaders continue to maintain that the Church that exists in the late 20th century is exactly the same Church, doctrinally and structurally, as that organized in 1830. It is their hermeneutic interpretation that the Gospel is as old as Adam that may contribute to this. The attempt to reconcile Latter-day Saint belief with historical evidence has often resulted in a distorted history of the Mormon Church.

The Church has taken great measures to protect the illusion of doctrinal continuity. They have removed canonized material which was no longer consistent with present Latter-day Saint thought. They have also used ambiguous statements of early Church members, and leaders, and reinterpreted these statements in light of present understanding. An example of this would be the present *Doctrine and Covenants* Section 79. This revelation given in 1832 is apparently the first time Joseph taught the plurality of Gods concept. In order to strengthen their argument, they refer to Joseph's claim of June 16, 1844, that he had always preached the plurality of Gods. Joseph Smith did not begin to teach the existence of a plurality of Gods until the 1840s. The apparent discrepancies are harmonized by using an ignorant masses theory. By saying that while Smith was aware of the concepts at an earlier date, the members were not yet prepared to receive the teachings when they were originally revealed. A classic example of this would be the polygamy teaching, apparently revealed to Joseph in 1832, to core members in 1843, and to the general Church in 1852.

Throughout this work, I have attempted to show that the introduction of new concepts, publicly, usually coincided with the origin of the concept. There may be one exception, that being the plurality of Gods. While Smith may have held to certain concepts privately at earlier dates (a plurality of Gods as early as 1842 as evidenced in his translation of the *Book of Abraham*), it was the introduction of the concept in 1844 that placed the concept into the realm of eternal truth for his followers.

Is it then fair to ask members of the Mormon Church what do Mormons believe? The question is not easily answered. In the Mormon Church, official doctrines, speculative theories, and personally held beliefs have always co-existed. For many outsiders this curious phenomenon defies explanation. Yet this phenomenon at the very least requires an explanation.

The Mormon Church is a religious institution that appears to be more concerned with orthopraxis than with orthodoxy. For members, it is not so much a matter of correct belief in the doctrines of the Church, as much as practical application of the doctrines, through the rituals and precepts of the Church.

As a result of this concern with orthopraxis, in the 20th century, a student of Mormonism will find it difficult to come to a consensus regarding the Mormon belief system, or its historical precursors. This work was an attempt to establish a chronological framework by which future students of Mormonism could define Latter-day Saint beliefs. While this work may not be inclusive, or totally representative of Mormonism in the last two centuries, it has provided some material that can be expanded upon at a future date.

The problem of not being able to work from an established narrative, or theological frame, has been difficult at times. Working through the midrash of speculative theology, theological commentary, and incomplete philosophical ideas has also been difficult. Several problems had to be overcome in order to establish a base chronological frame for the Latter-day Saints' development of the doctrine of God. Perhaps the most difficult problem was the reluctance of the Latter-day Saints' leaders to clearly define their beliefs, consistently. This reluctance, by the Church, has resulted in a "painted chair" effect. As new concepts were introduced, older concepts were not dispensed with. This resulted in a convoluted theology where divergent theological beliefs, such as modalism and cosmic henotheism, co-existed and were believed as accurate descriptions for the Latter-day Saint concept of God.

Appealing to the Latter-day Saints' canon for theological support has not been satisfactory. Contained within the Latter-day Saints' canon are works accepted as canonical at various points in Latter-day Saints' history. While some theological concepts have been removed or revised, the canon still contains both modalistic and henotheistic concepts.

For many of the Latter-day Saints, there appears to be no major difficulty in accepting the divergent concepts still present within their canon. There have been attempts by individuals within the Church to harmonize their past beliefs. The works of Orson Pratt, Parley P. Pratt, B. H. Roberts, John A. Widstoe, and James E. Talmage can be seen in this light. Of these, it is precisely the work of James E. Talmage that proved to be an important factor in harmonizing the beliefs of the Mormon Church. Perhaps, due to their isolationist policy, doctrinal divergency was not an important issue for 19th-century Latter-day Saints' officials. In the 20th century, several attempts at resolving the theological difficulties would be undertaken. This may be due to the emergence of several key intellectual figures within Mormonism. The early Latter-day Saints Church had within its membership several highly educated individuals. It was not the collection of rural illiterate converts that the Church has often portrayed in order to emphasize the work of God among them.

Since its early days, the Church had always valued secular education. In the 1840s knowledge came to be tied to the concept of eternal progression. The more an individual learns in any particular stage of the progression, the shorter the time of the progression. Smith, by the time of his death in 1844, was able to read three languages and was familiar with the majority of philosophical and theological theories of his day. Smith throughout most of his life surrounded himself with intellectuals. In 1835, the Church had employed Joshua Seixas to teach its elders Hebrew. As well, several early Latter-day Saint leaders were trained at some of the top universities in the country, such as Oberlin, Yale, and Union Theological Seminary.[61] For their time, Orson Spenser, Orson Pratt, and Sidney Rigdon were educated men. Apparently, at one time, self-educated Orson Pratt was believed to have been a world class scientist.[62]

It appears, however, that during the tenure of Brigham Young, the Church lost its zeal for intellectualism. Young's leadership of the Church was centered squarely on revelation, rather than reason. Under Brigham Young, the Saints resorted to a more practical approach to religion, favoring prophecy and ritual, to intellectual speculation and discussion.

Towards the end of the 19th century, intellectualism returned to Mormonism. The Latter-day Saints membership was surfacing from its long isolation in Utah. Its members were once again traveling abroad to the world's major universities. The resurgence in Latter-day Saints' intellectualism is seen in three individuals, B. H. Roberts, John A. Widstoe, and James Talmage. It would be these three individuals who would turn the midrash of 19th century speculative thought into, if not a coherent and logical belief system, at the very least, a semiconsistent one. Through the works of B. H. Roberts, John A. Widstoe, and James E. Talmage, Mormonism would undergo a revision in an attempt to reconcile past doctrinal teachings with then currently held views. Yet it would not be through any conscious effort that Mormonism would attempt a reconstruction of its past doctrinal history. The reconstruction would come about while addressing internal and external challenges.

The history of speculative theology within Mormonism had created several theological options for its followers. When the science versus religion controversy hit Mormonism in the early 20th century, Mormon intellectuals sought to rectify the controversy. It was really then an external pressure which forced the hand of the Church, rather than any conscious effort on the Church's part to reconcile its doctrinal inconsistencies.[63] The

Mormonism that emerged from the revision was a movement that claimed to have originated in 1830, but was far removed from that original movement. The movement had gone in a direction that left the 20th-century Church unrecognizable from its 19th-century counterpart. It is with this premise in mind that one should be lead to conclude that Mormonism is a product of the 20th century rather than of the nineteenth.

As a result of doctrinal development, the Church in the 20th century had removed itself so far from the original Church founded in 1830 that a drastic revision was needed to deal with the diverse teachings exhibited by the Latter-day Saints in the 20th century. This revision was undertaken by B. H. Roberts, John A. Widstoe, and James E. Talmage. In the end, it would be James Talmage's *Jesus the Christ* that would be the catalyst in synthesizing the past 70 years of doctrinal teachings. It follows then that Talmage's *Jesus the Christ* had a greater influence in shaping the present Mormon doctrine of God than either the *Book of Mormon* or the teachings of Joseph Smith and Brigham Young.

Before James Talmage, the teachings of Joseph Smith and Brigham Young had a form but lacked refined substance. Early 20th-century Mormon doctrine consisted of incomplete ideas, speculative thoughts, and theological options. James Talmage would bring these diverse thoughts and ideas together, resolving many of the theological inconsistencies that had emerged. It was not that Talmage, logically and with consistency, reduced the theological options available within Mormonism. Talmage resolved the inconsistencies by choosing one particular stream of theological interpretation, and attempted to harmonize some of the diverse theological teachings to that stream. Talmage's attempts were given additional weight. The Church hierarchy had specifically chosen him to do the task and accepted his resolutions as final, authoritative, and binding upon the Church's membership. Talmage's work, bringing unity from diversity, led to the birth of a new Mormonism in the 20th century.

NOTES

Introduction: Mormonism Yesterday and Today

1. References to the Mormons, Mormonism, the Mormon Church, the Latter-day Saints, the Saints, and the Church are to the people, beliefs, and institutions of The Church of Jesus Christ of Latter-day Saints with its headquarters in Salt Lake City, Utah. Unless specifically mentioned I do not intend to include within these categories other groups that are part of the greater Mormon movement or tradition.

2. *The Book of Mormon* (Salt Lake City: Deseret Book Co.,1981), 1 Nephi 13: 34. When referencing modern versions, Arabic numbers will be used for chapters and verses.

3. For a brief discussion of views on the concept of the restoration see Jan Shipps, *Mormonism: The Birth of a New Religious Tradition* (Urbana: University of Illinois Press, 1985), pp. 67–87, 119, 120, 122. Richard E. Bushman, *Joseph Smith and the Beginnings of Mormonism* (Urbana: University of Illinois Press, 1988), pp. 179–188.

4. We will examine the Mormon concept of the restoration in chapter 2 of this work.

5. Early Mormon services continuously exhibited prophecy and speaking in tongues. Smith attempted to curb the prophetic utterances by establishing his primacy as revelator by changing his title from "First Elder" to "President" in the spring of 1835. See *The Doctrine and Covenants of the Church of Jesus Christ of the Latter-day Saints* (Salt Lake City: Deseret Book Co., 1981), Section 107. Joseph Smith Jr., et al., *History of the Church of Jesus Christ of Latter-day Saints.* 7 Vols. (Salt Lake City: Deseret Book Co., 1951 [1971]), Vol. 4: 285, 287, 543. Milton V. Backman Jr., *The Heavens Resound: The History of the Church of Jesus Christ of Latter-day Saints in Ohio, 1830 –1838* (Salt Lake City: Deseret Book Co.,1983), pp. 284–309. Fawn M. Brodie, *No Man Knows My History: The Life of Joseph Smith the Mormon Prophet* (N.Y.: Alfred Knopf, 1945 [1982]), p. 161. Brodie also mentions, p. 159, that Smith's revelations became less frequent with time. Prior to 1835, Smith gave over 100 revelations. Between 1835 and 1844, he gave only thirteen. See *The Doctrine and Covenants*, section titled "Chronological Order of Contents." As well, initially speaking in tongues was seen as a gift of God in order to convert the unsaved from various cultures. By the 1840s speaking in tongues

had come to mean the ability to learn a foreign language in preparation for missionary endeavors. See sermon of December 26, 1842, in Smith Jr., *History of the Church*, Vol. 4: 485–486.

6. See Steven L. Shields, *Divergent Paths of the Restoration* (Bountiful: Restoration Inc., 1983). Kate B. Carter, *Denominations That Base Their Beliefs on the Teachings of Joseph Smith the Mormon Prophet* (Salt Lake City: Daughters of the Utah Pioneers, 1969).

7. See Bushman, *Joseph Smith and the Beginnings of Mormonism*, pp. 168–170.

8. See James B. Allen, "The Emergence of a Fundamental: The Expanding Role of Joseph Smith's 1st Vision in American Religious Thought," *Journal of Mormon History*, Vol. 7 (1980): 43–69. As well Marvin S. Hill, *Quest for Refuge: The Mormon Flight from American Pluralism* (Salt Lake City: Signature Books, 1989), pp. xi–xiii, 1–17, 26–27. Bushman, *Joseph Smith and the Beginnings of Mormonism*, pp. 149–159.

9. For much of the 1830s the Church was divided between Missouri and Ohio. Independence was the first Gathering place in Missouri. Upon their expulsion from Independence in 1833, a part of the Church moved to the northern Missouri counties. In 1838, a new Mormon center, Far West, was declared to be a Gathering place. It is estimated that between 8,000 to 10,000 came to Far West. See *The Doctrine and Covenants*, Section 115. Smith Jr., *History of the Church*, Vol. 3: 336–339. For discussion see Leonard J. Arrington, *The Great Basin Kingdom: Economic History of the Latter-day Saints 1830–1900* (Lincoln: University of Nebraska, 1955), pp. 11–15. The Saints left Missouri after the extermination order of Governor Lilburn Boggs. Smith Jr., *History of the Church*, Vol. 3: 175. The last of the Saints left Far West on April 20, 1839. See Smith Jr., *History of the Church*, Vol. 3: 326. George Albert Smith, recalling the event, estimates 12,000–15,000 people left Missouri, leaving behind an estimated 300,000 dollars in property. *Journal of Discourses of Brigham Young, His Counselors, and Other Church Leaders*. 26 Vols. (Liverpool: Latter-day Saints Book Depot, 1853–1886), Vol. 17: 60. Another participant in the Mormon exodus, Heber C. Kimball, recalls the events in his journal. Heber C. Kimball, *Journal* (Salt Lake City: Juvenile Instructors Office, 1882), pp. 61, 71–76.

10. Sidney Ahlstrom, *A Religious History of the American People* (New Haven: Yale University Press, 1972), pp. 141, 144, 147–150.

11. Shipps, *Mormonism: The Birth of a New Religious Tradition*, pp. 118–122. Hill, *Quest for Refuge*, pp. 6–9.

12. Smith's sermon of April 8, 1844, proclaimed all of the North American continent as Zion. See Smith Jr., *History of the Church*, Vol. 6: 318–320. Perhaps this was due to the continuing pressure from "Gentile" inhabitants of Illinois and Iowa, and the improbable return of the Saints to Independence, Missouri. See Gerald N. Lund, *The Coming of the Lord* (Salt Lake City: Bookcraft, 1971), pp. 100–118.

13. See *The Doctrine and Covenants*, Section 107: 53–57. See Lund, *The Coming of the Lord*. Lund's work, while not critical, provides a solid summary of Mormon eschatological views based upon the teachings of Mormon leaders.

14. *The Doctrine and Covenants*, Section 54, reveals Independence, Missouri, as Zion. The town of Adam Ondiamon was the site where Adam had made an altar to God after his expulsion from Eden. Far West had been the site were Cain had killed Abel. Smith Jr., *History of the Church*, Vol. 3: 35. *The Doctrine and Covenants*, Section 117: 8.

15. Mormonism's doctrine of God has been defined as being polytheistic because of the belief in distinct beings called Gods. While this appears to be the sentiment expressed by Joseph Smith in his sermon of April 7, 1844, there have been attempts to show that a unity exists among these beings. Mormonism does not follow Nicene Christological terminology (i.e., using essence and nature to define the unity of the beings). Rather, Mormonism chooses to concentrate on the distinctiveness of persons and unity of purpose among the beings. This concept attained its present status through the work of James E. Talmage. Essentially applying the term polytheism to Mormonism is inaccurate. While Mormons do believe that a plurality of Gods exist they do not worship a plurality of Gods. It is perhaps better to speak of Mormonism then as a henotheistic movement. That is to say, while there exist many Gods, Mormons worship only one God.

16. Throughout this work references to "the Prophet" are direct references to Joseph Smith Jr., the first prophet of the Mormon Church unless otherwise indicated.

17. *The Doctrine and Covenants*, Section 69.

18. The official history of the Church is published in seven volumes titled *History of the Church of Jesus Christ of Latter-day Saints*. This is a redacted work, including the histories recorded by Joseph Smith's personal scribes, William Clayton, Thomas Bullock, and William McIntire, Joseph Smith's personal diaries, and several private journals and diaries.

19. For brief self-description of its holdings, see T. A. Robinson, "Reports from Archives," *North American Religion*, Vol. 2 (1993): 232–247, pp. 235–236.

20. *Journal of Discourses*, Vol. 13: 95.

21. *The Doctrine and Covenants*, Section 68: 3.

22. *Ibid.*, Section 107.

23. The present *Articles of Faith* were part of the Wentworth Letter and appeared in 1842 in the *Times and Seasons*, 6 Vols. (Nauvoo, 1839–1846), Vol. 3: 709–710. The *Articles of Faith* can be found in many modern Church publications.

24. Many positions on the Church's origin have been promoted through the 19th century by several Mormon leaders. See *Journal of Discourses*, Vol. 21: 71, 196, 197; Vol. 6: 29, 335; Vol. 10: 129; Vol. 12: 334; Vol. 13: 78, 324; Vol. 20: 167.

25. There are many sources in support of this view. For a solid overview of these sources, consult Brodie, *No Man Knows My History*, Appendices A, B, pp. 427–456.

1. Ye Mountains Roll Down Your Thunder

1. Some sources seem to indicate that the total of 20,000 is high. The number would have to include a large number of LDS (Latter-day Saints) from around Nauvoo. The Wilford Woodruff journal entry for the date records 20,000, but then crosses out the number and places 10,000 in its place. Cited in Andrew F. Ehat and Lyndon W. Cook, eds., *The Words of Joseph Smith: The Contemporary Accounts of the Nauvoo Discourses of the Prophet Joseph Smith*, Vol. 6, Religious Studies Monograph Series (Provo: Brigham Young University Press, 1980), p. 343. Hereafter cited as *The Words of Joseph Smith*.

2. Apostasy and dissension had occurred in Kirtland during the 1830s. Smith left Kirtland in 1838 because of opposition. Backman, *The Heavens Resound*, pp. 127–128.

3. Smith Jr., *History of the Church*, Vol. 6: 618.

4. See Joseph Fielding, "They Might Have Known That He Was Not a Fallen Prophet: The Nauvoo Journal of Joseph Fielding," Andrew F. Ehat, ed., *Brigham Young University Studies* 19: 2 (1979): 133–166.

5. Smith Jr., *History of the Church*, Vol. 6: 448.

6. The text from the Nauvoo Charter is taken from Appendix B in David E. and Della S. Miller, *Nauvoo: The City of Joseph* (Santa Barbara: Peregrine Smith Inc., 1974), pp. 242–248, p. 243.

7. E. D. Howe, *Mormonism Unvailed: or, a Faithful Account of That Singular Delusion* (Painesville: E. D. Howe, 1834), p. 142.

8. John Whitmer, *History of the Church* (1831–1838), Chapter VIII, MSS. Typescript copy (Salt Lake City: Modern Microfilm), p. 5.

9. See Smith Jr., *History of the Church*, Vol. 1: 216, ftnt.

10. See Widmer, "Turbulence in Early Mormonism," p. 140. Lucy Mack Smith, the Prophet's mother, records in her book *Biographical Sketches of Joseph Smith the Prophet and His Progenitors For Many Generations* (Liverpool: Orson Pratt, 1853) that Smith had faced charges of treason against the state of Missouri. The trial of June 30, 1843, appears to have been transferred to the Nauvoo municipal court. See pp. 225 ff. The citation is in reference to Joseph's brother Hyrum making a defense of Joseph and the Mormons for their role in the Missouri troubles before the municipal court at Nauvoo.

11. Smith Jr., *History of the Church*, Vol. 6: 618.

12. Joseph saw himself as "one like unto Moses," see *The Doctrine and Covenants*, Section 107: 91.

13. Lyndon W. Cook, "William Law, Nauvoo Dissenter," *Brigham Young University Studies* 22: 1 (1982): 47–72.

14. See *Nauvoo Expositor* (Nauvoo: 1844), p. 2, cols. 3, 4. Widmer, "Turbulence in Early Mormonism," pp. 161, 164. Fawn Brodie in *No Man Knows My History* claims that the chief opposition to Smith made by the *Expositor* was surrounding polygamy. See p. 376.

15. Van Hale, "The Doctrinal Impact of the King Follett Discourse," *Brigham Young University Studies* 18: 2 (1978): 209–225, p. 212. Fawn Brodie, in *No

Man Knows My History, pp. 366, 376, attempts to explain the controversy surrounding the *Expositor*. Both hold a position that Smith did not introduce anything new in April of 1844.

16. William Law had been given a license to preach as an elder of the church at least three months prior to June 3, 1837. See *Latter Day Saints Messenger and Advocate*, 3 Vols. (Kirtland: 1835–1837),Vol. 3: 528. Hereafter cited as *Messenger and Advocate*. See also Donald Q. Cannon, "The King Follett Discourse: Joseph Smith's Greatest Sermon in Historical Perspective," *Brigham Young University Studies* 18: 2 (1978): 179–193, p. 187.

17. Hale, "The Doctrinal Impact of the King Follett Discourse," p. 223, states that five of Joseph Smith's sermons had been published prior to his death. I have only been able to uncover three sermons published prior to his death. These are the sermon of August 1832, published in *The Evening and Morning Star*, 3 Vols. (Kirtland and Independence: 1832–1834), Vol. 1: 3. The sermon of May 16, 1841, published in the *Times and Seasons*, Vol. 2: 429–430. The sermon of October 3, 1841, is published in the *Times and Seasons*, Vol. 2: 577–578. In contrast, the King Follett discourse had been published at least four times by the end of 1845.

18. See Backman, *The Heavens Resound*, pp. 127–128.

19. Present reconstructions (Fawn Brodie, p. 376, et al.) contends that the chief point of dissent was over the polygamy issue. Both Hale and Brodie see Joseph's progressive theology as developing from a core that existed in the early 1830s. See Brodie, *No Man Knows My History*, p. 366, 371; Hale, "The Doctrinal Impact of the King Follett Discourse," pp. 212–213, 223. The evidence does not support this view.

20. See Joseph Fielding Smith, ed., *Teachings of the Prophet Joseph Smith* (Salt Lake City: Deseret Book Co., 1976), pp. 369–376. Hereafter cited as *Teachings of the Prophet Joseph Smith*. See *The Words of Joseph Smith*, pp. 378–383.

21. *Teachings of the Prophet Joseph Smith*, pp. 342–346. *The Words of Joseph Smith*, pp. 340–362. The publication of the King Follet discourse began on August 15, 1844, in the *Times and Seasons*, Vol. 5: 612–617. The sermon used Thomas Bullock's account as the base text and the journal of William Clayton to flesh out additional areas. The discourse was never completely published at this time. The first full publication of the sermon appeared in 1857, in the July 8 *Deseret News*. It also appeared in 1859, in the *Journal of Discourses*, Vol. 6: 1–11. The text for the discourse was redacted by Johnathan Grisham in 1855 from contemporary accounts. The Grisham account remains the most widely used today. It was also published in the *Latter-day Saints Millennial Star*, 130 Vols. (Liverpool, 1840–1970), in 1863, Vol. 23: 245–280. Hereafter cited as *Millennial Star*. See B. H. Roberts, *A Comprehensive History of the Church of Jesus Christ of Latter-day Saints*, 6 Vols. (Provo: Brigham Young University Press, 1957), Vol. 2: 392. See Stan Larson, "The King Follett Discourse: A Newly Amalgamated Text," *Brigham Young University Studies* 18: 2 (1978): 193–208, p. 195.

22. See Allen, "The Emergence of a Fundamental," pp. 43–69.

23. See collection of essays in Gary J. Bergera, ed., *Line Upon Line: Essays on Mormon Doctrine* (Salt Lake City: Signature Books, 1989). Thomas G. Alexander,

"The Reconstruction of Mormon Doctrine: From Joseph Smith to Progressive Theology," *Sunstone* 10: 5 (1985): 8–18. Thomas G. Alexander, *Mormonism in Transition: A History of the Latter-day Saints 1890–1930* (Chicago: University of Illinois Press, 1986). Robert J. Matthews, "The New Translation of the Bible, 1830–1833: Doctrinal Development During the Kirtland Era," *Brigham Young University Studies* 11: 4 (1971): 400–422. T. Edgar Lyon, "Doctrinal Development of the Church During the Nauvoo Sojourn, 1839–1846," *Brigham Young University Studies* 15: 4 (1975): 425–438.

24. Joseph did not claim to translate the papyri of Abraham through revelation, as he had done with the *Book of Mormon*. Smith upon acquiring the papyrus began work on an alphabet and grammar to aid him in translating. This will be dealt with in chapter 5 of this work. See Brodie, *No Man Knows My History*, p. 170.

25. Joseph appeals to the Hebrew text and reason to support his views on a plurality of Gods. His argument from revelation plays a secondary role in the sermon. Smith Jr., *History of the Church*, Vol. 6: 302, 307. This will be dealt with in chapter 7 of this work.

26. See Brodie, *No Man Knows My History*, p. 159.

27. Hale, "The Doctrinal Impact of the King Follett Discourse," p. 212.

2. Out of the Ground a Voice Speaks

1. *Times and Seasons*, Vol. 3: 707–708. An earlier account is found in *The Elders Journal*, 1 Vol. (Kirtland and Far West, 1837–1838), Vol. 1: 43.

2. See B. H. Roberts, *New Witnesses for God*, 3 Vols. (Salt Lake City: The Deseret News Press, 1909), Vol. II, *The Book of Mormon*, pp. 134–227. Although dated, Roberts' monumental work is still relevant. Roberts gives a brief analysis of the history and geography of the *Book of Mormon* peoples, and makes an attempt to place *Book of Mormon* geography in its North American context, citing specific *Book of Mormon* lands with their modern American equivalents. Roberts, in seeing the *Book of Mormon* as history, makes claims that few since his day have attempted to make.

3. The Church of Christ was the original name of the Mormon Church.

4. E. D. Howe, *Mormonism Unvailed: or, A Faithful Account of That Singular Delusion* (Painesville: E. D. Howe, 1834). See *The Elders Journal*, Vol. 1: 50–51.

5. Ethan Smith, *The View of the Hebrews: or The Ten Tribes of Israel in America* (Poultney: Smith and Smith, 1825).

6. The Spalding theory had its origins in Howe's work, p. 278. The Spalding theory was again promoted in M. T. Lamb, *The Golden Bible: or, The Book of Mormon. Is It From God?* (New York: Ward and Drummond, 1887). Modern anti–Mormon literature for the most part appears to be based on the early arguments of Howe, Lamb, and J. B. Turner's *Mormonism in All Ages* (New York.: Platt and Peters, 1842).

7. B. H. Roberts, *A Book of Mormon Study*, MSS, Part 1, Chapter 1, pp. 1–4; Part 1, Chapter 13, pp. 1, 19–20; Chapter 14, pp. 1, 13. Typescript copy available from

Modern Microfilm in Salt Lake City. Roberts' unpublished work devoted over 170 pages to the parallels between Smith's *View of the Hebrews* and the *Book of Mormon*. Some of the parallels made by Roberts were published by Mervin B. Hogan in 1956 in the *Rocky Mountain Mason*, Vol. 10: (1956): 17–31. Roberts' manuscripts were eventually published in 1985 in *Studies of the Book of Mormon*, Brigham D. Madsen, ed., University of Illinois Press. See also Wesley P. Walters, "The Origin of the *Book of Mormon*," *Journal of Pastoral Practice*, Vol. 3: 3 (1979): 121–152.

8. The Mormon preoccupation with answering charges by critics that Smith, in writing the *Book of Mormon*, accessed contemporary sources continues in the 20th century. As an example of this see David A. Palmer, "A Survey of Pre–1830 Historical Sources Relating to the *Book of Mormon*," *Brigham Young University Studies* 17: 1 (1977): 101–109. See also Robert Paul, "Joseph Smith and the Manchester (New York) Library," *Brigham Young University Studies* 22: 3 (1982): 333–356.

9. The original criticism appeared in *Millennial Harbinger*, Vol. 2 (1831): 86–96. This quote is taken from Leonard J. Arrington and Davis Bitton, *The Mormon Experience: A History of the Latter-day Saints* (New York: Vintage, 1980), pp. 31–32.

10. Ahlstrom, A. *Religious History of the American People*, p. 450. Bushman, *Joseph Smith and the Beginnings of Mormonism*, pp. 179–183.

11. Hans Rollman, "The Early Baptist Career of Sidney Rigdon in Warren, Ohio," *Brigham Young University Studies* 21: 1 (1981): 37–50. See Bushman, *Joseph Smith and the Beginnings of Mormonism*, pp. 179–181. Hill, *Quest for Refuge*, p. 64.

12. Smith Jr., *History of the Church*, Vol 1: 119. Hill, *Quest for Refuge*, p. 64.

13. Howe, *Mormonism Unvailed*, p. 193.

14. Orson Spenser, *Letters*, N.D., N.P.

15. D. Michael Quinn, *Early Mormonism and the Magic World View* (Salt Lake City: Signature Books, 1987), p. 193. Richard Bushman cites that the Whitmers arrived in Fayette, New York, from Pennsylvania in 1809. Soon after, they joined the German Reformed Church in Fayette; Bushman, *Joseph Smith and the Beginnings of Mormonism*, p. 103.

16. See Laurence M. Yorgason, "Preview on a Study of the Social and Geographical Origins of Early Mormon Converts, 1830–1845," *Brigham Young University Studies* 10: 3 (1970): 279–282.

17. Hill, *Quest for Refuge*, pp. 1–16.

18. See Arrington and Bitton, *The Mormon Experience*, pp. 31–34. As well Cannon, "The King Follett Discourse: Joseph Smith's Greatest Sermon in Historical Perspective," p. 188.

19. Frederick J. Voros Jr., "Was the *Book of Mormon* Buried with King Follett?" *Sunstone* 11: 6 (1986): 15–19, intimates that the theology of the *Book of Mormon* was an expression of the experiential and theological environment of early 19th-century America. See as well Thomas G. Alexander, "The Place of Joseph Smith in the Development of American Religion: A Historiographical Inquiry," *Journal of Mormon History*, Vol. 5 (1978): 3–17, p. 11.

20. Philip Barlow, *Mormons and the Bible: The Place of the Latter-day Saints in American Religion* (London: Oxford University Press, 1991), pp. 11–73.

21. Whitney Cross, *The Burned-over District: The Social and Intellectual History of Enthusiastic Religion in Western New York, 1800–1850* (Ithaca: Cornell University Press, 1950), pp. 138–150.

22. See Lucy Mack Smith, *Biographical Sketches of Joseph Smith the Prophet and His Progenitors For Many Generations* (Liverpool: Orson Pratt, 1853), p. 74. See as well pp. 70–87 where she relates several incidents surrounding the foundation of the Church. See as well Hill, *Quest for Refuge*, pp. 4–6, 14–17.

23. Brodie, *No Man Knows My History*, p. 83.

24. We will examine Smith's religious experience and its impact upon Mormonism in chapter 6 of this work.

25. Jerald and Sandra Tanner, *3,913 Changes in the Book of Mormon* (Salt Lake City: Utah Light House, N.D.).

26. Milton V. Backman Jr., *American Religions and the Rise of Mormonism* (Salt Lake City: Deseret Book Co., 1970), pp. 241, 331. Channing did not view Jesus as divine but rather as an angelic being. Channing's thought may have laid the ground work for the theological milieu which Smith could have accessed. Richard Bushman provides evidence that the Smith family was familiar with deistic thought through Asael Smith, the paternal grandfather of Joseph Smith. Bushman, *Joseph Smith and the Beginnings of Mormonism*, pp. 28, 38.

27. See Claude Welch, *Protestant Thought in the Nineteenth Century*, 2 Vols. (New Haven: Yale University Press, 1989), Vol. 1, pp. 127–137.

28. Emerson's work can be found in various collections. Perhaps one of the best is the Brooks Atkinson edited volume, *The Selected Writings of Ralph Waldo Emerson* (New York: The Modern Library, 1968).

29. For a short treatment on Emerson and the Transcendentalists see Welch, *Protestant Thought in the Nineteenth Century*, 2 Vols. (New Haven: Yale University Press, 1989), Vol. 1, pp. 177–183.

30. See selections in Atkinson, *The Selected Writings of Ralph Waldo Emerson* (New York: The Modern Library, 1968).

31. Sabellianism confounds the three persons making no distinction between the three persons in the godhead.

32. Noetic Christology is another variant of Sabellianism. The Christology of Origen and Dionysius of Alexandria would be considered tritheistic. For an excellent treatment of varying Christologies in the history of Christianity, see Edmund J. Fortman, *The Triune God: A Historical Study of the Doctrine of the Trinity* (Grand Rapids: Baker Book House, 1982), pp. 58–61.

33. The use of the term's heterodox and orthodox are not intended to carry any value judgments. By heterodox I intend to imply other, or a different, Christological interpretation than that represented by the majority, as determined by the ecumenical councils of the Christian tradition. The term orthodox thereby would represent the views of the majority as determined by the same councils.

34. See sermon of April 7, 1844, *Teachings of the Prophet Joseph Smith*, pp. 343–347. Sermon of May 2, 1844, *Teachings of the Prophet Joseph Smith*, pp. 364–365, 368. Sermon of June 16, 1844; *Teachings of the Prophet Joseph Smith*, pp. 371–373.

35. Klaus J. Hansen in *Mormonism and the American Experience* (Chicago: University of Chicago, 1971), pp. 45–83, provides a great introduction into the background of early 19th-century American culture.

36. See Hill, *Quest for Refuge*, pp. 14–17.

37. By use of the term church, I intend to be inclusive of all Christian churches, Protestants and Catholics alike. As early Mormons saw all of Christendom as consisting in a dichotomy, the term would include all those that did not belong to the LDS Church.

38. Hill, *Quest for Refuge*, pp. 7–8.

39. Boyd Kirkland, "The Development of the Mormon Doctrine of God," in Gary J. Bergera, ed., *Line Upon Line: Essays on Mormon Doctrine* (Salt Lake City: Signature Books, 1989), pp. 35–52, p. 36.

40. See Van Hale, "Defining the Contemporary Mormon Concept of God," in Gary J. Bergera, ed., *Line Upon Line: Essays on Mormon Doctrine* (Salt Lake City: Signature Books, 1989), pp. 7–15. As well Dan Vogel, "The Earliest Mormon Concept of God," in Gary J. Bergera, ed., *Line Upon Line: Essays on Mormon Doctrine* (Salt Lake City: Signature Books, 1989), pp. 17–34.

41. Early versions of the *Book of Mormon*, from 1830 until the 1880s, were not divided into chapter and verse references. In referencing these earliest versions it is easiest to quote page numbers, and the chapters will be cited using Roman numerals.

42. See modern version of the text, *Book of Mormon*, 1 Nephi 11:18, 21.

43. See modern version 1 Nephi 12:18.

44. The revised passage is found in modern versions at 1 Nephi 11:32.

45. The vision of the brother of Jared, by Mormon accounts, would predate the Mosaic vision of Mt. Sinai.

46. Thomas G. Alexander, "The Reconstruction of Mormon Doctrine: From Joseph Smith to Progressive Theology," *Sunstone* 10:5 (1985): 8–18, p. 9. As well see Vogel, "The Earliest Mormon Concept of God," pp. 21–24.

47. Kirkland, "The Development of the Mormon Doctrine of God," pp. 36–37. See also Boyd Kirkland, "Jehovah as the Father," *Sunstone* 10: 2 (1985): 36–44, p. 37.

48. *A Book of Commandments for the Government of the Church of Christ* (Zion: W. W. Phelps, 1833). Very few copies of this work exist. When the presses of the *Evening and Morning Star* were destroyed a large part of the uncut sheets on which the book was printed were destroyed as well. Hereafter cited as *A Book of Commandments*.

49. See Lyndon W. Cook, ed., *The Revelations of the Prophet Joseph Smith: A Historical and Biographical Commentary on the Doctrine and Covenants* (Salt Lake City: Deseret Book Co., 1985), pp. 31–32.

50. This statement of faith was first published in the *Evening and Morning Star* in June of 1832.

51. *The Doctrine and Covenants of the Church of the Latter Day Saints* (Kirtland: F. G. Williams, 1835). Hereafter cited as 1835, *Doctrine and Covenants*. The statement is found in Section II. The revision changed the words "which Father, and Son, and Holy Ghost is one God," to "which Father, and Son, and Holy Ghost are one God."

52. *A Book of Commandments,* Chapter 24, pp. 49–50.

53. See "Account of Mormonism: A New Extravaganza in America." *The Christian Reformer, or New Evangelical Miscellany,* Vol. 18 (1832): 456–462. Howe, *Mormonism Unvailed.* LaRoy Sunderland, *Mormonism Exposed and Refuted* (New York: Piercy and Reed, 1838). William Swartzell, *Mormonism Exposed* (Pittsburgh: Pekin O., 1840). Compare these earlier works to John C. Bennett, *The History of the Saints: or, An Expose of Joe Smith and Mormonism* (Boston: Leland and Whiting, 1842). Henry Caswell, *City of the Mormons: or, Three Days at Nauvoo in 1842* (London: J. G. F. & J. Rivington, 1842). Henry Caswell, *Prophet of the Nineteenth Century* (London: J. G. F. & J. Rivington, 1843). Turner, *Mormonism in All Ages,* and Lamb, *The Golden Bible.*

54. L. M. Smith, *Biographical Sketches of Joseph Smith,* p. 146. An exchange of letters on the relevance of spiritual gifts appears in *The Elders Journal,* Vol. 1: 224–27. The Mormons claim the gifts are relevant.

55. Vogel, "The Earliest Mormon Concept of God," p. 25. An extract from a Post letter appeared in *The Elders Journal,* Vol. 1: 49–50. A brief statement of belief is found in *The Elders Journal,* 1: 44.

56. *The Book of Mormon* (Palmyra: E. B. Grandin, 1830), p. 32.

57. *Ibid.,* pp. 536–537.

58. Smith Jr., *History of the Church,* Vol 1: 215.

59. On tongues, see Smith Jr., *History of the Church,* Vol. 1: 296, 297, 323, 369, 409, 419, 422; Vol. 2: 292, 376, 392. On healings see Smith Jr., *History of the Church,* Vol 1: 431; Vol. 2: 95, 354; Vol. 4: 5, 414.

60. "The Father and the Son: A Doctrinal Exposition by the First Presidency and the Twelve," Appendix II, James Talmage, *A Study of the Articles of Faith: Being a Consideration of the Principal Doctrines of the Church of Jesus Christ of Latter-day Saints* (Salt Lake City: Deseret Book Co., 1982), pp. 466–473.

61. The ninth *Article of Faith* states: "We believe all that God has revealed, all that He does now reveal, and we believe that He will yet reveal many great and important things pertaining to the Kingdom." A similar statement was made by Oliver Cowdery in response to the recently acquired Egyptian papyri, which became the *Book of Abraham.* See *Messenger and Advocate,* Vol. 2: 234.

62. This concept appears to have been introduced to Mormonism in late 1830, through Smith's revision of Genesis. See *Joseph Smith's New Translation of the Bible* (Independence: Herald House, 1970), Genesis 5:26–7:86.

3. Knowing the Only True God

1. *A Book of Commandments,* Chapter 24, pp. 49–50. This statement of faith was first published in the *Evening and Morning Star* in June of 1832. See Cook, *The Revelations of the Prophet Joseph Smith,* pp. 31–32. The Church changed its name to the Church of the Latter Day Saints in 1834, and took on its present name

in 1838. The document was the original statement of faith for the Mormon Church. An additional statement of faith known as the "Articles of Faith" appeared in 1842, in Joseph Smith's letter to John Wentworth. The letter was published in the *Times and Seasons*, Vol. 3: 709–710.

2. Joseph Smith Jr., *The Pearl of Great Price: Being a Choice Selection From the Revelations, Translations, and Narrations of Joseph Smith; First Prophet, Seer and Revelator to the Church of Jesus Christ of Latter-day Saints* (Liverpool: F. D. Richards, 1851). Hereafter cited as *The Pearl of Great Price*.

3. Robert L. Millett, "Joseph Smith's Translation of the Bible: A Historical Overview," in Monte S. Nyman and Robert L. Millett, eds., *The Joseph Smith Translation: The Restoration of Plain and Precious Truths*, Vol. 12, Religious Studies Monograph Series (Provo: Brigham Young University, 1985), pp. 23–50, p. 45.

4. See Backman, *The Heavens Resound*, pp. 91–92.

5. Throughout this chapter and remaining chapters, the revelations of 1830 will be referenced by their collective and published name of the *Book of Moses*, unless specifically individualized.

6. *Evening and Morning Star*, Vol. 1: 44–47.

7. *Ibid.*, Vol. 1: 145.

8. *Ibid.*, Vol. 1: 161–162.

9. *Times and Seasons*, Vol. 4: 71–73.

10. *Millennial Star*, Vol. 13: 90–93.

11. The original revelation, found in the *Evening and Morning Star*, corresponds to Moses Chapter 2. The chapter and verse designation appear to have been added, by James Talmage, complete with references in the 1902 compilation of *The Pearl of Great Price*.

12. *Joseph Smith's New Translation of the Bible*, p. 12.

13. *Ibid.*, pp. 14–16.

14. *Ibid.*, p. 19.

15. *Ibid.*, pp. 11–12.

16. See Robert L. Millett, "Joseph Smith's Translation of the Bible: Impact on Mormon Theology," *Religious Studies* 8 (1987): 43–53, p. 46.

17. *Joseph Smith's New Translation of the Bible*, pp. 17–23.

18. See Millett, "Joseph Smith's Translation of the Bible: Impact on Mormon Theology," pp. 47 ff.

19. *Joseph Smith's New Translation of the Bible*, Genesis, Chapters 1–2.

20. See Millett, "Joseph Smith's Translation of the Bible: Impact on Mormon Theology," p. 49. George A. Horton Jr., "Insights into the Book of Genesis," in Monte S. Nyman and Robert L. Millett, eds., *The Joseph Smith Translation: The Restoration of Plain and Precious Truths*, Vol. 12, Religious Studies Monograph Series (Provo: Brigham Young University, 1985), pp. 51–70, pp. 55–63.

21. Hale, "The Doctrinal Impact of the King Follett Discourse," pp. 213–215, 224.

22. See relevant texts in both versions of the Bible.

23. Matthews, "The New Translation of the Bible, 1830–1833: Doctrinal Development During the Kirtland Era," p. 400.

24. See *Joseph Smith's New Translation of the Bible*, pp. 11–12.

25. Matthews, "The New Translation of the Bible, 1830–1833: Doctrinal Development During the Kirtland Era," pp. 414–415. As well see *Joseph Smith's New Translation of the Bible,* pp. 8–9.

26. *Joseph Smith's New Translation of the Bible*, pp. 8–9.

27. Smith Jr., *History of the Church*, Vol. 4: 187. As well, see Matthews, "The New Translation of the Bible, 1830–1833: Doctrinal Development During the Kirtland Era," p. 415.

28. Barlow, *Mormons and the Bible*, pp. 46–50.

29. See David Whitmer, *An Address to All Believers in Christ* (Richmond: N.P., 1887), pp. 32–35. See also David Whitmer, *An Address to All Believers in the Book of Mormon* (Richmond: N.P., 1887).

30. Alexander, "The Reconstruction of Mormon Doctrine: From Joseph Smith to Progressive Theology," p. 9.

31. Arrington and Bitton, *The Mormon Experience*, p. 32.

32. Claude Welch, *Protestant Thought in the Nineteenth Century*, 2 Vols. (New Haven: Yale University Press, 1989), Vol. 1, pp. 132–137.

33. See Ahlstrom, *A Religious History of the American People*, pp. 445–451.

34. Yorgason, "Preview on a Study of the Social and Geographical Origins of Early Mormon Converts, 1830–1845," p. 282.

35. The article entitled "On Marriage" was included in the 1835 *Doctrine and Covenants* as Section 101. In 1838 they also denied that the Church practiced polygamy. See *The Elders Journal*, Question 7, Vol. 1:43.

36. Smith Jr., *History of the Church*, Vol. 4: 187. As well see Matthews, "The New Translation of the Bible, 1830–1833: Doctrinal Development During the Kirtland Era," p. 420.

37. Joseph Fielding Smith, *Blood Atonement and the Origin of Plural Marriage* (Independence: Press of Zions' Printing and Publishing Co., 1905).

38. Robert J. Matthews, "Major Doctrinal Contributions of the JST," in Monte S. Nyman and Robert L. Millett, eds., *The Joseph Smith Translation: The Restoration of Plain and Precious Truths*, Vol. 12, Religious Studies Monograph Series, (Provo: Brigham Young University, 1985), pp. 271–290. Matthews, "The New Translation of the Bible, 1830–1833: Doctrinal Development During the Kirtland Era," pp. 400–422.

4. Among the School of the Prophets in Ohio

1. See Backman, *The Heavens Resound*, p. 311. Arrington and Bitton, *The Mormon Experience*, pp. 37, 38, 47.

2. Backman, *The Heavens Resound*, pp. 327–329. Arrington and Bitton, *The Mormon Experience*, pp. 46–50, 88.

3. The school of instruction was known by several names including School of the Elders, School of the Prophets, and "school of mine apostles." See Cook, *The Revelations of Joseph Smith*, p. 185.

4. The theological treatises are referred to in literature as the *Lectures on Faith*, and the *Lectures of Faith*. We will use the original 1835 wording, *Lectures of Faith*, and the term *Lectures* to denote the treatises.

5. Cook, *The Revelations of Joseph Smith*, p. 185.

6. On early Mormon education in Kirtland, see Backman, *The Heavens Resound*, pp. 262–268.

7. Cook, *The Revelations of Joseph Smith*, p. 188.

8. *Ibid.*, p. 190.

9. See Smith Jr., *History of the Church*, Vol. 2: 176–180. As well Robert L. Millett, "The Supreme Power Over All Things: The Doctrine of the Godhead in the *Lectures on Faith*," in Larry E. Dahl and Charles D. Tate Jr., eds., *The Lectures on Faith in Historical Perspective*, Vol. 15, Religious Studies Monograph Series (Provo: Brigham Young University, 1990), pp. 221–240.

10. Cook, *The Revelations of Joseph Smith*, p. 189.

11. Kirkland, "Jehovah as the Father: The Development of the Mormon Jehovah Doctrine," p. 37.

12. James E. Talmage, *Jesus the Christ* (Salt Lake City: The Church, 1915), p. 32. For views of the godhead expressed in the 19th century, see the following— Jehovah as God: Smith Jr., *History of the Church*, Vol. 1: 278, 280, 313, 466; Vol. 2: 104, 114, 126; Vol. 3: 118, 329, 330, 420; Vol. 4: 55, 267, 376, 377; Vol. 5: 107, 108, 143, 144; *Journal of Discourses*, Vol. 1: 16, 51, 116, 119, 154; Vol. 5: 206, 275; Vol. 7: 38, 49, 208, 211. Jehovah as the Father: Smith Jr., *History of the Church*, Vol. 1: 289, Vol. 2: 11, 18, 175, 420, 422, 423; Vol. 4: 128, 256, Vol. 5: 127; *Journal of Discourses*, Vol. 1: 72, 123, 238; Vol. 2: 30, 78; Vol. 8: 195, 228; Vol. 11: 27. Jehovah as Jesus: Smith Jr., *History of the Church*, Vol. 2: 17, 435; Vol. 6: 254; *Journal of Discourses*, Vol. 6: 355; Vol. 26: 300.

13. Elohim as the Father: see Smith Jr., *History of the Church*, Vol. 5: 94, 127, 248, 499; Vol. 6: 294, 295, 303; *Journal of Discourses*, Vol. 1: 153, 372, 375; Vol. 9: 165, 236, 278, 279, 341; Vol. 10: 50; Vol. 14: 269, 337. Elohim as member of Council of Gods: Smith Jr. *History of the Church*, Vol. 5: 2; Vol. 6: 475, 476; *Journal of Discourses*, Vol. 1: 51, 356; Vol. 25: 213.

14. See Smith Jr., *History of the Church*, Vol. 2: 176–180.

15. See Larry E. Dahl, "Authorship and History of the *Lectures on Faith*," in Larry E. Dahl and Charles D. Tate Jr., eds., *The* Lectures on Faith *in Historical Perspective*, Vol. 15, Religious Studies Monograph Series (Provo: Brigham Young University, 1990), pp. 1–22.

16. *Ibid.*, p. 13.

17. *Ibid.*, p. 10.

18. *Ibid.*, p. 8–10.

19. Backman, *The Heavens Resound*, p. 269. In the preface of modern versions of *The Doctrine and Covenants* this argument is also made.

20. Smith Jr., *History of the Church*, Vol. 2: 176. Roberts cites the meeting of August 17, 1835, to support his argument.

21. The minutes of the assembly were included in the 1835 *Doctrine and Covenants*, pp. 255–257.

22. Dahl, "Authorship and History of the *Lectures on Faith*," p. 15.
23. *Ibid.*, p.p. 14–15.
24. Smith Jr., *History of the Church*, Vol. 2: 165. The minutes of the September 24 meeting was included in the 1835 *Doctrine and Covenants*, p. 255.
25. Leland H. Gentry, "What of the *Lectures on Faith?*" *Brigham Young University Studies* 24: 1 (1984): 5–18, p. 16. As well see introduction to 1835 *Doctrine and Covenants*.
26. The Mormon Church has undergone several name changes over the years. It was incorporated as the Church of Christ in 1830. During the early 1830s it was known as the Church of the Latter Day Saints. In 1838 it took on its present name.
27. See Dahl, "Authorship and History of the *Lectures on Faith*," pp. 16–19. Gentry, "What of the *Lectures on Faith?*" p. 16.
28. See Backman, *The Heavens Resound*, pp. 217, 232, 269. Backman does not mention the *Lectures* decanonization but rather questions, like Roberts, whether the *Lectures* were ever part of the canon.
29. Dahl, "Authorship and History of the *Lectures on Faith*," pp. 12–13, argues against the use of the *Lectures* in the School of the Prophets.
30. Smith Jr., *History of the Church*, Vol. 2: 176.
31. Kirkland, "Jehovah as the Father: The Development of the Mormon Jehovah Doctrine," p. 37.
32. *Doctrine and Covenants*, 1835, pp. 52–58.
33. *Ibid.*, p. 52.
34. *Ibid.*, pp. 52–54.
35. Vern G. Swanson, "The Development of the Concept of the Holy Ghost in Mormon Theology," in Gary J. Bergera, ed., *Line Upon Line: Essays on Mormon Doctrine* (Salt Lake City: Signature Books, 1989), pp. 89–102, pp. 90–91.
36. *Doctrine and Covenants*, 1835, p. 55.
37. *Ibid.*, p. 56.
38. For example, see Backman, *The Heavens Resound*, p. 232. The contention is that the confused nature of the godhead in this period would still allow for a harmonious understanding between Kirtland and Nauvoo theological perspectives on the godhead.
39. Backman, *The Heavens Resound*, p. 232.
40. *Doctrine and Covenants*, 1835, p. 56–57.
41. *Ibid.*, p. 57.
42. Smith Jr., *History of the Church*, Vol. 2: 300.
43. *Ibid.*, Vol. 2: 318.
44. The correspondence between Piexotto and the Mormons is recorded in Joseph Smith's diary. See Dean C. Jesse, *The Papers of Joseph Smith: Autobiographical and Historical Writings* (Salt Lake City: Deseret Book Co., 1989), pp. 207–208.
45. Smith Jr., *History of the Church*, Vol. 2: 319.
46. *Ibid.*, Vol. 2: 355–356. Also, Cook, *The Revelations of Joseph Smith*, p. 319 ftnt. 27.
47. Smith Jr., *History of the Church*, Vol. 2: 356, 368.

48. Joshua Seixas, *Manual Hebrew Grammar: For Beginners*, 2nd ed. (Andover: Gould and Newman, 1834). See Backman, *The Heavens Resound*, p. 271.

49. See Backman, *The Heavens Resound*, p. 272.

50. Kirkland, "The Development of the Mormon Doctrine of God," pp. 36–37.

51. Smith Jr., *History of the Church*, Vol. 6: 305–308. J. F. Smith, *Teachings of the Prophet Joseph Smith*, pp. 343–344. *The Words of Joseph Smith*, pp. 341, 343, 348, 356.

52. We have discussed this in chapter 2 of this work.

53. See Parley P. Pratt, *An Answer to Mr. William Hewitt's Tract* (Manchester: W. R. Thomas, 1840), p. 9. Also Hale, "The Doctrinal Impact of the King Follett Discourse," pp. 213–215, 219 ftnt. 57.

54. See Pratt, *An Answer to Mr. William Hewitt's Tract,* p. 9. Also Hale, "The Doctrinal Impact of the King Follett Discourse," pp. 213–215, 219 ftnt.# 57.

55. Allen, "The Emergence of a Fundamental," p. 47.

5. In the Grand Council of the Gods

1. See Backman, *The Heavens Resound*, pp. 218–221.

2. J. Reuben Clark, *The Story of the* Pearl of Great Price (Salt Lake City: Bookcraft, 1955), p. 142. Milton R. Hunter, Pearl of Great Price *Commentary* (Salt Lake City: Bookcraft, 1951), p. 9.

3. Henry Caswell, in his visit to Nauvoo in 1842, reports that he brought with him a Greek psalter to test Smith's translating ability. He records that the mummies were put on display and visitors were charged admission to see the mummies. See Caswell, *City of the Mormons*, pp. 22–23. As well see Backman, *The Heavens Resound*, p. 220.

4. Clark, *The Story of the* Pearl of Great Price, p. 73 ff.

5. See Smith Jr., *History of the Church*, Vol. 2: 235–236. The meeting is not contained in Smith's diaries and journals. The quote in the *History of the Church* must come from a secondary source.

6. Smith Jr., *History of the Church*, Vol. 2: 235.

7. Bushman, *Joseph Smith and the Beginnings of Mormonism*, p. 87.

8. Smith Jr., *History of the Church*, Vol. 2: 236.

9. Joseph Smith Jr., *Egyptian Alphabet and Grammar* (c. 1835–1838).

10. *Ibid.*, pp. J, K, L, M, Q, P, O.

11. Roberts, *Comprehensive History of the Church*, Vol. 2: 395.

12. Smith Jr., *Egyptian Alphabet and Grammar*, pp. J, K, L, M, Q, P, O.

13. See Scott F. Faulring, ed., *An American Prophet's Record: The Diaries and Journals of Joseph Smith* (Salt Lake City: Signature Books, 1989), pp. 35, 38, 39, 40, 42, 65, 66, 69, 72, 75, 77, 78, 91, 127, 128, 131–134, 183. Smith Jr., *History of the Church*, Vol. 2: 286, 349; Vol. 4: 519, 520, 543; Vol. 5: 11. As well see Roberts, *Comprehensive History of the Church*, Vol. 2: 126–129; 136–139.

14. Hugh Nibley, "The Meaning of the Kirtland Egyptian Papers," *Brigham Young University Studies* 11: 4 (1971): 350–399.

15. Louis C. Zucker, "Joseph Smith as a Student of Hebrew," *Dialogue: A Journal of Mormon Thought*, 3:2 (1969):41–56.

16. Joseph Smith Jr., *"The Book of Abraham,"* in the *Times and Seasons*, Vol. 3: 703–706, 719–722. The 1842 edition of the work does not follow modern verse configurations. The shift occurs between chapter 3 and 4 in modern editions. The shift occurs mid paragraph of verse 23 on p. 720 in the 1842 *Times and Seasons* edition.

17. Joseph Smith Jr., "The *Book of Abraham,"* in *Times and Seasons*, Vol. 3: 703–706, 719–722.

18. Smith Jr., *History of the Church*, Vol. 2: 519–520. See Backman, *The Heavens Resound*, p. 220.

19. Smith worked on translating the records from 1835 to 1842. See Smith Jr., *History of the Church*, Vol. 2: 286, 349; Vol. 4: 519, 520, 543; Vol. 5: 11. As well see Roberts, *Comprehensive History of the Church*, Vol. 2: 126–129; 136–139. See Faulring, *An American Prophet's Record*, pp. 35, 38, 39, 40, 42, 65, 66, 69, 72, 75, 77, 78, 91, 127, 128, 131–134, 183. In Smith's diaries the texts are referred to as the "Egyptian records," or as "ancient records." There is confusion over whether these references are to the texts themselves, or to the *Alphabet and Grammar*, which appears to have been used to translate the *Book of Abraham*.

20. Smith Jr., *History of the Church*, Vol. 4: 458.

21. See Clark, *The Story of the* Pearl of Great Price, pp. 172–173.

22. Roberts, *Comprehensive History of the Church*, Vol. 2: 395.

23. *Messenger and Advocate*, Vol. 2: 235–238.

24. *Ibid.*

25. See introduction to *Book of Abraham* in the *Times and Seasons*, Vol. 3: 703. Some editions of the *Pearl of Great Price* include the original introduction which describes the work as "purporting to be the writings of Abraham."

26. The *Book of Abraham* appeared in England in the *Latter-day Saints Millennial Star* in July and August of 1842. Editorials by Church officials preceding and accompanying the publication asserted that the book was of great antiquity and that it taught certain truths. See *Millennial Star*, Vol. 3: 32, 46, 71–72.

27. There appears to be a reference to the *Book of Abraham* and the role of the "Gods" in the creation of man dated July 9, 1843. Given the context of the quote, it appears the reference to God's image should be seen in a possessive context rather than as a plurality of Gods; i.e., God's image, not Gods image. See *Words of Joseph Smith*, p. 231.

28. J. F. Smith, *Teachings of the Prophet Joseph Smith*, p. 373.

29. *Ibid.*, pp. 369–376.

30. *Ibid.*, pp. 372–373.

31. Both Fawn Brodie, *No Man Knows My History*, p. 366, and Van Hale, "Doctrinal Impact of the King Follett Discourse," p. 212, maintain that the King Follett discourse contained no new doctrines. Full documentation will be presented in a future chapter. While the discourse and the *Book of Abraham* deal with the plurality of Gods, there is no indication that the *Book of Abraham* was accepted as a doctrinal work between 1842 and 1844. At this time the *Lectures of Faith* would still have been accepted as binding upon the Latter-day Saints.

32. A modern version of the *Book of Abraham* is used.
33. Abraham 3:24.
34. Seixas, *Manual Hebrew Grammar*, 2nd ed., 1834.
35. Zucker, "Joseph Smith as a Student of Hebrew," pp. 41–56.
36. Pratt, *An Answer to Mr. William Hewitt's Tract*, p. 9. Pratt had defended Mormon doctrine in the late 1830s against LaRoy Sunderland's allegations in *Mormonism Exposed and Refuted*. In his *Mormonism Unveiled: Zion's Watchman, Unmasked; and its Editor, Mr. L. R. Sunderland, Exposed: Truth Vindicated: The Devil Mad and Priestcraft in Danger* (New York: Parley P. Pratt, 1838), Pratt had defended the Mormon position that individuals would be joint heirs with Christ, partaking of all the same rights and privileges.
37. Smith Jr., *History of the Church*, Vol. 5: 127.
38. Kirkland, "The Development of the Mormon Doctrine of God," p. 38.
39. *The Words of Joseph Smith*, pp. 343, 358–359, 379.
40. Zucker, "Joseph Smith as a Student of Hebrew," p. 54
41. J. F. Smith, *Teachings of the Prophet Joseph Smith*, pp. 371–372.
42. James B. Allen and Glen Leonard, *The Story of the Latter-day Saints* (Salt Lake City: Deseret Book Co., 1980), p. 34. Zucker, "Joseph Smith as a Student of Hebrew," p. 47.
43. Jesse, *The Papers of Joseph Smith: Autobiographical and Historical Writings*, p. 459.
44. *Times and Seasons*, Vol. 3: 723–724.
45. Zucker, "Joseph Smith as a Student of Hebrew," pp. 41–56.
46. Smith Jr., *History of the Church*, Vol. 4: 458.
47. H. Donl Peterson, "Sacred Writings from the Tombs of Egypt," in H. Donl Peterson and Charles D. Tate Jr., eds., *The* Pearl of Great Price: *Revelations from God,* Vol. 14, Religious Studies Monograph Series (Provo: Brigham Young University, 1989), pp. 137–154, p. 152.
48. See Allen, "The Emergence of a Fundamental," pp. 43–69
49. Turner, *Mormonism in All Ages*, pp. 240–243. Caswell, *City of the Mormons*, p. 35. Caswell, *Prophet of the Nineteenth Century*, p. 95.
50. See "George Laub's Nauvoo Journal," Eugene England, ed., *Brigham Young University Studies* 18: 2 (1978): 151–177, p. 171. The Laub account is from memory. Given the context of the sermon it is likely that Laub mistook the years 1843 for 1844. *Times and Seasons*, Vol. 4: 89, 121.
51. *The Doctrine and Covenants*, Section 132, seems to teach a plurality of Gods and a nascent concept of exaltation. The revelation while dated originally to July 12, 1843, was not published until 1852. The original copy, recorded by William Clayton, was burned by Emma Smith. Joseph C. Kingsbury made an additional copy from the Clayton original. The present Section 132 was based on the Kingsbury copy. It is difficult to assess the provenance of the section in question. With that in mind I have not included Section 132 in the discussion. See Cook, *The Revelations of Joseph Smith*, pp. 293–295.
52. *Times and Seasons*, Vol. 1: 99–104.
53. *Times and Seasons*, Vol. 1: 103.

54. *Millennial Star*, Vol. 17: 52–56.
55. Cook, *The Revelations of Joseph Smith*, p. 239.
56. See reprint of original letter in Dean C. Jesse, ed., *Personal Writings of Joseph Smith* (Salt Lake City: Deseret Book Co., 1985). Jesse includes the verses. Secondhand accounts of individuals who have seen the letter provide no conclusive evidence either way. See Koury, *The Truth and the Evidence*, pp. 25–27.
57. *Times and Seasons*, Vol. 4: 84.
58. Caswell, *City of the Mormons*, pp. 9, 17.
59. *Ibid.*, pp. 4, 63.
60. *Ibid.*, p. 35.
61. The work was Pratt's *Truth Vindicated*.
62. Turner, *Mormonism in All Ages*, p. 240.
63. Caswell, *Prophet of the Nineteenth Century*, p. 95.
64. Edward H. Ashment, "Reducing Dissonance: The *Book of Abraham* as a Case Study," in Dan Vogel, ed., *The Word of God: Essays on Mormon Scripture* (Salt Lake City: Signature Books, 1990), pp. 237–264, pp. 250–251.
65. *Ibid.*, pp. 245–246.

6. *If Any Man Lack Wisdom*

1. The term First Vision or 1st Vision is used to distinguish the initial appearance of heavenly beings to Joseph Smith from the heavenly being, or angel, that presented Smith with the golden plates from which the *Book of Mormon* was translated.
2. *Times and Seasons*, Vol. 3: 727–728, 748–749.
3. The earliest accounts are found in Smith's diaries in 1832, 1835, and his history for 1839. Pratt's account dates from 1840. Orson Hyde published an account in German in 1842. The *Times and Seasons* account dates from 1842. Smith gave an account to David White in 1843. Daniel Rupp records an account in his history of Illinois. As well, Smith's German tutor, Alexander Neibauer, records an account. Both accounts are dated 1844. All accounts are contained in Jesse, *The Papers of Joseph Smith: Autobiographical and Historical Writings*.
4. Orson Pratt, *A Interesting Account of Some Remarkable Visions, and of the Late Discovery of Ancient American Records Giving an Account of the Commencement of the Work of the Lord in This Generation* (Edinburgh, 1840). Reprinted in Jesse, *The Papers of Joseph Smith: Autobiographical and Historical Writings*, pp. 387–401.
5. James B. Allen, "The Significance of Joseph Smith's 1st Vision in Mormon Thought," in *Dialogue: A Journal of Mormon Thought*, Vol. 1: 3 (1966): 29–45, p. 29.
6. *Journal of Discourses*, Vol. 24: 340–341, 371–372.
7. The angel has appeared as both Nephi and Moroni in LDS sources. Official accounts point to Moroni as the angel that appeared to Smith with the golden plates.

8. Bushman, *Joseph Smith and the Beginnings of Mormonism*, pp. 43–78.

9. Allen, "The Significance of Joseph Smith's 1st Vision in Mormon Thought," p. 30.

10. *Ibid.*, p. 31. The arguments of early anti–Mormons have been brought out in earlier sections of this work.

11. Jesse, *The Papers of Joseph Smith: Autobiographical and Historical Writings*, pp. xxii–xxiv.

12. *Ibid.*, p. xiv.

13. *Ibid.*, pp. xxii–xxiii.

14. Quinn, *Early Mormonism and the Magic World View*, pp. 113, 114, 117.

15. See Whitmer, *An Address to All Believers in Christ*, p. 33. Whitmer, the third person to join the infant Church, points this out.

16. *Times and Seasons*, Vol. 3: 703–734.

17. Dean C. Jesse in his *The Papers of Joseph Smith: Autobiographical and Historical Writings* records the known versions of the First Vision. Jesse draws upon Smith's diary accounts and early secondary accounts. Some controversy exists on the dating of the official Vision as to whether it was recorded in 1838 or 1839. See Milton V. Backman Jr., "Verification of the 1838 Account of the First Vision," in H. Donl Peterson and Charles D. Tate Jr., eds., *The Pearl of Great Price: Revelations from God*, Vol. 14, Religious Studies Monograph Series (Provo: Brigham Young University, 1989), pp. 237–248. Jesse dates the Vision to 1839 based upon the scribe, James Mulholland, and it being a continuation of the original history begun by Smith in 1838. The Vision is not contained in the original draft to the history.

18. The official version is based upon the 1839 account. This version was prepared by Smith for a Church history.

19. Backman, in "Verification of the 1838 Account of the First Vision," dismisses this.

20. See Joseph Smith Jr., *Diaries of Joseph Smith* (1832–1834), pp. 4–7. Faulring, *An American Prophet's Record*, pp. 5–6. Jesse, *The Papers of Joseph Smith: Autobiographical and Historical Writings*, pp. 3–5.

21. See Joseph Smith Jr., *Diaries of Joseph Smith* (1835–1836), pp. 23–25. Faulring, *An American Prophet's Record*, pp. 51–52. Jesse, *The Papers of Joseph Smith: Autobiographical and Historical Writings*, pp. 125–127.

22. Milton V. Backman Jr., *Joseph Smith's First Vision: The First Vision in Historical Context* (Salt Lake City: Bookcraft, 1976), p. 158, states that the scribe is Mathias Cowdery (Oliver's brother). Sources seem to indicate that it was Warren Parrish who recorded the 1835 account for Smith. See Smith Jr., *Diaries of Joseph Smith* (1835–1836), pp. 23. Faulring, *An American Prophet's Record*, pp. 51–52. Jesse, *The Papers of Joseph Smith: Autobiographical and Historical Writings*, pp. 125–127.

23. See Whitmer, *An Address to All Believers in Christ*, pp. 32–34.

24. Smith Jr., *History of the Church*, Vol. 6: 408–409.

25. See sermons of May 2, June 13, and June 16, 1844. Smith is attempting to vindicate his position. Smith's earlier sermons would display a servant attitude. *Teachings of the Prophet Joseph Smith*, pp. 364–376.

26. *Doctrine and Covenants*, 1835, preface.

27. Jesse, *The Papers of Joseph Smith: Autobiographical and Historical Writings*, p. 127.

28. *Ibid.*, pp. 272–273. The text comes from the narrative history of Joseph Smith. James Mulholland is the scribe for this account. See p. 265.

29. The 1839 account and the official account are identical. See Backman, "Verification of the 1838 Account of the First Vision," pp. 237–248.

30. In Jesse, *The Papers of Joseph Smith: Autobiographical and Historical Writings*, pp. 439–440.

31. *Ibid.*

32. Backman, *The Heavens Resound*, pp. 327–329. Brodie, *No Man Knows My History*, pp. 194–207.

33. Pratt, *An Answer to Mr. William Hewitt's Tract*, p. 9. Hale, "Doctrinal Impact of the King Follett Discourse," p. 219.

34. Brodie, *No Man Knows My History*, pp. 194–207. Backman, *The Heavens Resound*, pp. 326–329.

35. See *Nauvoo Expositor*, Widmer, "Turbulence in Early Mormonism." See as well Ehat, "The Nauvoo Journal of Joseph Fielding," pp. 133–166.

36. See as well the discourse of June 13 in Smith Jr., *History of the Church*, Vol. 6: 461–462, and *Teachings of the Prophet Joseph Smith*, pp. 368–369.

37. Jesse, *The Papers of Joseph Smith: Autobiographical and Historical Writings*, pp. 266–267.

38. Smith began the history shortly after his release from the Liberty jail. Perhaps the events surrounding his imprisonment had persuaded him to concentrate on the history. The basis for the history was a draft prepared in Nauvoo in early 1839. It was a continuation of a history begun while Smith was in Far West in 1838. See Jesse, *The Papers of Joseph Smith: Autobiographical and Historical Writings*, p. 230–264.

39. The problems I have in mind are the failures of Smith and the Church to meet its members' expectations. These would be leaving New York, the failure of the economic ventures in Kirtland, and the several attempts to establish the Church in Missouri.

40. See Allen, "The Emergence of A Fundamental," pp. 43–69.

41. See Quinn, *Early Mormonism and the Magic World View*, pp. 80–81, 129.

42. Pratt, *A Interesting Account of Some Remarkable Visions*, reprint, pp. 387–401.

43. Orson Hyde, *Ein Ruf aus der Wüste, Einne Stimme aus dem Schoose der Erde*, Frankfurt, 1842. Reprinted in Dean C. Jesse, ed., *The Papers of Joseph Smith: Autobiographical and Historical Writings*, pp. 402–426.

44. Welch, *Protestant Thought in the Nineteenth Century*, Vol. 1, pp. 127–137.

45. See Erich Robert Paul, *Science, Religion, and Mormon Cosmology* (Chicago: University of Illinois Press, 1992), pp. 22–32.

46. The science and religion debate had an indirect impact on Mormon doctrinal development. The debate caused the Church to reevaluate its doctrinal positions in the 20th century and form concrete doctrinal statements. We will deal with this in the final chapter of this work.

7. And Ye Shall Be Gods

1. "Prospectus," *The Nauvoo Expositor*.
2. *The Nauvoo Expositor*, p. 3.
3. *The Nauvoo Expositor*, p. 2. Widmer, "Turbulence in Early Mormonism," pp. 164, 166, 167.
4. Joseph, in his diary, records that he met with Robert Foster on June 7, and made an attempt to bring him back into the fold. See Faulring, *An American Prophet's Record*, p. 488.
5. Smith Jr., *History of the Church*, Vol. 7: 57; 6: 210. Robert Bruce Flanders, *Nauvoo, Kingdom on the Mississippi* (Urbana: University of Illinois, 1975), p. 308. Flanders estimates that there were about 200 dissenters that united with the Laws.
6. Flanders, *Nauvoo, Kingdom on the Mississippi*, p. 308.
7. Lyndon W. Cook, "William Law, Nauvoo Dissenter," *Brigham Young University Studies* 22: 1 (1982): 47–72, p. 61 ff.
8. *The Doctrine and Covenants*, Section 124: 91–95.
9. Smith Jr., *History of the Church*, Vol. 6:152.
10. Cook, "William Law, Nauvoo Dissenter," p. 67.
11. See "Circuit Court," *Nauvoo Expositor*, p. 3. Smith Jr., *History of the Church*, Vol. 6: 437.
12. See Hill, *Quest for Refuge*, pp. 144–145.
13. See Smith Jr., *History of the Church*, Vol. 6: 437.
14. The "Prospectus" first appeared in Nauvoo on May 10. It is reprinted in the June 7, 1844, edition of the *Nauvoo Expositor*. The "Prospectus" was distributed to inhabitants of the city of Nauvoo, as well it was carried in several local newspapers.
15. Faulring, *An American Prophet's Record*, p. 488. See Allen and Leonard, *The Story of the Latter-day Saints*, p. 191.
16. Smith Jr., *History of the Church*, Vol. 6: 434–44, 448. Hill, *Quest for Refuge*, p. 145.
17. Section 25 of the Nauvoo Charter had granted the Mormons the right to bear arms. This right was carried out through the Nauvoo Legion. Section 25 says: "The said Legion shall perform the same amount of military duty as is now, or may be hereafter, required of the regular Militia of the State, and shall be at the disposal of the Mayor in executing the laws and ordinances of the City Corporation, and the laws of the State, and at the disposal of the Governor for public

defense, and in the execution of the laws of the State, or the United States, and shall be entitled to their proportion of the Public Arms..." Miller and Miller, *Nauvoo: City of Joseph*, pp. 244–245. Charges of treason were levied against Smith for the use of public arms against its own citizens after declaring martial law in Nauvoo. Robert Flanders estimates the size of the Legion in 1844 at around 4,000 to 5,000. Flanders, *Nauvoo, Kingdom on the Mississippi*, p. 109.

18. See Arrington and Bitton, *The Mormon Experience*, p. 78.
19. Section 14, Miller and Miller, *Nauvoo: City of Joseph*, p. 244.
20. The antilibel law suggested heavy financial penalties for contravening the law, with destruction of the libelous institution as a final resort. There was only one dissenting voice on the Nauvoo city council.
21. Roberts, *Comprehensive History of the Church*, Vol. 2: 237 ff, relates this incident in detail. See also Hill, *Quest for Refuge*, p. 146. Section 17 of the Nauvoo Charter; granted the Municipal Court of Nauvoo the "power to grant writs of habeas corpus in all cases arising under ordinances of the City Council." Miller and Miller, *Nauvoo: City of Joseph*, p. 244.
22. See Section 17 of Nauvoo Charter, Miller and Miller, *Nauvoo: City of Joseph*, p. 244. As well see Allen and Leonard, *The Story of the Latter-day Saints*, pp. 191–193.
23. Flanders, *Nauvoo, Kingdom on the Mississippi*, p. 309.
24. Text of the Nauvoo Charter in Miller and Miller, *Nauvoo: City of Joseph*, pp. 242–248.
25. Miller and Miller, *Nauvoo: City of Joseph*, p. 243.
26. Miller and Miller, *Nauvoo: City of Joseph*, p. 244.
27. L. M. Smith, *Biographical Sketches of Joseph Smith*, pp. 225 ff.
28. Smith Jr., *History of the Church*, Vol. 6: 480–488, also Hill, *Quest for Refuge*, pp. 147–148,
29. Arrington and Bitton, *The Mormon Experience*, p. 79.
30. Howe, *Mormonism Unvailed*, p. 142.
31. *Ibid.*, pp. 142–144.
32. Smith Jr., *History of the Church*, Vol. 6: 498, 538, 582. See also Hill, *Quest for Refuge*, p. 146.
33. All of these individuals published the reasons for their apostasy from the Church at one time in their life.
34. For full discussion see Cook, "William Law, Nauvoo Dissenter," pp. 56–66.
35. Smith Jr., *History of the Church*, Vol. 6: 408–409.
36. *Ibid.*, Vol. 6: 288–291.
37. The number of individuals in Nauvoo to hear the sermon has been disputed. Robert Flanders estimates the number of Mormons in Hancock County to be around 25,000. Flanders, *Nauvoo, Kingdom on the Mississippi*, p. 117. Wilford Woodruff in his journal cites that 20,000 attended the meeting. He crosses out that number and places 10,000 in its place. See "Wilford Woodruff Journal" in *The Words of Joseph Smith*, p. 343. Willard Richards' journal records 10,000 were present at the conference. *The Words of Joseph Smith*, p. 362.

38. The existing accounts of the sermon are found in *The Words of Joseph Smith*, pp. 340–362. The standard text for the sermon is the Johnathan Grisham redaction of 1855. It was published in the *Deseret News* in 1857.
39. Smith Jr., *History of the Church*, Vol. 6: 303.
40. See *The Words of Joseph Smith*, pp. 343, 362.
41. Smith Jr., *History of the Church*, Vol. 6: 305–306.
42. *Ibid.*, Vol. 6: 307–308.
43. See *Teachings of the Prophet Joseph Smith*, pp. 369, 370–376. *The Words of Joseph Smith*, 378–383.
44. Hale, "The Doctrinal Impact of the King Follett Discourse," pp. 224–225. Brodie, *No Man Knows My History*, p. 366.
45. See Chapter Five in this work.
46. The four concepts would be: 1) Men can become Gods; 2) A plurality of Gods exists; 3) A hierarchy of Gods exists; 4) God is an exalted man.
47. See *The Words of Joseph Smith*, pp. 59–61. See also *Teachings of the Prophet Joseph Smith*, p. 181.
48. *The Words of Joseph Smith*, pp. 172–173. Ehat and Cook state that Richards was not present, and was given the information either by Smith, or Clayton, see p. 267. Cook, *The Revelations of Joseph Smith* p. 288.
49. *The Words of Joseph Smith*, pp. 169–170. Faulring, *An American Prophet's Record*, p. 341.
50. Cook, *The Revelations of Joseph Smith*, p. 291.
51. *The Words of Joseph Smith*, pp. 209–216. Faulring, *An American Prophet's Record*, pp. 383–387. *Teachings of the Prophet Joseph Smith*, p. 307–312.
52. *The Words of Joseph Smith*, p. 214. Faulring, *An American Prophet's Record*, pp. 386. *Teachings of the Prophet Joseph Smith*, p. 312.
53. In the sermon of January 5, 1841, Smith cites that the word "create" should be translated "formed and fashioned." See *The Words of Joseph Smith*, p. 60. *Teachings of the Prophet Joseph Smith*, p. 181.
54. *Teachings of the Prophet Joseph Smith*, pp. 364–365. See Smith Jr., *History of the Church*, Vol. 6: 363 ff.
55. Smith Jr., *History of the Church*, Vol. 6: 408–409.
56. *Times and Seasons*, Vol. 5: 612–617.

8. Adam Our Father and Our God

1. *Times and Seasons*, Vol. 5: 651, 683. For a narrative see Flanders, *Nauvoo, Kingdom on the Mississippi*, pp. 312–316.
2. The Quorum of the Twelve Apostles was a traveling High Council, or a missionary group which chose lower-level leaders in specific geographical regions to do missionary work. From their origination in 1835, until the death of Smith, the Apostles were the Church's itinerant evangelists. See *The Doctrine and Covenants*, Section 107: 23, 28–35. They were accountable to the presidency of the Church and held no authority over the other quorums, see Section 107: 21–26.

3. William Smith, *A Proclamation and Faithful Warning to all the Saints Scattered around in Boston, Philadelphia, New York, Salem, New Bedford, Lowell, Peterborough, Gilsom, St. Louis, Nauvoo, and Elsewhere in the United States; Also, to Those Residing in the Different Parts of Europe and in the Islands of the Seas* (Warsaw: Wm. Smith, 1845). No copies of the original are known to have survived. The tract was reprinted in the *Warsaw Signal*, October 29, 1845. I have used a reprint of the tract from the *Warsaw Signal*.

4. See Koury, *The Truth and the Evidence*, pp. 82–84.

5. See Allen and Leonard, *The Story of the Latter-day Saints*, p. 213. *Times and Seasons*, Vol. 5: 638. For arguments from additional Mormon groups on the right of succession see Shields, *Divergent Paths of the Restoration,* and Koury, *The Truth and the Evidence*, pp. 67–90.

6. Koury, *The Truth and the Evidence*, pp. 14–15, 101.

7. As an example see Koury, *The Truth and the Evidence*, pp. 16–34.

8. See Allen and Leonard, *The Story of the Latter-day Saints*, pp. 213–225. Arrington, *The Great Basin Kingdom*, pp. 40–50. Arrington and Bitton, *The Mormon Experience*, pp. 162–163.

9. Arrington and Bitton, *The Mormon Experience*, p. 163.

10. *Times and Seasons*, Vol. 5: 615.

11. See Smith Jr., *History of the Church*, Vol. 3: 388. Ogden Kraut, *Michael-Adam* (N.P., N.D.), pp. 80–97. Cully K. Christensen, *The Adam God Maze* (Scottsdale: Independent Publishers, N.D.), pp. 131–149. Joseph Musser, *Michael Our Father and Our God* (Salt Lake City: Truth, 1963), pp. 38, 50–57.

12. See Kraut, *Michael-Adam*, pp. 80–97; Christensen, *The Adam God Maze*, pp. 131–138; Musser, *Michael Our Father and Our God*, pp. 38, 43–46. Mormon fundamentalists still hold to the view of Adam-God as taught by Brigham Young.

13. Gary J. Bergera, "The Orson Pratt–Brigham Young Controversies: Conflict Within the Quorums 1853–1868," *Dialogue: A Journal of Mormon Thought*, Vol. 13: 2 (1983): 7–49, p. 42.

14. See Gary J. Bergera, "The Orson Pratt–Brigham Young Controversies: Conflict Within the Quorums 1853-1868." *Dialogue: A Journal of Mormon Thought,* Vol. 13: 2 (1983): 7–49. Barlow, *Mormons and the Bible*, pp. 90–92.

15. *Journal of Discourses*, Vol. 1: 51.

16. *Journal of Discourses*, Vol. 2: 6; Vol. 3: 319; Vol. 5: 331; Vol. 6: 285; Vol. 8: 58, 208, 244. The latest reference to Adam-God, from Young, is dated to February 7, 1877. See Fred C. Collier, *Unpublished Revelations of the Prophets and Presidents of the Church of Jesus Christ of Latter-day Saints*, Vol. 1 (Salt Lake City: Collier Publishing Co., 1979), pp. 113–118. As well see the unpublished sermons of February 19, 1854, and especially the sermon of October 8, 1854, which is the clearest expression of the concept. Brigham Young Collection, LDS Church Archives.

17. *Deseret News*, June 18, 1873, p. 308.

18. The original is found under the date of February 7, 1877, in the John L. Nuttall Diary. References are from the copy contained in Collier, *Unpublished Revelations*, pp. 113–118.

19. Gary J. Bergera, "The Orson Pratt–Brigham Young Controversies: Conflict Within the Quorums 1853–1868," *Dialogue: A Journal of Mormon Thought* Vol. 13: 2 (1983): 7–49, p. 37.
20. *Ibid.*, p. 36.
21. *Ibid.*, p. 30.
22. *Ibid.*, p. 27.
23. *Ibid.*, p. 37.
24. Barlow, *Mormons and the Bible*, pp. 90–92.
25. Paul, *Science, Religion, and Mormon Cosmology*, p. 128.
26. See *Messenger and Advocate*, Vol. 2: 77; *Evening and Morning Star*, Vol. 1: 113. For discussion, see Van Hale, "The Origin of the Human Spirit in Early Mormon Thought," in Gary J. Bergera, ed., *Line Upon Line: Essays on Mormon Doctrine* (Salt Lake City: Signature Books, 1989), pp. 115–126; pp. 116–120. Blake Ostler, "The Idea of Pre-existence in Mormon Thought," in Gary J. Bergera, ed., *Line Upon Line: Essays on Mormon Doctrine* (Salt Lake City: Signature Books, 1989), pp. 127–144, pp. 130–134.
27. Pratt's first attempts are dated as early as 1845. For brief discussion see Hale, "The Origin of the Human Spirit in Early Mormon Thought," pp. 119–120.
28. For discussion see Barlow, *Mormons and the Bible*, p. 93.
29. Orson Pratt, ed., *The Seer*, 2 Vols. (Washington D.C.: 1853-54), Vol. 1: 24.
30. *The Seer*, Vol. 1: 103.
31. *Ibid.*
32. *Ibid.*, Vol. 1: 102–103, 131–132.
33. *Ibid.*, Vol. 1: 132.
34. *Ibid.*, Vol. 1: 117
35. See Hale, "The Origin of the Human Spirit in Early Mormon Thought," pp. 115–126. Ostler, "The Idea of Pre-existence in Mormon Thought," pp. 127–144.
36. *Journal of Discourses*, Vol. 2: 6; 3: 319; 7: 285.
37. See *Times and Seasons*, Vol. 6: 1039. Linda P. Wilcox, "The Mormon Concept of a Mother in Heaven," in Gary J. Bergera, ed., *Line Upon Line: Essays on Mormon Doctrine* (Salt Lake City: Signature Books, 1989), pp. 103–114; pp. 103–104. Ostler, "The Idea of Pre-existence in Mormon Thought," p. 133. Hale, "The Origin of the Human Spirit in Early Mormon Thought," pp. 120–121.
38. *The Seer*, Vol. 1: 18–19, 23, 54–57.
39. For full discussion see Ostler, "The Idea of Pre-existence in Mormon Thought," pp. 133–136.
40. Smith dealt with this in the *Book of Moses* and the *Book of Abraham*. The two works attempt to resolve the conflict in the biblical text in Genesis 1:26–27, and Genesis 2:5. Other statements by Smith had addressed the question of pre-mortal existence in classic Christian terms. See *Messenger and Advocate*, Vol. 2: 77; *Evening and Morning Star*, Vol. 1: 113.

NOTES—CHAPTER 8

41. Official declarations are found in J. Reuben Clark, *Messages of the First Presidency*, 6 Vols. (Salt Lake City: Bookcraft, 1971), Vol. 2: 214–224, 229–240. See Ostler, "The Idea of Pre-existence in Mormon Thought," p. 135. Bergera, "The Orson Pratt–Brigham Young Controversies," pp. 7–49. See Wilford Woodruff journal entry for December 29, 1856, and January 27, 1860, in Wilford Woodruff, *Journals 1833–1898*, Lyndon W. Cook and Scott Kenney, eds., 9 Vols. (Midvale: Signature Books, 1983–1985).

42. Ostler, "The Idea of Pre-existence in Mormon Thought," pp. 127–144. Ostler defines the differences between Young and Pratt as differing perspectives of God; finitist and absolutist positions.

43. See "Minutes of Council of Twelve," April 4–5, 1860, MSS, LDS Church Archives. For full narrative of the event see Bergera, "The Orson Pratt–Brigham Young Controversies," pp. 7–49.

44. See "Minutes of the Council of Twelve," April 4–5, 1860, MSS.

45. Several members in the Quorum of the Twelve held to either of the views expressed above. This inconsistency led to tension in the Quorum's and the Church's leadership. We will give some time to this in the next chapter under the heading "Discord Among the Lords Anointed."

46. *The Words of Joseph Smith*, p. 351. Smith Jr., *History of the Church*, Vol. 5: 392–393.

47. See Cannon, "The King Follett Discourse," pp. 179–193. Voros, "Was the *Book of Mormon* Buried with King Follett?" pp. 15–19.

48. The "plan of exaltation" is fundamental to Mormon theology today. Briefly it is: the relationship of God to man in his origin and destiny. The destiny is described as exaltation, or elevation to divinity through following established precepts and laws as all divine beings have done through the ages.

49. See for example Voros, "Was the *Book of Mormon* Buried with King Follett?" pp. 15–19.

50. The concept of the Holy Ghost in Mormon theology has been addressed at different times in Mormon history. The concept of the Holy Ghost was addressed in the *Lectures of Faith* in 1835. The first major treatment was in 1855, in Parley P. Pratt, *Science, With Key to Theology* (Liverpool: Millennial Star, 1855). The most extensive treatment was given in 1917. See Alexander, *Mormonism in Transition*, p. 280. See also Swanson, "The Development of the Concept of the Holy Ghost in Mormon Theology," pp. 89–102. For collection of primary sources on the Holy Ghost, see Smith, Joseph, Jr., et al., *Discourses on the Holy Ghost.* Compiled by N. B. Lundwall (Salt Lake City: Bookcraft, 1959).

51. We have argued in previous chapters that some of the shifts in Mormon theology were the result of dissent in the Church, directed against the prophetic claim of Smith.

52. The Church's early educational endeavors are dealt with in an earlier chapter. We can see strong 19th-century influences in the *Book of Moses* and the *Book of Abraham*. Possible relationships can exist between Mormon thought and the philopophy of Thomas Dick, Immanuel Kant, and Thomas Paine.

53. *The Doctrine and Covenants*, Section 68: 4.

54. Smith Jr., *History of the Church*, Vol. 1: 296; Vol. 2: 428; Vol. 7: 558. *Journal of Discourses*, Vol. 2: 111; Vol. 4: 2, 218; Vol. 13: 264; Vol. 16: 46.

9. Unity from Diversity

1. John A. Widstoe, *A Rational Theology* (Salt Lake City: Deseret Book Co., 1915).
2. James E. Talmage, *Jesus the Christ: A Study of the Messiah According to the Holy Scriptures* (Salt Lake City: The Church, 1915).
3. See Hale, "The Origin of the Human Spirit in Early Mormon Thought," pp. 120-123. As well see Orson Pratt, *The Absurdities of Immaterialism: or A Reply To T. W. P. Taydlers Pamphlet Entitled "The Materialism of The Mormons or Latter-day Saints Examined and Refuted"* (Liverpool: R. James, 1849). See also P. Pratt, *Science, With Key To Theology*, pp. 32-38.
4. *Times and Seasons*, Vol. 5: 612-617.
5. The Grimshaw text is the most common version of the sermon. It is based on additional accounts of the sermon besides the William Clayton and Thomas Bullock accounts which comprised the *Times and Seasons* version. Hale, "The Origin of the Human Spirit in Early Mormon Thought," p. 123. Larson, "The King Follett Discourse: A Newly Amalgamated Text," p. 195.
6. The Grimshaw text was used in the 1859 publication of the *Journal of Discourses*. See *Journal of Discourses*, Vol. 6: 1-11.
7. *Journal of Discourses*, Vol. 26: 18-30.
8. Ostler, "The Idea of Pre-existence in Mormon Thought," p. 136.
9. *Journal of Discourses*, Vol. 26: 23.
10. Ostler, "The Idea of Pre-existence in Mormon Thought," p. 136.
11. *Ibid.*, p. 136.
12. Alexander, *Mormonism in Transition*, p. 273.
13. Ostler, "The Idea of Pre-existence in Mormon Thought," p. 137. Barlow, *Mormons and the Bible*, p. 114.
14. Ostler, "The Idea of Pre-existence in Mormon Thought," p. 137.
15. *Ibid.*
16. Roberts had included the Grimshaw redaction in the manuscript. Penrose favored the original *Times and Seasons* account as his view was based upon the reading of that text.
17. Ostler, "The Idea of Pre-existence in Mormon Thought," p. 138.
18. *Ibid.*, pp. 138-139.
19. For brief discussion see Hale, "The Origin of the Human Spirit in Early Mormon Thought," pp. 123-124.
20. Alexander, *Mormonism in Transition*, p. 287. Ostler, "The Idea of Pre-existence in Mormon Thought," p. 139.
21. See Paul, *Science, Religion, and Mormon Cosmology*, pp. 148, 157-160.
22. The articles from the *Improvement Era* have been compiled in John A. Widstoe, *Evidences and Reconciliations* (Salt Lake City: Bookcraft, 1960).

23. Alexander, *Mormonism in Transition*, p. 279. Ostler, "The Idea of Pre-existence in Mormon Thought," pp. 138–139.
24. Alexander, *Mormonism in Transition*, p. 279.
25. *Ibid.*, p. 278.
26. See Widstoe, *A Rational Theology*, pp. 15, 17, 24.
27. *Ibid.*, pp. 15–19. Ostler, "The Idea of Pre-existence in Mormon Thought," pp. 138-139. Alexander, *Mormonism in Transition*, p. 278.
28. Alexander, *Mormonism in Transition*, p. 279.
29. See Widstoe, *A Rational Theology*, pp. 15, 17, 24, 25.
30. See Paul, *Science, Religion, and Mormon Cosmology*, pp. 157–160.
31. Alexander, *Mormonism in Transition*, p. 278.
32. The articles would be compiled as John A. Widstoe, *Evidences and Reconciliations* (Salt Lake City: Bookcraft, 1960).
33. Alexander, *Mormonism in Transition*, pp. 279-280.
34. *Ibid.*, p. 273.
35. James E. Talmage, *A Study of the* Articles of Faith: *Being a Consideration of the Principal Doctrines of the Church of Jesus Christ of Latter-day Saints* (Salt Lake City: The Church of Jesus Christ of Latter-day Saints, 1982).
36. Thomas Alexander, "The Reconstruction of Mormon Doctrine," in Gary J. Bergera ed., *Line Upon Line: Essays on Mormon Doctrine* (Salt Lake City: Signature Books, 1989), pp. 53–66, p. 60.
37. Alexander, *Mormonism in Transition*, p. 281
38. Talmage, *A Study of the* Articles of Faith, p. 39.
39. *Ibid.*, p. 40.
40. *Ibid.*, p. 41.
41. Despite Talmage's assertion, Mormonism still holds that an intelligence can only achieve exaltation through a material body, yet the Holy Ghost has only a spirit body. The declaration of the Holy Ghost as a person is a revision of the earlier thought, dating from 1835, that the Holy Ghost was the mind of the Father and the Son, and the 1850s' teaching that the Holy Ghost was the fluid that allowed God to be omnipresent.
42. Alexander, *Mormonism in Transition*, pp. 280–281.
43. Alexander, "The Reconstruction of Mormon Doctrine," p. 60. Alexander, *Mormonism in Transition*, p. 280.
44. See Kirkland, "The Development of the Mormon Doctrine of God," p.
45. Alexander, "The Reconstruction of Mormon Doctrine," pp. 60–62.
45. Talmage, *Jesus the Christ*, p. 32.
46. Talmage, *Jesus the Christ*, p. 38.
47. See Kirkland, "The Development of the Mormon Doctrine of God," p. 46.
48. "The Father and the Son: A Doctrinal Exposition by the First Presidency and the Twelve," Appendix II, in Talmage, *A Study of the* Articles of Faith, pp. 466–473.
49. "The Father and the Son: A Doctrinal Exposition," pp. 466–473.
50. *Ibid.*, p. 467.
51. *Ibid.*, pp. 467–471.

52. *Ibid.*, pp. 471–473.

53. The ninth *Article of Faith* states: We believe all that God has revealed, all that He does now reveal and we believe that He will yet reveal many great and important things pertaining to the Kingdom.

54. See Talmage, *Jesus the Christ*, p. 32. Kirkland, "The Development of the Mormon Doctrine of God," p. 48.

55. Alexander, *Mormonism in Transition*, p. 281.

56. See Larry E. Dahl, "Authorship and History of the *Lectures on Faith*," in Larry E. Dahl and Charles D. Tate Jr., eds., *The Lectures on Faith in Historical Perspective*, Vol. 15, Religious Studies Monograph Series (Provo: Brigham Young University, 1990), pp. 1–22, pp. 16–19. Also Gentry, "What of the *Lectures on Faith?*" pp. 5–12.

57. See Alexander, "The Reconstruction of Mormon Doctrine," p. 63. Alexander, *Mormonism in Transition*, p. 282.

58. See 1835 edition of *The Doctrine and Covenants*, pp. 255–257.

59. *Ibid.*, 575. See as well Dahl, "Authorship and History of the *Lectures on Faith*," pp. 16–19.

60. Alexander, "The Reconstruction of Mormon Doctrine," p. 63.

61. Arrington and Bitton, *The Mormon Experience*, p. 29.

62. Erich Robert Paul cites that English astronomer Richard Proctor considered Pratt one of the top seven astronomers of the 19th century. Paul, *Science, Religion, and Mormon Cosmology*, p. 140.

63. Alexander, *Mormonism in Transition*, p. 296.

Bibliography

Primary Sources

Books, Tracts, Diaries, Journals

"Account of Mormonism: A New Extravaganza in America." *The Christian Reformer, or New Evangelical Miscellany*. Vol. 18 (1832): 456–462.

Bennett, John C. *The History of the Saints: or, An Expose of Joe Smith and Mormonism*. Boston: Leland and Whiting, 1842.

A Book of Commandments for the Government of the Church of Christ. Zion: W. W. Phelps, 1833.

The Book of Mormon. Palmyra: E. B. Grandin, 1830.

The Book of Mormon. Kirtland: F. G. Williams and Co., 1837.

The Book of Mormon. Salt Lake City: Church of Jesus Christ of Latter-day Saints, 1981.

Campbell, Alexander. *Millennial Harbinger*. Vol. 2 (1831): 86–96.

Caswell, Henry. *City of the Mormons: or, Three Days at Nauvoo in 1842*. London: J. G. F. & J. Rivington, 1842.

___. *The Prophet of the Nineteenth Century*. London: J. G. F. & J. Rivington, 1843.

Clark, J. Reuben. *Messages of the First Presidency*. 6 Vols. Salt Lake City: Bookcraft, 1971.

Clayton, William. *Journal*. Salt Lake City: Clayton Family Association, 1921.

Collier, Fred C. *Unpublished Revelations of the Prophets and Presidents of the Church of Jesus Christ of Latter-day Saints*. Vol. 1. Salt Lake City: Collier Publishing Co., 1979.

Cook, Lyndon W., ed. *The Revelations of the Prophet Joseph Smith: A Historical and Biographical Commentary on the Doctrine and Covenants*. Salt Lake City: Deseret Book Co., 1985.

The Doctrine and Covenants of the Church of Jesus Christ of the Latter-day Saints. Salt Lake City: Church of Jesus Christ of Latter-day Saints, 1981.

The Doctrine and Covenants of the Church of the Latter Day Saints. Kirtland: F. G. Williams and Co., 1835.

Ehat, Andrew F., ed. "They Might Have Known That He Was Not a Fallen Prophet: The Nauvoo Journal of Joseph Fielding." *Brigham Young University Studies* 19: 2 (1979): 133–166.

___, and Lyndon W. Cook, eds., *The Words of Joseph Smith: The Contemporary Accounts of the Nauvoo Discourses of the Prophet Joseph Smith*. Vol. 6. Religious Studies Monograph Series. Provo: Brigham Young University Press, 1980.

England, Eugene, ed. "George Laub's Nauvoo Journal." *Brigham Young University Studies* 18: 2 (1978): 151–177.

Faulring, Scott F., ed. *An American Prophet's Record: The Diaries and Journal of Joseph Smith*. Salt Lake City: Signature Books, 1989.

Hancock, Mosiah. *Journal*. MSS.

Howe, E. D. *Mormonism Unvailed: or, A Faithful Account of That Singular Delusion*. Painesville: E. D. Howe, 1834.

Hyde, Orson. *Ein Ruf aus der Wüste, Einne Stimme aus dem Schoose der Erde*. Frankfurt, 1842. Reprinted in Dean C. Jesse, ed. *The Papers of Joseph Smith: Autobiographical and Historical Writings*. Salt Lake City: Deseret Book Co., 1989, pp. 402–426.

Jesse, Dean C., ed. *The Papers of Joseph Smith: Autobiographical and Historical Writings*. Salt Lake City: Deseret Book Co., 1989.

___, ed. *The Papers of Joseph Smith, Vol. 2, Journal 1832–1842*. Salt Lake City: Deseret Book Co., 1992.

___, ed. *Personal Writings of Joseph Smith*. Salt Lake City: Deseret Book Co., 1985.

Journal of Discourses of Brigham Young, His Counselors, and Other Church Leaders. 26 Vols. Liverpool: Latter-day Saints Book Depot, 1853–1886.

Kimball, Heber C. *Journal*. Salt Lake City: Juvenile Instructors Office, 1882.

Lamb, M. T. *The Golden Bible: or, The Book of Mormon. Is It From God?* New York: Ward and Drummond, 1887.

Larson, Stan. "The King Follett Discourse: A Newly Amalgamated Text." *Brigham Young University Studies* 18: 2: (1978): 193–208.

Ludlow, Daniel H., ed. and arr. *Latter-day Prophets Speak: Selections from the Sermons and Writings of the Church Presidents*. Salt Lake City: Bookcraft, 1948.

The Pearl of Great Price: A Selection from the Revelations, Translations, and Narrations of Joseph Smith; First Prophet, Seer and Revelator to the Church of Jesus Christ of Latter-day Saints. Salt Lake City: Church of Jesus Christ of Latter-day Saints, 1981.

The Pearl of Great Price: Being a Choice Selection from the Revelations, Translations, and Narrations of Joseph Smith; First Prophet, Seer and Revelator to the Church of Jesus Christ of Latter-day Saints. Liverpool: F. D. Richards, 1851.

Pratt, Orson. *The Absurdities of Immaterialism: or A Reply To T. W. P. Taylders Pamphlet Entitled "The Materialism of the Mormons or Latter-day Saints Examined and Exposed."* Liverpool: R. James, 1849.

___. "Angels." In *The New York Messenger*, October 18, 1845. Reprinted in *The Essential Orson Pratt*. Salt Lake City: Signature Books, 1991, pp. 42–47.

___. *Divine Authority of the* Book of Mormon: *Evidences of the* Book of Mormon *and the Bible Compared.* Liverpool: R. James, 1850.

___. *Divine Authority of the* Book of Mormon: *Introduction; To Expect More Revelation Is Not Unscriptural, To Expect More Revelation Is Not Unreasonable.* Liverpool: R. James, 1850.

___. *Divine Authority of the* Book of Mormon: *More Revelation Is Indispensibly Necessary.* Liverpool: R. James, 1850.

___. *Divine Authority of the* Book of Mormon: *or, The Question Was Joseph Smith Sent By God?* Liverpool: R. James, 1848.

___. *Divine Authority of the* Book of Mormon: *Prophetic Evidence in Favour of the* Book of Mormon. R. James, N.D.

___. *Divine Authority of the* Book of Mormon: *The Bible and Tradition Without Further Revelation, an Insufficient Guide.* Liverpool: R. James, 1850.

___. *Divine Authority of the* Book of Mormon: *The* Book of Mormon *Confirmed by Miracles.* Liverpool: R. James, 1851.

___. *The Essential Orson Pratt.* Salt Lake City: Signature Books, 1991.

___. *Great First Cause, or the Self Moving Forces of the Universe.* Liverpool: R. James, 1851.

___. *A Interesting Account of Some Remarkable Visions, and of the Late Discovery of Ancient American Records Giving an Account of the Commencement of the Work of the Lord in This Generation.* Edinburgh: Ballantyne and Hughes, 1840. Reprinted in Dean C. Jesse, ed. *The Papers of Joseph Smith: Autobiographical and Historical Writings.* Salt Lake City: Deseret Book Co., 1989, pp. 387–401. Also reprinted in *The Essential Orson Pratt.* Salt Lake City: Signature Books, 1991, pp. 1–23.

___. *The Key to the Universe, Or a New Theory of its Mechanism.* Salt Lake City: Orson Pratt, 1879.

___. *The Kingdom of God.* 4 Parts. Liverpool: R. James, 1848–1849.

___. "Mormon Philosophy: Space, Duration, and Matter." In *The New York Messenger*, September 13, 1845. Reprinted in *The Essential Orson Pratt.* Salt Lake City: Signature Books, 1991, pp. 31–36.

___. *New Jerusalem: or, The Fulfillment of Modern Prophecy.* Liverpool: R. James, 1849.

___. "Questions on the Origin of Man." In *The New York Messenger*, September 6, 1845. Reprinted in *The Essential Orson Pratt.* Salt Lake City: Signature Books, 1991, pp. 29–31.

___. "Questions on the Present State of Man." In *The New York Messenger*, September 27, 1845. Reprinted in *The Essential Orson Pratt.* Salt Lake City: Signature Books, 1991, pp. 36–42.

___. *Remarkable Visions.* Liverpool: R. James, 1848.

___. *Reply: To a Pamphlet Printed in Glasgow, With the Approbation of Clergymen of Different Denominations Entitled, "Remarks on Mormonism."* Liverpool: R. James, 1849.

___. *A Series of Pamphlets.* Liverpool: F. D. Richards, 1852.

___. *Works Vol. 1. 1848–1851.* Salt Lake City: P. P. Robinson [1945].

___, ed. *The Seer.* 2 Vols. Washington, D.C., 1853–1854.
Pratt, Parley P. *An Answer to Mr. William Hewitt's Tract.* Manchester: W. R. Thomas, 1840.
___. *Mormonism Unveiled: Zion's Watchman, Unmasked; and its Editor, Mr. L. R. Sunderland, Exposed: Truth Vindicated: The Devil Mad and Priestcraft in Danger.* New York: Parley P. Pratt, 1838.
___. *Science, With Key To Theology.* Liverpool: Millennial Star, 1855.
Roberts, B. H. "Book of Mormon Difficulties: A Study." *Studies of the* Book of Mormon. Brigham D. Madsen, ed. University of Illinois Press, 1985, pp. 61–148.
___. A *Book of Mormon* Study. MSS. Salt Lake City: Modern Microfilm.
___. "A *Book of Mormon* Study." *Studies of the* Book of Mormon. Brigham D. Madsen, ed. Chicago: University of Illinois Press, 1985, pp.149–320.
___. *A Comprehensive History of the Church of Jesus Christ of Latter-day Saints.* 6 Vols. Provo: Brigham Young University Press, 1957.
___. *The Gospel.* Salt Lake City: The Contributor, 1888.
___. *The Mormon Doctrine of Deity.* Salt Lake City: The Deseret News Press, 1903.
___. *New Witnesses for God.* 3 Vols. Salt Lake City: The Deseret News Press, 1909.
___. "A Parallel." Mervin B. Hogan, ed. *Rocky Mountain Mason.* Vol. 10: (1956): 17–31.
___. "A Parallel." *Studies of the* Book of Mormon. Brigham D. Madsen, ed. Chicago: University of Illinois Press, 1985, pp. 321–344.
Seixas, Joshua. *Manual Hebrew Grammar: For Beginners.* 2nd ed. Andover: Gould and Newman, 1834.
Smith, Eliza R. Snow. *Biography and Family Record of Lorenzo Snow.* Salt Lake City: Deseret News, 1884.
Smith, Ethan. *View of the Hebrews: or The Ten Tribes of Israel in America.* Poultney: Smith and Smith, 1825.
Smith, Hyrum M., and J. M. Sjodahl. *The Doctrine and Covenants, Containing Revelations Given to Joseph Smith Jr. the Prophet: With an Introduction and Historical and Exegetical Notes.* Salt Lake City: Deseret Book Co., 1920.
Smith, Joseph, Jr. *Diaries of Joseph Smith.* MSS. 1832–1842.
___. *Egyptian Alphabet and Grammar.* MSS. c. 1835–1838.
___. *Joseph Smith's New Translation of the Bible.* Independence: Herald House, 1970.
___, et al. *Discourses on the Holy Ghost.* Compiled by N. B. Lundwall. Salt Lake City: Bookcraft, 1959.
___, et al. *History of the Church of Jesus Christ of Latter-day Saints.* B. H. Roberts, ed., 7 Vols. Salt Lake City: Deseret Book Co. 1951 [1971].
Smith, Joseph Fielding. *Blood Atonement and the Origin of Plural Marriage.* Independence: Press of Zion's Printing and Publishing Co., 1905.
___. *Gospel Doctrine: Selections from the Sermons and Writings of Joseph F. Smith.* Salt Lake City: Deseret Book Co., 1919 [1961].
___, ed. *Teachings of the Prophet Joseph Smith.* Salt Lake City: Deseret Book Co., 1976.

Smith, Lucy Mack. *Biographical Sketches of Joseph Smith the Prophet and His Progenitors For Many Generations.* Liverpool: Orson Pratt, 1853.
Smith, William. *A Proclamation and Faithful Warning to All the Saints Scattered Around in Boston, Philadelphia, New York, Salem, New Bedford, Lowell, Peterborough, Gilsom, St. Louis, Nauvoo, and Elsewhere in the United States; Also, to Those Residing in the Different Parts of Europe and in the Islands of the Seas.* Warsaw: Wm. Smith, 1845.
Spenser, Orson. *Letters.* N.D., N.P.
Sunderland, LaRoy. *Mormonism Exposed and Refuted.* New York: Piercy and Reed, 1838.
Swartzell, William. *Mormonism Exposed.* Pittsburgh: Pekin O., 1840.
Talmage, James E. *The Great Apostasy.* Independence: Press of Zion's Printing and Publishing Co., 1909.
___. *Jesus the Christ: A Study of the Messiah According to the Holy Scriptures Both Ancient and Modern.* Salt Lake City: The Church, 1915.
___. *A Study of the* Articles of Faith: *Being a Consideration of the Principal Doctrines of the Church of Jesus Christ of Latter-day Saints.* Salt Lake City: Deseret Book Co., 1890 [1982].
Turner, J. B. *Mormonism in All Ages.* New York: Platt and Peters, 1842.
Whitmer, David. *An Address to All Believers in Christ.* Richmond: N.P., 1887.
___. *An Address to All Believers in the* Book of Mormon. Richmond: N.P., 1887.
Whitmer, John. *History of the Church.* MSS. 1831–1838.
Widstoe, John A., ed. *Discourses of Brigham Young.* Salt Lake City: Deseret Book Co., 1951.
___. *Evidences and Reconciliations.* Salt Lake City: Bookcraft, 1960.
___. *Joseph Smith as Scientist.* Salt Lake City: YMMIA General Board, 1909.
___. *A Rational Theology.* Salt Lake City: Deseret Book Co., 1915.
Woodruff, Wilford. *Journals 1833–1898.* Cook, Lyndon W., and Scott Kenney, ed. 9 Vols. Midvale: Signature Books, 1983–1985.
Young, Brigham. Unpublished Sermons: *February 19, 1854; October 8, 1854.* MSS. Brigham Young Collection, LDS Church Archives.

NEWSPAPERS, PERIODICALS, COUNCIL MINUTES

The Deseret News. 1850–present.
The Elders Journal. 1 Vol. Kirtland and Far West, 1837–1838.
The Evening and Morning Star. 3 Vols. Kirtland and Independence: 1832–1834.
Kirtland Council Minutes. MSS. 1832–37.
Kirtland Revelation Book. MSS. 1831–34.
The Latter Day Saints Messenger and Advocate. 3 Vols. Kirtland: 1834–1837.
The Latter-day Saints Millennial Star. 130 Vols. Liverpool: 1840–1970.
Minutes of the Council of the Twelve Apostles. MSS. 1860.
Nauvoo Expositor. Nauvoo: 1844.
Nauvoo High Council Minutes. MSS. 1839–1845.
Times and Seasons. 6 Vols. Nauvoo: 1839–1846.

Secondary Sources

BOOKS AND PAMPHLETS

Ahlstrom, Sidney. *A Religious History of the American People.* New Haven: Yale University Press, 1972.

Alexander, Thomas G. *Mormonism in Transition: A History of the Latter-day Saints 1890–1930.* Urbana: University of Illinois Press, 1986.

Allen, James B., and Glen Leonard. *The Story of the Latter-day Saints.* Salt Lake City: Deseret Book Co. 1980.

Andrus, Hyrum L. *Doctrinal Commentary on the* Pearl of Great Price. Salt Lake City: Deseret Book Co., 1972.

Arrington, Leonard J. *The Great Basin Kingdom: Economic History of the Latter-day Saints 1830–1900.* Lincoln: University of Nebraska, 1955.

___, and Davis Bitton. *The Mormon Experience: A History of the Latter-day Saints.* New York: Vintage, 1980.

Backman, Milton V., Jr. *American Religions and the Rise of Mormonism.* Salt Lake City: Deseret Book Co., 1970.

___. *The Heavens Resound: The History of the Church of Jesus Christ of Latter-day Saints in Ohio, 1830–1838.* Salt Lake City: Deseret Book Co., 1983.

___. *Joseph Smith's First Vision: The First Vision in Historical Context.* Salt Lake City: Bookcraft, 1976.

Barlow, Phillip. *Mormons and the Bible: The Place of the Latter-day Saints in American Religion.* London: Oxford University Press, 1991.

Bergera, Gary J., ed. *Line Upon Line: Essays on Mormon Doctrine.* Salt Lake City: Signature Books, 1989.

___, ed. *New Views of Mormon History: A Collection of Essays in Honor of Leonard J. Arrington.* Salt Lake City: University of Utah Press, 1987.

Berrett, Wm. E. *Teachings of the Doctrine and Covenants.* Salt Lake City: Deseret Book Co., 1961.

Brodie, Fawn. *No Man Knows My History: The Life of Joseph Smith the Mormon Prophet.* New York: Alfred Knopf, 1945 [1982].

Bushman, Richard E. *Joseph Smith and the Beginnings of Mormonism.* Urbana: University of Illinois Press, 1988.

Carter, Kate B. *Denominations That Base Their Beliefs on the Teachings of Joseph Smith the Mormon Prophet.* Salt Lake City: Daughters of the Utah Pioneers, 1969.

Clark, J. Reuben. *The Story of the* Pearl of Great Price. Salt Lake City: Bookcraft, 1955.

Christensen, Cully K. *The Adam God Maze.* Scottsdale: Independent Publishers, N.D.

Cross, Whitney. *The Burned-over District: The Social and Intellectual History of Enthusiastic Religion in Western New York, 1800–1850.* Ithaca: Cornell University Press, 1950.

Dahl, Larry E., and Charles D. Tate Jr., eds. *The* Lectures on Faith *in Historical Perspective.* Vol. 15, Religious Studies Monograph Series. Provo: Religious Studies Center, Brigham Young University, 1990.
Durham, Homer, ed. *The Gospel Kingdom: Writings and Discourses of John Taylor.* Salt Lake City: Bookcraft, 1943.
Durham, Reed C., and Jack Adamson. *No Help for the Widow's Son.* Nauvoo: Martin Publishing Co., 1980.
Flanders, Robert B. *Nauvoo, Kingdom on the Mississippi.* Urbana: University of Illinois, 1975.
Griggs, Wilfred C. ed. *Apocryphal Writings and the Latter-day Saints.* Vol. 13, Religious Studies Monograph Series. Provo: Religious Studies Center, Brigham Young University, 1986.
Hampshire, Annette P. *Mormonism in Conflict: The Nauvoo Years.* Lewiston: Edwin Mellen Press, 1985.
Hansen, Klaus J. *Mormonism and the American Experience.* Chicago: University of Chicago, 1971.
___. *Quest For Empire: The Political Kingdom of God and the Council of Fifty in Mormon History.* Ann Arbor: Michigan State Press, 1967.
Hill, Donna. *Joseph Smith: The First Mormon.* New York: Doubleday, 1977.
Hill, Marvin S. *Quest for Refuge: The Mormon Flight from American Pluralism.* Salt Lake City: Signature Books, 1989.
Hunter, Milton R. *The Gospel Through the Ages.* Salt Lake City: Stevens and Wallis, 1945.
___. Pearl of Great Price *Commentary.* Salt Lake City: Bookcraft, 1951 [1958].
Kirkham, Francis. *A New Witness for Christ.* 2 Vols. Independence: Zion's Press, 1947.
Koury, Aleah. *The Truth and the Evidence: A Comparison Between Doctrines of the Reorganized Church of Jesus Christ of Latter Day Saints and the Church of Jesus Christ of Latter-day Saints.* Independence: Herald House, 1965.
Kraut, Ogden. *Blood Atonement.* Salt Lake City: Pioneer Press, N.D.
___. *Michael-Adam.* N.P., N.D.
Lund, Gerald N. *The Coming of the Lord.* Salt Lake City: Bookcraft, 1971.
Lundwall, N. B. *The Vision.* Salt Lake City: Bookcraft, N.D.
McKiernan, F. Mark, Alma Blair, and Paul M. Edwards, eds. *The Restoration Movement: Essays in Mormon History.* Lawrence: Coronado Press, 1972.
Miller, David E., and Della S. Miller. *Nauvoo: The City of Joseph.* Santa Barbara: Peregrine Smith Inc., 1974.
Musser, Joseph. *Celestial or Plural Marriage.* Salt Lake City: Truth Publishing, 1944.
___. *Michael Our Father and Our God.* Salt Lake City: Truth Publishing, 1963.
Nyman, Monte S., and Robert L. Millett, eds. *The* Joseph Smith Translation: *The Restoration of Plain and Precious Truths.* Vol. 12, Religious Studies Monograph Series. Provo: Religious Studies Center, Brigham Young University, 1985.
Paul, Erich Robert. *Science, Religion, and Mormon Cosmology.* Chicago: University of Illinois Press, 1992.

Peterson, H. Donl, and Charles D. Tate Jr., eds. *The Pearl of Great Price: Revelations from God.* Vol. 14, Religious Studies Monograph Series. Provo: Religious Studies Center, Brigham Young University, 1989.

Quinn, D. Michael. *Early Mormonism and the Magic World View.* Salt Lake City: Signature Books, 1987.

Shields, Steven L. *Divergent Paths of the Restoration.* Bountiful: Restoration Inc., 1983.

Shipps, Jan. *Mormonism: The Birth of a New Religious Tradition.* Urbana: University of Illinois Press, 1985.

Sperry, Sidney B. *Doctrine and Covenants Compendium.* Salt Lake City: Bookcraft, 1960.

Tanner, Jerald, and Sandra Tanner. *3,913 Changes in the* Book of Mormon. Salt Lake City: Utah Light House, N.D.

Vogel, Dan, ed. *The Word of God: Essays on Mormon Scripture.* Salt Lake City: Signature Books, 1990.

Welch, Claude. *Protestant Thought in the Nineteenth Century.* 2 Vols. New Haven: Yale University Press, 1989.

West, Emmerson R. *Profiles of the Presidents.* Salt Lake City: Deseret Book Co., 1972.

White, Kendall O., Jr., *Mormon Neo-orthodoxy: A Crisis Theology.* Salt Lake City: Signature Books, 1987.

Articles

Alexander, Thomas G. "The Place of Joseph Smith in the Development of American Religion: A Historiographical Inquiry." *Journal of Mormon History.* Vol. 5 (1978): 3–17.

___. "The Reconstruction of Mormon Doctrine: From Joseph Smith to Progressive Theology." *Sunstone.* Vol. 10: 5 (1985): 8–18.

___. "The Reconstruction of Mormon Doctrine." Gary J. Bergera, ed. *Line Upon Line: Essays on Mormon Doctrine.* Salt Lake City: Signature Books, 1989, pp. 53–66.

Allen, James B. "The Emergence of a Fundamental: The Expanding Role of Joseph Smith's 1st Vision in American Religious Thought." *Journal of Mormon History.* Vol. 7 (1980): 43–69.

___. "The Significance of Joseph Smith's 1st Vision in Mormon Thought." *Dialogue: A Journal of Mormon Thought.* Vol. 1: 3 (1966): 29–45.

Ashment, Edward H. "Reducing Dissonance: The *Book of Abraham* as a Case Study." Dan Vogel, ed. *The Word of God: Essays on Mormon Scripture.* Salt Lake City: Signature Books, 1990, pp. 231–264.

Backman, Milton V. "Verification of the 1838 Account of the First Vision." H. Donl Peterson and Charles D. Tate Jr., eds. *The* Pearl of Great Price: *Revelations from God.* Vol. 14, Religious Studies Monograph Series. Provo: Religious Studies Center, Brigham Young University, 1989, pp. 237–248.

Barney, Kevin, L. "The *Joseph Smith Translation* and Ancient Texts of the Bible." Dan Vogel, ed. *The Word of God: Essays on Mormon Scripture*. Salt Lake City: Signature Books, 1990, pp. 143–160.

___. "The *JST* and Ancient Texts of the Bible." *Dialogue: A Journal of Mormon Thought*. Vol. 19: 3 (1986): 85–102.

Bergera, Gary J. "The Orson Pratt–Brigham Young Controversies: Conflict Within the Quorums 1853–1868." *Dialogue: A Journal of Mormon Thought*. Vol. 13: 2 (1983): 7–49.

Cannon, Donald Q. "The King Follett Discourse: Joseph Smith's Greatest Sermon in Historical Perspective." *Brigham Young University Studies* 18: 2 (1978): 179–193.

Charles, Melodie Moench. "The Mormon Christianizing of the Old Testament." Dan Vogel, ed. *The Word of God: Essays on Mormon Scripture*. Salt Lake City: Signature Books, 1990, pp. 131–142.

Cook, Lyndon W. "William Law, Nauvoo Dissenter." *Brigham Young University Studies* 22:1 (1982): 47–72.

Curtis, Susan. "Early Nineteenth-Century America and the Book of Mormon." Dan Vogel, ed. *The Word of God: Essays on Mormon Scripture*. Salt Lake City: Signature Books, 1990, pp. 81–96.

Gentry, Leland H. "What of the *Lectures on Faith*?" *Brigham Young University Studies* 24: 1 (1984): 5–12.

Godfrey, Kenneth W. "The History of Intelligence in Latter-day Saint Thought." H. Donl Peterson and Charles D. Tate Jr., eds. *The* Pearl of Great Price: *Revelations from God*. Vol. 14, Religious Studies Monograph Series. Provo: Religious Studies Center, Brigham Young University, 1989, pp. 213–236.

Hale, Van. "Defining the Contemporary Mormon Concept of God." Gary J. Bergera, ed. *Line Upon Line: Essays on Mormon Doctrine*. Salt Lake City: Signature Books, 1989, pp.7–16.

___. "The Doctrinal Impact of the King Follett Discourse." *Brigham Young University Studies* 18: 2 (1978): 209–225.

___. "The Origin of the Human Spirit in Early Mormon Thought." Gary J. Bergera, ed. *Line Upon Line: Essays on Mormon Doctrine*. Salt Lake City: Signature Books, 1989, pp. 115–126.

Hansen, Klaus J. "Mormonism and American Culture." F. Mark McKiernan, Alma Blair, and Paul M. Edwards, eds. *The Restoration Movement: Essays in Mormon History*. Lawrence: Coronado Press, 1980, pp. 1–25.

Hogan, Mervin B. "A Parallel: A Matter of Chance Versus Coincidence." *The Rocky Mountain Mason*. Vol. 10 (1956): 17–31.

Horton, George A., Jr., "Insights into the Book of Genesis." Monte S. Nyman and Robert L. Millett, eds. *The* Joseph Smith Translation: *The Restoration of Plain and Precious Truths*. Vol. 12, Religious Studies Monograph Series. Provo: Religious Studies Center, Brigham Young University, 1985, pp. 51–70.

Howard, Richard P. "Latter Day Saint Scriptures and the Doctrine of Propositional Revelation." Dan Vogel, ed. *The Word of God: Essays on Mormon Scripture*. Salt Lake City: Signature Books, 1990, pp. 1–18.

Jesse, Dean C. "Joseph Knight's Recollection of Early Mormon History." *Brigham Young University Studies* 17: 1 (1979): pp. 29–39.

___. "New Documents and Mormon Beginnings." *Brigham Young University Studies* 24: 4 (1984): 397–428.

___. "The Writing of Joseph Smith's History." *Brigham Young University Studies* 11: 4 (1970): 439–473.

Kimball, Stanley B. "Heber C. Kimball and Family: The Nauvoo Years." *Brigham Young University Studies* 15: 4 (1975): pp. 447–479.

___. "Sources on the History of the Mormons in Ohio: 1830–1838." *Brigham Young University Studies* 11: 4 (1971): 524–540.

Kirkland, Boyd. "The Development of the Mormon Doctrine of God." Gary J. Bergera, ed. *Line Upon Line: Essays on Mormon Doctrine.* Salt Lake City: Signature Books, 1989, pp. 35–52.

___. "Elohim and Jehovah in Mormonism and the Bible." *Dialogue: A Journal of Mormon Thought* 19: 1 (1986): 79–93.

___. "Eternal Progression and the Second Death in the Theology of Brigham Young." Gary J. Bergera, ed. *Line Upon Line: Essays on Mormon Doctrine.* Salt Lake City: Signature Books, 1989, pp. 171–182.

___. "Jehovah as the Father: The Development of the Mormon Jehovah Doctrine." *Sunstone.* 10: 2 (1985): 36–44.

Lancaster, James E. "The Translation of the *Book of Mormon.*" Dan Vogel, ed. *The Word of God: Essays on Mormon Scripture.* Salt Lake City: Signature Books, 1990, pp. 97–112.

Lyon, T. Edgar. "Doctrinal Development of the Church During the Nauvoo Sojourn, 1839–1846." *Brigham Young University Studies* 15: 4 (1975): 425–438.

Matthews, Robert J. "Major Doctrinal Contributions of the *JST.*" Monte S. Nyman and Robert L. Millett, eds. *The* Joseph Smith Translation: *The Restoration of Plain and Precious Truths.* Vol. 12, Religious Studies Monograph Series. Provo: Religious Studies Center, Brigham Young University, 1985, pp. 271–290.

___. "The New Translation of the Bible, 1830–1833: Doctrinal Development During the Kirtland Era." *Brigham Young University Studies* 11: 4 (1971): 400–422.

___. "A Study of the Text of Joseph Smith's Inspired Version of the Bible." *Brigham Young University Studies* 9: 1 (1969): 3–16.

McConkie, Joseph F. "Premortal Existence, Foreordinations, and Heavenly Councils." Wilfred C. Griggs, ed. *Apocryphal Writings and the Latter-day Saints.* Vol. 13, Religious Studies Monograph Series. Provo: Religious Studies Center, Brigham Young University, 1986, pp. 173–198.

Millett, Robert L. "Joseph Smith's Translation of the Bible: A Historical Overview." Monte S. Nyman and Robert L. Millett, eds. *The* Joseph Smith Translation: *The Restoration of Plain and Precious Truths.* Vol. 12, Religious Studies Monograph Series. Provo: Religious Studies Center, Brigham Young University, 1985, pp. 23–50.

___. "Joseph Smith's Translation of the Bible: Impact on Mormon Theology." *Religious Studies.* Vol. 8 (1987): 43–53.

___. "The Supreme Power Over All Things: The Doctrine of the Godhead in the *Lectures on Faith*." Larry E. Dahl and Charles D. Tate Jr., eds. *The Lectures on Faith in Historical Perspective*. Vol. 15, Religious Studies Monograph Series. Provo: Religious Studies Center, Brigham Young University, 1990, pp. 221–240.

Nibley, Hugh. "The Meaning of the Kirtland Egyptian Papers." *Brigham Young University Studies* 11: 4 (1971): 350–399.

Olson, Earl E. "The Chronology of the Ohio Revelations." *Brigham Young University Studies* 11: 4 (1971): 329–349.

Ostler, Blake. "The Idea of Pre-existence in Mormon Thought." Gary J. Bergera, ed. *Line Upon Line: Essays on Mormon Doctrine*. Salt Lake City: Signature Books, 1989, pp. 127–144.

Palmer, David A. "A Survey of Pre–1830 Historical Sources Relating to the *Book of Mormon*." *Brigham Young University Studies* 17: 1 (1977): 101–109.

Parker, Arthur C. "The Code of Handsome Lake, the Seneca Prophet." *New York State Museum Bulletin*. 1912, pp. 6–139.

Parkin, Max H. "Kirtland, a Stronghold for the Kingdom." F. Mark McKiernan, Alma Blair, and Paul M. Edwards, eds. *The Restoration Movement: Essays in Mormon History*. Lawrence: Coronado Press, pp. 63–98.

Paul, Robert. "Joseph Smith and the Manchester (New York) Library." *Brigham Young University Studies* 22: 3 (1982): 333–356.

Peterson, H. Donl. "Sacred Writings from the Tombs of Egypt." H. Donl Peterson and Charles D. Tate Jr., eds. *The* Pearl of Great Price: *Revelations from God*. Vol. 14, Religious Studies Monograph Series. Provo: Religious Studies Center, Brigham Young University, 1989, pp. 137–154.

Porter, Larry C. "The Church in New York and Pennsylvania." F. Mark McKiernan, Alma Blair, and Paul M. Edwards, eds. *The Restoration Movement: Essays in Mormon History*. Lawrence: Coronado Press, 1980, pp. 27–61.

Rich, Russell R. "Where Were the Moroni Visits?" *Brigham Young University Studies* 18: 4 (1978): 255–258.

Richards, Stephen L. "Continuing Revelation and Mormon Doctrine." Gary J. Bergera, ed. *Line Upon Line: Essays on Mormon Doctrine*. Salt Lake City: Signature Books, 1989, pp. 183–186.

Robinson, T. A. "Reports from Archives." *North American Religion*. Vol. 2 (1993): 232–247.

Rollman, Hans. "The Early Baptist Career of Sidney Rigdon in Warren, Ohio." *Brigham Young University Studies* 21: 1 (1981): 37–50.

Shoemaker, Thaddeus E. " Speculative Theology: Key to a Dynamic Faith." Gary J. Bergera, ed. *Line Upon Line: Essays on Mormon Doctrine*. Salt Lake City: Signature Books, 1989, pp. 1–6.

Stott, G. St. John. "Joseph Smith's 1823 Vision: Uncovering the Angel Message." *Religion*. Vol. 18: (1988): 347–362.

Swanson, Vern G. "The Development of the Concept of the Holy Ghost in Mormon Theology." Gary J. Bergera, ed. *Line Upon Line: Essays on Mormon Doctrine*. Salt Lake City: Signature Books, 1989, pp. 89–102.

Thomas, Mark D. "Scholarship and the *Book of Mormon.*" Dan Vogel, ed. *The Word of God: Essays on Mormon Scripture.* Salt Lake City: Signature Books, 1990, pp. 63–80.

Turner, Rodney. "The Doctrine of the Firstborn and Only Begotten." H. Donl Peterson and Charles D. Tate Jr., eds. *The* Pearl of Great Price: *Revelations from God.* Vol. 14, Religious Studies Monograph Series. Provo: Religious Studies Center, Brigham Young University, 1989, pp. 91–118.

___. "The Imperative and Unchanging Nature of God." Larry E. Dahl and Charles D. Tate Jr., ed. *The* Lectures on Faith *in Historical Perspective.*" Vol. 15, Religious Studies Monograph Series. Provo: Religious Studies Center, Brigham Young University, 1990, pp. 199–220.

Vogel, Dan. "The Earliest Mormon Concept of God." Gary J. Bergera, ed. *Line Upon Line: Essays on Mormon Doctrine.* Salt Lake City: Signature Books, 1989, pp. 17–34.

___, and Brent Lee Metcalfe. "Joseph Smith's Scriptural Cosmology." Dan Vogel, ed. *The Word of God: Essays on Mormon Scripture.* Salt Lake City: Signature Books, 1990, pp. 187–220.

Voros, Frederick J., Jr. "Was the *Book of Mormon* Buried with King Follett?" *Sunstone.* Vol. 11: 2 (1986): pp. 15–19.

Walters, Wesley P. "The Origin of the *Book of Mormon.*" *Journal of Pastoral Practice.* Vol. 3: 3 (1979): 121–152.

Wellnitz, Marcus Von. "The Catholic Liturgy and the Mormon Temple." *Brigham Young University Studies* 21: 1 (1981): 3–35.

Widmer, Kurt. "Turbulence in Early Mormonism and the Death of Joseph Smith: The Nauvoo Expositor (1844)." *North American Religion.* Vol. 2: (1993): 135–201.

Wilcox, Linda P. "The Mormon Concept of a Mother in Heaven." Gary J. Bergera, ed. *Line Upon Line: Essays on Mormon Doctrine.* Salt Lake City: Signature Books, 1989, pp. 103–114.

Yorgason, Laurence M. "Preview on a Study of the Social and Geographical Origins of Early Mormon Converts, 1830–1845." *Brigham Young University Studies* 10: 3 (1970): pp. 279–282.

Zucker, Louis C. "Joseph Smith as a Student of Hebrew." *Dialogue: A Journal of Mormon Thought.* Vol. 3: 2 (1969): 41–56.

INDEX

Abraham, the Patriarch 3; in Egypt 72, 73
Adam 3, 5, 41, 45, 65, 89, 105, 126, 131, 132, 133, 135, 137, 138, 139; as Father of Spirits 138
Adam-God 105, 133, 137, 138, 155
Adams, John Q. 30
Alsace, France 82
America: culture of early 19th century 30, 38; early 19th century 51, 52
Ancient of Days 127
Anthon, Charles 72
anthropocentrism 106
anti–Mormon literature 8, 85, 88, 93
apocalyptic expectations 18
apostasy: first apostates 17; in Kirtland 17, 19; in Nauvoo 19, 110, 116; in New York 17; of Christianity 89; of David Whitmer 51; of Latter-day Saints after April 7, 1844 15; of prominent members 115; of the Twelve Apostles 19; of William Law 19, 110
apotheosis 49, 122
Arizona 128
The Articles and Covenants of the Church of Christ 36, 42, 43
The Articles of Faith 12, 41, 150; impact of 151
Austria 104
authority: of revelation 10; of scripture 12; of *The Book of Abraham* 83, 88; of the First Presidency 12; of the General Authorities 10, 12; of the High Councils 12; of *The Joseph Smith Translation* 50; of *The Lectures of Faith* 62; of the Prophets 12; of the Twelve Apostles 12

Barstow, John 92
Bauer, F. C. 135
Bennett, John C. 115
Bettisworth, David 112
The Bible 9; Joseph Smith revises 36; polytheistic passages removed 49; The Apocrypha 47; *The Authorized Version* 12, 44, 47, 48; *The Inspired Version* 46; *The Joseph Smith Translation* 36, 46; truths restored in *The Joseph Smith Translation* 50; use of in early Mormonism 143; use of in King Follett discourse 120
Bidamon, Lewis: marries Emma Smith 128
binatarianism 6, 59, 67, 68, 69, 79, 82, 96, 99, 116
The Book of Abraham 9, 19, 22, 58, 67, 68, 69, 70, 72, 73, 74, 75, 76, 77, 78, 79, 80, 81, 82, 83, 84, 85, 86, 87, 88, 89, 90, 95, 157; canonization of 78
A Book of Commandments for the Government of the Church of Christ 36, 43, 44, 84
The Book of Mormon 4, 5, 9, 12, 13, 20, 21, 22, 23, 24, 25, 26, 27, 28, 30, 32, 33, 34, 35, 36, 37, 38, 39, 40, 41, 43, 45, 46, 48, 49, 50, 51, 52, 53, 56, 63, 67, 68, 69, 71, 72, 76, 83, 84, 92, 93, 94, 95, 97, 98, 99, 103, 104, 105, 106, 108, 143, 152, 154, 160, 161; as a second witness to Christ 98; as history of American continent 24; as history of Amerindians 25; Christology of 30; early criticisms towards 28; early uses 23; message of 39; monotheism of 21; origin of 8, 23, 26; revision of 32, 35; teachings of 25
The Book of Moses 9, 36, 43, 44, 45, 46, 47, 51, 53, 56, 73, 88, 97, 105, 135, 154; authority of 43; creation in 45; modalism of 49
Booth, Ezra 115; as Methodist preacher 27; early apostate 17; early missionary in Missouri 17; early writings 25; letters in *The Ohio Star* 17; letters sent from Kirtland 17

Bullock, Thomas 8, 118; records King Follett discourse 118, 145

California 128
Campbell, Alexander 37, 135; criticisms of *The Book of Mormon* 26
Canada 94, 104
Cannon, George Q.: on the nature of God 146; role in First Vision 93
canon 9, 12, 19, 21, 32, 43, 46, 62, 64, 67, 88, 99, 105, 143; authority of 10; process of canonization 9, 88; the Mormon 21
Cardston, Alberta 128
Carthage, Illinois 15, 17, 112, 114, 116, 126
Caswell, Henry 88
Champollion, Jean-François 71, 72
Chandler, Michael H. 70, 71, 72
Channing, William Ellery 29, 38, 52; Christology of 29; *Likeness of God* 29; *Unitarian Christianity* 29
charismatic gifts 142; gifts of the Holy Spirit 103, 104; healings 4, 8, 20, 40, 103, 104; miracles 20, 40; prophecy 4, 8, 20, 103, 104; speaking in unknown tongues 4, 8, 40, 103, 104, 114
The Chicago Democrat 24, 92
Christ 87
Christian Church 99
The Christian Palladium 38
Christianity 4; apostasy of 4; early 19th century 32; New Testament 4; 19th Century 3; primitive 4; restoration of 4; Christology 106; Arianism 53; Chalcedonian 31, 52; early Mormon 20, 31, 32; early 19th century 38; in *The Book of Mormon* 35; modalism 30, 53; modalism in early Mormon Church 22; modalism in *The Book of Mormon* 38; Mormon 7; Nicene 30, 31, 52; Noetic 30; of *The Joseph Smith Translation* 50; Patripassianism 30, 38, 53; Sabellianism 30, 53; *The Book of Mormon* defined 30; Trinitarian 30, 31; tritheism 30
Circuit Court of Hancock County 113
City of New Jerusalem 5, 58
The City of the Mormons 86
Clark, J. Reuben 71
Clayton, William 8, 118, 122, 123; records King Follett discourse 118, 145
Columbia University 72
competing theologies 12
Constitution of the United States 16
continuing revelation 3
converts: beliefs of 27; to early Mormonism 27; to early Mormonism from Baptists 27; to early Mormonism from Disciples of Christ 27; to early Mormonism from Mennonites 27; to early Mormonism from Methodists 27
cosmic henotheism 96
cosmology 78; during late 1800s 135; of *The Book of Abraham* 73
Council in Heaven 48, 85
Council of Gods 15, 86, 90, 119, 121, 125, 126, 131
Council of Spirits 123
Council of the Twelve 147
Cowdery, Oliver 17, 46, 47, 63, 66, 102, 115
creation: in *The Book of Abraham* 79; in *The Book of Moses* 46, 48; in *The Joseph Smith Translation* 48
creation accounts 88, 90

Darwin, Charles 135
denominations, Mormon 4
Deseret, State of 128
Disciples of Christ 26; relation to early Mormons 26
dissent: in Kirtland 19; in Missouri 16; in Nauvoo 15, 18, 110, 116; throughout Mormon history 16
Doctrinal Exposition on the Father and the Son 155
The Doctrine and Covenants 9, 10, 11, 12, 36, 37, 43, 44, 46, 47, 48, 49, 54, 56, 58, 59, 61, 62, 63, 64, 84, 85, 99, 123, 139, 153, 157, 161

early polemics 8
Edinburgh, Scotland 92
Egypt 70, 72, 76
Egyptian: grammar 72, 75; hieroglyphics 71, 73; mummies 72; papyrus 73
Elijah 97, 98
Eloah 79
Elohim 36, 60, 64, 66, 67, 68, 69, 74, 79, 80, 81, 82, 99, 131, 133, 155; as God superior to Jehovah 61, 67; as God the Father 60; as head of the Council of Gods 60; as the Council of Gods 61, 131; as the Father of Jehovah 61; in the thought of James Talmage 152; role in creation 132
Elohim Jehovah controversy 60, 64
Elohist 88
Emerson, Ralph Waldo 29, 38, 135; *An American Scholar* 29; concept of apotheosis 29; *Nature* 29; *Self Reliance* 29; *The Over Soul* 29

Emmons, Sylvester 111
Enoch 3; prophecy of 44
eschatology, Mormon 18
Eternal Father 23, 33, 34, 39, 146
Eternal God 33, 36, 85
eternal progression 15, 119, 129, 140; in the thought of B. H. Roberts 137; in the thought of Brigham Young 137; in the thought of Charles Penrose 137; in the thought of Orson Pratt 137
evangelical Christians 98
evangelicalism 28, 38, 53
The Evening and Morning Star 16, 37, 43, 44, 49, 84; destruction of 43, 114
Everlasting Father 33
Evidences and Reconciliations 148, 149
evolution 106

Far West, Missouri 5
Fielding, Joseph 15; records King Follett discourse 118
Finney, Charles G. 30, 38, 102
first missionary proclamation 5
First Presidency 11, 12, 127
First Vision 4, 9, 69, 84, 92, 93, 94, 95, 96, 99, 100, 101, 102, 103, 104, 105, 106; role of in Mormon history 92
Ford, Thomas 112, 114
Foster, Charles 15
Foster, Robert D. 5, 109, 110, 126
fullness of the Gospel 95

Garden of Eden 5, 127; location of 6
Gathering 5; purpose of 58; to Kirtland, Ohio 57, 58
General Authorities 150
General Church Conference 11, 12
Genesis 79
German 27, 81, 82, 104, 125
German mission 104
Germany 104
God 90, 95, 98, 100, 102, 105, 118, 127, 128, 149; as Elohim 60, 67; as Elohim and Jehovah 67; as Jehovah 60, 67, 81; as the Father 81, 122; as the Father and the Son 49; as the Holy Ghost 81; as the Only Begotten 45; as the Son 81; as three personages 66; co-equal with man 119, 129; competing views of 21; concept of in early 19th-century America 52; distinctiveness of Father and Son 66; during the Kirtland period 69; early Mormon view 21; has a material body 122, 123, 135, 145; in *The Book of Mormon* 49; in *The Book of Moses* 46, 49; in *The Lectures of Faith* 64; in the thought of B. H. Roberts 146; in the thought of Brigham Young 139; in the thought of Charles W. Penrose 145; in the thought of George Q. Cannon 146; in the thought of James Talmage 150; in the thought of John A. Widstoe 146; in the thought of Orson Pratt 139, 145; man may become 15, 50, 109, 119, 125, 126, 129; mysteries of 30; nature and character of 41, 29, 135, 140; no distiction between Father and Son 31; once a man 73, 119, 122, 129; origin and nature of 139; progression of 135; resurrection of 124, 138; role in creation 45; sectarian concept of 122; the Father 60; the Holy Ghost 59; the Holy Spirit 59; the Son 60; Trinitarian view 21; true nature revealed 119; truths of 118
God the Father 31, 38, 87, 96, 97, 99, 100, 101; in *Lectures of Faith* 65
God the Holy Ghost 38, 87, 100
God the Holy Spirit, in *Lectures of Faith* 65
God the Son 31, 38, 87, 96, 97, 99, 100, 101; in *Lectures of Faith* 65
The Godhead 99, 101, 124
Gods 73, 87, 120, 121, 137; Council of 119; hierarchy of 109, 123; in *The Book of Abraham* 75; plurality of 9, 15, 18, 19, 49, 50, 60, 70, 73, 74, 75, 76, 77, 78, 79, 84, 85, 86, 87, 88, 89, 90, 101, 106, 119, 121, 122, 123, 125, 126, 131, 133, 137, 138, 139
The Gospel 89; as old as Adam 45, 48
Gospel of John 98
Göttingen 148
Great Salt Lake 115, 128
Greek 59, 66, 81, 82, 125

Hancock County, Illinois 16
Harris, Martin 72
Harvard 148
Hawes, H. M. 59
Heaven, in *The Book of Abraham* 73
Hebrew 36, 49, 52, 58, 59, 60, 66, 67, 68, 69, 74, 79, 80, 81, 82, 89, 99, 119, 121, 125
Hebrew instructors: Parker, Lucius 67; Piexotto, Daniel 66; Seixas, Joshua 67
henotheism 6, 7, 21, 22, 52, 66, 68, 77, 78, 82, 90, 99, 105, 116, 121, 122, 130, 140, 141; nascent 6, 77
hierarchy of Gods 123, 126
hieroglyphics 71
Higbee, Chauncey 15

INDEX

Higbee, Francis 15
High Councils: in Kirtland 12; in Missouri 12
historical criticism 10
history of Joseph Smith 23
Holy Ghost 12, 26, 32, 33, 35, 37, 42, 59, 61, 64, 80, 87, 98, 100, 123, 138, 141; in the thought of James Talmage 150; indwelling of 123
Holy Spirit 11, 60, 65, 66, 118, 119, 123, 125
Howe, E. D. 17, 25
Hume, David 135
Hyde, Orson 104

Idaho 128
Illinois State Legislature 16, 113
The Improvement Era 149
Independence, Missouri 5, 16, 43, 114
The Inspired Version of the Bible 46
intelligences 138, 139
Ivins, Anthony 153
Ivins, Charles 109

Jackson, Andrew 30, 53
Jackson County, Missouri 17
Jehovah 36, 60, 64, 66, 67, 68, 69, 80, 81, 99, 117, 131, 133, 152, 155; as God of Israel 67; as member of the Council of Gods 131; as Father 67, 151; as Father explained 152; as God of Old Testament 143; role in creation of 132; Jesus Christ 93, 96, 98, 99, 102, 120, 121, 126
Jesus the Christ 151, 153, 156, 160; impact of 151, 152, 154, 155; teachings in 151; John the Apostle 126
Joseph, in Egypt 72
"Joseph Smith History" 9
The Joseph Smith Translation 36, 46, 48, 50, 53, 97; authority of work 50; modalism of 49
The Journal of Discourses 11

King Follett discourse 7, 9, 56, 58, 64, 68, 77, 78, 79, 84, 86, 88, 89, 90, 100, 108, 109, 115, 116, 118, 119, 122, 123, 124, 125, 126, 128, 129, 130, 135, 139, 140, 141, 145, 147, 154, 155; first publication of 145; Grimshaw redaction 145; henotheism of 22; impact of 14; teachings of 119, 144
Kirtland, Ohio 5, 12, 17, 19, 43, 48, 51, 52, 55, 56, 58, 59, 60, 62, 64, 65, 67, 68, 69, 70, 71, 74, 81, 94, 99, 100, 102, 103, 141, 154

Kirtland Anti-Banking Society 100
Kirtland High Council 62
Kirtland Temple 94
Kolob 73

Lamb of God 34
languages: Greek 47, 51; Hebrew 47, 51, 52, 82; Latin 59, 81, 82, 125
The Latter-day Saints Millennial Star 3, 44, 83, 85, 90, 131
Law, William 77, 110, 126; as Prophet, Seer and Revelator 110; as Second Counsellor 15, 109; begins seperate Church 110; editor of *The Nauvoo Expositor* 15; excommunication of 110; following destruction of *Nauvoo Expositor* 18; rift with Joseph Smith 18; role in death of Joseph Smith 15
"Lecture Before the Veil" 132
Lectures of Faith 10, 32, 46, 49, 58, 59, 60, 61, 62, 63, 64, 67, 76, 77, 99, 105, 153; as doctrine portion of *Doctrine and Covenants* 62; authority of 62; contents of 63; description of 61; inclusion in 1835 *Doctrine and Covenants* 62; Lecture Fifth 64; part of *Doctrine and Covenants* 61; taught during 1834-35 59; the decanonization of 64, 144
Liberty, Missouri 85; jail in 86
literature, early anti–Mormon 27
Lucifer 49; member of the Council of Gods 131
Lund, Anthon H. 147, 149
Luther, Martin 51

mankind, pre-mortal existence of 48
The Manuscript Story 25–26
Massachusetts Bay Colony 5
McIntire, William 122, 123
Melchizedek, Prince of Jerusalem 73
The Messenger and Advocate 61, 76
Methodism 104; criticisms against Mormon Church 38
Mexico 128
Michael: as father of Jehovah 133; as father of Jesus 133; as God the Father 133; as member of the Council of Gods 131; becomes Adam 131; brings wife to Earth 133; comes to Earth as Adam 133; role in creation 132
Michael, the Archangel 127
Michael-Adam 131
Millard, David 38
migration to Missouri 17

The Millennial Harbinger 26
Millennium 3, 5
missionary activity, early 5 17; in Indian territory 17; in Mentor, Ohio 58
Missouri, expulsion from 17, 100, 114; migration to 17
modalism 6, 22, 30, 31, 32, 33, 34, 35, 36, 38, 40, 41, 45, 49, 50, 52, 53, 59, 66, 67, 68, 82, 96, 97, 99, 105, 140, 143, 152, 154
modern prophecy 105
monotheism 6, 21, 73, 80, 141; in *The Book of Abraham* 75
Mormon Church: early apocalyptic belief 18; early converts' beliefs 5; early converts to 5, 20; opposition from Methodism 38; reasons for conversion to 20
Mormon denominations 4
Mormon eschatology 5
Mormon migration to Missouri 17
Mormon sects 4
Mormonism in All Ages 86
Mormonism Unvailed 17, 25
Mormons: in Illinois 16; in Missouri 16
Moses 97, 118; the revelations of 43, 44
Mother in Heaven 138

Nauvoo, Illinois 5, 14, 78, 88, 109, 115, 124, 125, 126, 131, 141, 154; many stay behind 128
The Nauvoo Charter 15, 16, 111, 112, 113; Section 11 15; Section 16 16
Nauvoo Circuit Court 109
Nauvoo City Council 16
Nauvoo City Ordinances 111
The Nauvoo Expositor 15, 17, 18, 19, 55, 77, 108, 109, 110, 111, 112, 113, 114, 115, 121, 125, 126; critique of Joseph Smith 18; critique of April 7, 1844, sermon 18; declared public nuisance 15; the destruction of 17, 111; publication of 15
The Nauvoo Legion 17, 111, 112
Nauvoo Lyceum 122
Nauvoo Municipal Court 111, 113; power of 112
The Nauvoo Neighbor 111
Neibauer, Alexander 81, 82
Nevada 128
New Hampshire 92
The New Testament 50, 121
New Witnesses for God 26, 147
newspapers: *Chicago Democrat* 23; *Evening and Morning Star* 16, 17, 43, 49; *Latter-day Saints Millennial Star* 3, 44, 83; *Messenger and Advocate* 61, 76; *Nauvoo Expositor* 15, 77; *Nauvoo Neighbor* 111; *Ohio Star* 16, 25; *Pittsburgh Gazette* 100; *Times and Seasons* 44, 75, 76, 82, 84, 85, 86, 90, 92, 109, 110, 111
Noah, the Patriarch 3

Oberlin 159
The Ohio Star 17, 25
The Old Testament 50
origin myth 106
origin of the Mormon Church: myths surrounding 13; official position 13

Paine, Thomas 52, 53; *Age of Reason* 135
Parker, Theodore 38
Parrish, Warren 97
Paul, the Apostle 97, 98, 126
The Pearl of Great Price 9, 23, 43, 44, 73, 84, 90
Penrose, Charles W. 147; and the concept of Eternal progression 137
Peter, the Apostle 97, 98, 126
Phelps, W. W. 102, and the First Vision 94
The Pittsburgh Gazette 100
plain and precious parts of the Gospel 4
plain and precious truths 53
plurality of Gods 30, 45, 46, 48, 49, 69, 74, 75, 95, 105, 115, 116, 119, 121, 122, 124, 125, 126, 128, 153, 156, 157; denied by RLDS 128; origin of 135
plurality of worlds 73
polemics, early 8
polygamy 109
polytheism 82; removed from the Bible 49
Pratt, Orson 21, 55, 92, 104, 130, 131, 133, 134, 135, 136, 137, 138, 139, 140, 148, 155, 158, 159; and evolutionary pantheism 139; and the concept of Eternal progression 137; and the First Vision 92; materialism of God 145; on the nature of God 145; teachings on God 130, 138; use of King Follett discourse 145
Pratt, Parley P. 80, 87, 102, 158; and the First Vision 94; concept of God 100
predestination 106
preexistence 90; in Mormon thought 137; in the thought of Orson Pratt 136
Preston, England 82
primitive Christianity 48, 65, 88, 89
progressive revelation 105
The Prophet of the Nineteenth Century 86, 87
prophets 5, 125; modern 3
Protestant churches 94

Quorum of the Seventies (Seventy) 11
Quorum of the Twelve Apostles 11, 127; missionary work of 130; apostasy of while in Kirtland 19

Ramus, Illinois 123
A Rational Theology 148, 149
Reorganized Church of Jesus Christ of Latter Day Saints 46, 128
restoration 4, 30, 38, 40, 41, 89, 98; message of 41; of modalism 53; of plain and precious truths 53
revelation, used in the writing of *Book of Mormon* 22
Richards, George F. 153
Richards, Willard 123; records King Follett discourse 118
Rigdon, Sidney 26, 47, 58, 61, 63, 110, 148, 159; excommunication of 128; following death of Joseph Smith 127; revises Bible 50; sermon of April 1844 118
Roberts, B. H. 21, 26, 55, 62, 73, 75, 76, 134, 137, 141, 144, 147, 148, 149, 154, 156, 158, 159, 160; and the concept of eternal progression 137; comments on *Book of Mormon* origins 26
Rosetta stone 71

San Bernardino, California 128
Schleiermacher, Friederich 135
School of the Elders 59; operates in Independence 59
School of the Prophets 58, 59, 141; formation of 59; purpose of 59
Scripture 11
Second Great Awakening 28, 51
sects, Mormon 4
seers 5
The Seer 134, 136
Seixas, Joshua 59, 67, 80; arrives in Kirtland 67; lectures at Oberlin 67; *Manual Hebrew Grammar: For Beginners* 67
Smith, Adam 135
Smith, Alvin, joins Methodist and Presbyterian churches 28
Smith, Emma, widow of Prophet remarries 128
Smith, Ethan 26
Smith, Hyrum 61, 113; joins Methodist and Presbyterian churches 28
Smith, John 62
Smith, Joseph F. 43, 148, 149
Smith, Joseph Fielding (son of Joseph F. Smith) 71

Smith, Joseph, III (son of Joseph Smith Jr.): leads splinter group 128; son of the Prophet 128
Smith, Joseph, Jr. 4, 5, 7, 8, 9, 10, 11, 12, 13, 14, 15, 17, 19, 20, 21, 23, 24, 26, 27, 28, 30, 36, 43, 45, 46, 47, 48, 49, 50, 51, 52, 53, 55, 56, 58, 59, 60, 61, 62, 63, 64, 66, 69, 70, 71, 79, 81, 84, 85, 91, 92, 93, 94, 96, 97, 98, 99, 101, 103, 104, 105, 108, 109, 110, 112, 113, 114, 115, 117, 118, 122, 123, 124, 126, 127, 128, 129, 130, 132, 133, 135, 136, 137, 138, 139, 140, 143, 145, 150, 153, 155, 156, 157, 160; and the destruction of *The Nauvoo Expositor* 17; arrest for destruction of press 17; arrest of 112; as alleged false Prophet 15, 19; as fallen prophet 15, 100, 125; as founder 4; as Mayor of Nauvoo 15, 17; as Prophet of God 89, 92, 95, 101, 118; as Prophet of the Restoration 98; as Prophet, Seer and Revelator 6, 89; as religionist 13; as restorationist 13, 89; as the Second Witness 98; as the Testator 98; as translator 51, 70; called to translate *The Book of Mormon* 51; calling of 51; charged with destruction of private property 17; charged with treason 17; claims to be Prophet of God 119; death of 6, 17, 115; declares martial law 112; diaries of 8, 74, 123; early theological convictions 27; finds golden plates 23; First Vision 69; flees Nauvoo 114; learns Hebrew 58; letter from Liberty Jail 85; Nauvoo theology of 139; origin of *The Book of Mormon* 24; receives revelations from God 119; revelations of 42; revises Bible 50; sermon of April 2, 1843 124; sermon of January 5, 1841 124; sermon of June 11, 1843 124; sermon of June 16, 1844 100, 125, 126; sermons of 94; teaches the existence of a Mother in Heaven 138; teachings of 6; trial in Carthage, Illinois 17; use of Greek 82; use of Hebrew 82; uses inspiration to revise Bible 47; uses powers granted under Nauvoo Charter 17
Smith, Lucy Mack 113; joins Methodist and Presbyterian churches 28
Smith, Sophronia, joins Methodist and Presbyterian churches 28
Smith, William, Patriarch of the Church 128
Smith family: converts to Mormonism 28; converts to Protestantism 28

Snow, Eliza R. 67, 137, 138, 139; concept of Mother in heaven 137
Snow, Lorenzo 3
"Sola Scriptura" 51
Son of God 99
Spalding, Solomon 26
Spencer, Herbert 135; relation to Mormonism 149
Spenser, Orson 26, 159
spirit intelligences 145, 147, 149; autonomous 147
Spirit of God 119
spirit offspring 136, 137, 139
"Standard Works" 9, 12
Stone, J. Barton 52, 135
Strauss, David 135
succession 11
Swedenborg, Emmanuel 102
Switzerland 104

Talmage, James E. 7, 21, 40, 60, 141,149, 150, 152, 153, 154, 155, 156, 158, 159, 160; his *Jesus the Christ* 143, 144
Taylor, John, materialism of God 145; use of King Follett discourse 145
The Church of Jesus Christ of Latter-day Saints 3, 5, 8, 11
Thebes, Egypt 70
theophany 94, 100, 101
The Times and Seasons 44, 75, 76, 82, 84, 85, 90, 92, 110, 126, 138
Trancendentalists 29, 38
Trinitarianism 30, 37, 52, 53, 59, 123
Trinity 87
True Church 104
Turner, J. B. 88

Union Theological Seminary 159
Unitarianism 52
United Order 100

Utah 104, 128

View of the Hebrews 25
"Vision of the Glories" 48

Wasatch Mountains 128
Wentworth, John 23, 92
White, David 100
Whitmer, David 51, 115; apostasy of 51
Whitmer, John 8, 17; early Mormon historian 17
Widstoe, John A. 12, 141, 144, 148, 149, 154, 156, 158, 159, 160; his *A Rational Theology* 144; on progression of God 149
Williams, Frederick G. 61, 63
Winthrop, John 5
Woodruff, Wilford 123; records King Follett discourse 118
Wyoming 128

Yahweh 97
Yahwist 88
Yale 159
Young, Brigham 11, 133, 140, 144, 156, 159, 160; and the concept of Eternal progression 137; establishes foothold in Great Salt Lake Valley 129; leads Saints to Utah 128; sermon of April 9, 1852 127; succeeds Joseph Smith as leader 128; teaches Adam-God 131; teachings on God 130

Zion 5, 58; Center Stake at Independence 17, 58; early Mormon concept of 5; establishment of 5; Gathering to 5; located in Missouri 5; North America as 5; pattern of 48
The Zohar 82